Validation in Psychology

Validation in Psychology

Hadyn Ellis
Neil Macrae

Editors

Transaction Publishers
New Brunswick (U.S.A.) and London (U.K.)

Library of Congress Catalog Number: 00-064816
ISBN: 0–7658–0647–9
Printed in the United States of America

Library of Congress Cataloging-in-Publication Data

Validation in psychology : research perspectives/[edited by] Hadyn Ellis and Neil Macrae.
    p. cm.
    "Originally published in 1999 as an issue of Current psychology, spring 1999, volume 18, number 1"—T.p. verso.
    Includes bibliographical references.
    ISBN 0-7658-0647-9 (pbk. : alk. paper)
    1. Face perception. 2. Body image. I. Ellis, Hadyn. II. Macrae, Neil.

BF242. V35 2000
153. 7'5—dc21

00-064816

Contents

Tribute to
John W. Shepherd

The reasons for dedicating this collection of papers to John Shepherd are that not only has he made significant contributions to the research themes of People, Paradigms, and Psychology, but he has influenced and guided so many others in their research. As an experimental social psychologist John Shepherd has inspired generations of students at Aberdeen University. With his committed teaching they have learned to appreciate an empirical approach to social psychology, to design well-constructed and meaningful experiments, and to analyze their data in the most elegant ways possible.

His colleagues have also benefited from his erudition and incisiveness, always conveyed with humility and humor. As a research collaborator, John Shepherd is a pleasure to work with as he can listen to the most half-baked idea and help turn it into a useful and viable study. He has a knack of rescuing the most hopeless-looking results so that, from a morass of information, patterns can be discerned that can be meaningfully related to the original hypothesis. In short, for almost forty years John Shepherd has been a shining example of academic devotion and all who have had the pleasure of knowing him have been enriched by the experience.

Born in 1932, John Shepherd left school to become a clerical officer with London County Council before carrying out National Service with the RAF. After this he trained as a teacher at the City of Leeds Training College (where he met his wife Jean). While teaching in Croyden, John studied psychology part-time at Birkbeck College, graduating in 1961 with a first class degree. He was immediately offered the position of Assistant in the Department of Psychology Aberdeen University where he has worked ever since. From 1993 to 1997 John was head of the Department of Psychology.

John Shepherd's achievements are many; often, however, they have involved his spending endless hours teaching undergraduates and supervising postgraduate students—tasks he has always relished and to which unfailingly he has applied himself with great enthusiasm, enormous industry, and enviable talent. His more public activities have largely centred upon his research into person recognition and recall. He helped to initiate the British movement in face processing some twenty-six years ago and has been actively involved in this throughout that period. Most of his work has been funded more or less continuously for more than twenty years by the Police Scientific Research Development Branch, and he and Jean are still working on computerised face composite technique. To mark John's contribution to this field, half of the papers in this special issue of *Current Psychology* are devoted to face processing. Some of them concern the topic of social influences on face perception which has long been of special interest to John and where he has made some of his most important findings.

The other papers in this special issue cover a wide range of areas—all of which John Shepherd has either worked in or to which he has contributed. These include health psychology, crime, organizational safety and, above all, person perception. The latter, undoubtedly, is the overreaching and abiding passion linking most of John Shepherd's principal interests. He has long been concerned with the way we respond to others—both to their physical appearances and to their personalities—and we hope that he will find much to interest him in this issue of *Current Psychology*, which is dedicated to his own unique contributions to People, Paradigms, and Psychology.

Hadyn Ellis
Neil Macrae

Assessing the State of Organizational Safety— Culture or Climate?

KATHRYN J. MEARNS and RHONA FLIN

This article explores the concepts of safety culture and safety climate in an attempt to determine which is the more useful for describing an organization's "state of safety." From a review of the literature purporting to measure safety culture or safety climate, it is argued that, although the two terms are often interchangeable, they are actually distinct but related concepts and should be treated accordingly. The term "safety climate" best describes employees' perceptions, attitudes, and beliefs about risk and safety, typically measured by questionnaire surveys and providing a "snapshot" of the current state of safety. "Safety culture" is a more complex and enduring trait reflecting fundamental values, norms, assumptions and expectations, which to some extent reside in societal culture. The expression of these "cultural" elements, perhaps, can be seen through safety management practices which are reflected in the safety climate. Basically, measurement of safety culture requires in-depth investigation including an analysis of how organizational members interact to form a shared view of safety.

INTRODUCTION

In the field of safety research, empirical studies and theories about the nature and measurement of "safety culture" have reached something of a hiatus. Indeed, a special edition of the journal *Work and Stress* (Cox and Flin, 1998) has been entirely devoted to exploring the validity and applicability of the concept—this at a time when practical textbooks on how to improve safety culture (Reason, 1997; Cooper, 1998) are reaching the bookshelves.

In line with current thinking in organizational research, the time has come to assess what is actually meant by "safety culture" and whether

5

it is the same as, or different from, the associated concept of "safety climate." For too long, the concepts have been used synonymously and interchangeably, a state of affairs which has led to confusion and misunderstanding amongst both safety practitioners and researchers alike.

A discussion already exists within the organizational literature about the nature, validity, and applicability of the concepts of "culture" and "climate" (Schneider, 1975, 1990; Schein, 1984; Cooke and Rousseau, 1988). Despite this ongoing debate, safety managers and academics immediately took the concept of "safety culture" to heart as a valid construct, assuming that its measurement and development would lead to improved safety performance throughout a range of industries.

But what precisely is safety culture, and how do you measure it? Is it any different from the concept of safety climate and, if so, how? Furthermore, how do you know whether you have a good safety culture (or climate) within your organization? Can you link the prevailing safety culture to individual accident rates, for example, or does the absence of a good safety culture only become apparent after a major disaster?

Given the history of the development of "safety culture," the latter scenario would appear to be the case, since current interest in the topic appears to have stemmed from the Chernobyl disaster in 1986. Here, the identification of a "poor safety culture" as a factor contributing to the accident by the OECD Nuclear Agency (1987) led to a plethora of studies searching for safety culture in a number of different high-risk, high-hazard industries. However, as Pidgeon (1995) points out, the search for "safety culture" has been reduced to the measurement of individual attitudes and practices within a hazardous work context that more closely matches the concept of "safety climate."

This article will explore whether or not this claim is correct and also whether measurements of safety culture or climate can be linked to the accident rate within an organization or are there possibly other measures to which one can link employees' attitudes to and perceptions about safety? For example, are "leading indicators" of the state of safety, as opposed to "lagging indicators" (i.e., injury and accident rates), of relevance? The meaning of culture and climate in organizational research is presented before discussing some of the existing studies on the definition and measurement of safety climate and culture. In the final section, a model of safety culture and climate is outlined as well as a consideration of how leading safety performance indicators can help ascertain an organization's "state of safety."

THE MEANING OF CULTURE AND CLIMATE IN
ORGANIZATIONAL RESEARCH

As mentioned above, the concepts of "culture" and "climate" have been widely debated within the organizational literature, and researchers have been at pains to make clear distinctions between them (Ashforth, 1985; Rousseau, 1988; Schneider and Gunnarson, 1996). Glick (1985) has argued that whereas climate developed from Lewin's (1951) social psychology of person/situation interaction, culture was derived from symbolic interactionism and has its roots in sociology and social anthropology (Mead, 1934). According to Moran and Volkwein (1992), social psychologists have focused on how the individual apprehends and discriminates attributes of the organization through perceptions, perceptual processes, cues, and cognitions. The cultural approach analyses the underlying structure of symbols, myths, social drama, and rituals manifested in the shared values, norms, and meanings of groups.

Denison has extensively discussed the differences and similarities between culture and climate, concluding that on the surface the distinctions appear to be quite clear.

> Climate refers to a situation and its link to thoughts, feelings and behaviours of organisational members. Thus it is temporal, subjective and often subject to direct manipulation by people with power and influence, Culture, in contrast, refers to an evolved context (within which a situation may be embedded). Thus, it is rooted in history, collectively held, and sufficiently complex to resist many attempts at direct manipulation. (1996)

However, when Denison compared the individual studies that make up the two literatures, these distinctions disappeared leading to the conclusion that the two research traditions should be viewed as differences in *interpretation* rather than differences in the *phenomenon*. In fact, according to Denison, culture/climate research actually addresses a common phenomenon, namely, "the creation and influence of social contexts in organizations" (1996). He calls for an integration between the two traditions, in order better to serve the future study of organizational *contexts*.

In their review of how "culture" forms and informs organizational climate, Moran and Volkwein concluded that climate and culture overlap as "components of the expressive, communicative, socially-constructed dimensions of organizations" (1992), but differ in that climate reflects the attitudes and behavior of organizational members, which are directly observable to outsiders, whereas culture is about assumptions, expectations, and outlooks that are taken for granted by organizational members and are therefore not immediately interpretable by outsiders. Culture and climate are also related through the way in which the historically-constructed values and meanings of the organization's culture determine the attitude and practices of its current climate.

Schneider and Gunnarson (1996) also applied these notions in their analysis of the psychology of the workplace through organizational climate and culture. They define culture in terms of assumptions, values, and philosophies that tend to concern human nature and the role of work in life. These map, respectively, onto climate "dimensions" such as practices, procedures, and rewarded behavior, namely the themes which employees believe describe their organization. They argue that climate tells us "what" happens in an organization, whereas culture helps explain "why" things happen in a particular way. Is this the case then for safety culture and climate? Do the empirical studies carried out to date make this subtle distinction? The following section will outline how "safety climate" and "safety culture" have been defined and measured, before considering how the concepts should be measured in the future.

THE CONCEPT OF CLIMATE AND CULTURE IN SAFETY RESEARCH

Psychological research into industrial safety during the 1990s has been dominated by studies attempting to measure safety culture or safety climate. A proliferation of definitions and methods has resulted in a mass of research lacking a coherent theoretical framework. Consulting the broader organizational literature suggested that it was possible and useful to distinguish climate from culture when studying dimensions of organizational life such as creativity, productivity or

TABLE 1
Definitions of Safety Culture

Turner, Pidgeon, Blockley, and Toft (1989)	The set of beliefs, norms, attitudes, roles, and social and technical practices that are concerned with minimising the exposure of employees, managers, customers, and members of the public to conditions considered dangerous or injurious.
International Nuclear Safety Advisory Group (1991)	That assembly of characteristics and attitudes in organisations and individuals that establishes that, as an overriding priority, nuclear plant safety issues receive the attention warranted by their significance.
Advisory Committee for Safety in Nuclear Installations (ACSNI) (1993)	The product of individual and group values, attitudes, perceptions, competencies, and patterns of behavior that determine commitment to, and the style and proficiency of, an organisation's health and safety management.

safety. The following discussion presents a brief review of the relevant safety research that deals with the fundamental social context for safety and its manifestations as an underlying culture or more transient work climate.

From a theoretical perspective, safety culture has been described in terms of values, beliefs, attitudes, social mores, norms, rules, practices, competencies, and behavior (see Table 1). Cox and Cox (1996) maintain that, as a result, there is a danger these definitions may become a catch-all for social-psychological and human-factor issues, and the very broadness of the definitions weakens their scientific utility. They also note that there is a distinct lack of empirical data showing what characterises a good safety culture, and few studies have been designed to capture all the aspects of safety culture implied in its definition.

Pidgeon (1991) is more optimistic about the validity and utility of the concept of safety culture, claiming that it might prove to be a useful heuristic tool in risk management strategy. He suggests that safety culture can be grouped under three headings:

(1) Norms and rules for dealing with risk;
(2) Safety attitudes; and
(3) The capacity to reflect on safety practices.

However, as we shall see, most studies that allegedly measure safety culture have only measured safety attitudes with little, if any, attention paid to how the organization deals with risks through norms and rules or whether the organization has the capacity to reflect on safety practices. Thus, as Pidgeon (1995) claims, the search for "safety culture" has been reduced to the measurement of individual attitudes and practices within a hazardous work context, more closely matching the concept of "safety climate."

MEASUREMENT OF SAFETY

Zohar (1980) was one of the first to describe what he called a "climate for safety" in twenty Israeli industrial organizations. His measure of safety climate was a summary of molar perceptions employees shared about their work environment and the relative importance of safety behavior. Based on questionnaires completed by over 400 employees, Zohar concluded the following organizational practices, procedures, and rewarded behaviors were linked to an organization's safety level (measured in terms of safety inspectors' ratings).

1. Importance of safety training;
2. Effects of required work pace on safety;
3. Status of safety committee;
4. Status of safety officer;
5. Effects of safe conduct on promotion;
6. Level of risk at the work place;
7. Management attitudes to safety; and
8. Effect of safe conduct on social status.

Unfortunately, Zohar did not have the opportunity to link these climate measures with actual accident rates at the plants. However, in 1986, Brown and Holmes attempted to validate Zohar's safety climate model on a sample of 425 American production workers, and they also related their measures of safety climate to actual safety performance (i.e., employees with accidents versus no accidents). They found that the original eight-factor climate model reduced to three factors:

1. Management attitudes, i.e., employee perception of how concerned management is with their well-being;
2. Management actions, i.e., employee perception of how active management is in responding to their concerns; and
3. Level of risk, i.e., the physical risk perception of employees.

Furthermore, their results indicated that, whereas the climate *structures* did not differ between the accident and non-accident groups, differences in climate perceptions were detected between the two groups. This would seem to indicate that as far as accident versus non-accident groups are concerned, there are no differences in the general *phenomenon* of safety within the organizations, but there are differences in *interpretations* about safety (Denison, 1996).

More recently, Williamson, Feyer, Cairns, and Biancotti (1997) developed a sixty-seven-item measure of safety climate based on perceptions and attitudes about safety, many of which were borrowed from existing questionnaires. This instrument was completed by 660 Australian workers (42% response rate) from seven workplaces (ranging from heavy through light manufacturing industry and outdoor workers). Factor analysis of a reduced scale revealed five factors: personal motivation for safe behaviour; positive safety practice; risk justification; fatalism; and optimism. Williamson et al. did not have any data on accident rates with which to compare their safety climate measures, however. Their most surprising finding was that so many items reflected a high level of consensus amongst respondents, no matter which company they came from. Furthermore, the skew in the items tended to be in the direction of "good" safety. These results suggested either that the skewed items reflect shared positive safety attitudes that have been generated by consistently good conditions in the companies or that the questions were not phrased in such a way that would emphasise individual differences. It is worth noting that in this study most of the skewed items were attitudinal, whereas perceptual or reality-based questions were not. Is this, then, where a distinction between "safety culture" and "safety climate" comes into its own? If attitudinal items are skewed, this perhaps indicates that this sample of Australian workers from a variety of occupations *share* common attitudes and beliefs with respect to safety. The differing perceptions and experiences of day-to-day safety were based, however, on practices, procedures, and rewarded behavior, which employees believed described their organization.

SAFETY ATTITUDES AS A MEASURE OF SAFETY CULTURE

Cox and Cox appear to have been among the first to measure employee attitudes to safety, pointing out that "the idea is that safety cultures reflect the attitudes, beliefs, perceptions and values that employees share in relation to safety" (1991). The study measured 630 employees' attitudes to safety in a European company in order to identify the common architecture of those attitudes across occupations, occupational levels, and countries. The framework for investigation concentrated on attitudes to safety software, people, and risk. It did not cover employee attitudes to safety hardware and specific hazards. The results revealed five orthogonal factors underpinning the employee attitudes to safety, which together described 50 percent of the variance. These were personal scepticism, individual responsibility, the safety of the work environment, the effectiveness of arrangements for safety, and personal immunity. Cox and Cox (1991) developed a model from these data that emphasises the shared aspects of employee attitudes to safety, providing what they claimed to be a *partial description* of the company's safety culture. However, they did not attempt to link these measures with accident rates within the various departments, occupations, or countries in which the company was operating.

In a later study, based in an oil company, Alexander, Cox, and Cheyne (1995), collected questionnaire data from 1080 employees (offshore and onshore) in an attempt to measure safety culture. They also tried to link safety attitudes with prior accident involvement. The authors reported that a measure of the safety culture could not be reliably demonstrated, but they identified six key factors that underpinned employee attitudes to safety: overt management commitment; personal need for safety; personal appreciation of risk; attributions of blame; conflict and control; and supportive environment. Regarding factor 5 (conflict and control), Alexander et al., report that those with managerial and supervisory responsibility appeared less reluctant to take risks and compromise safety than those without such responsibilities. Furthermore, managers and supervisors seemed more convinced that a "no blame" culture existed within the company and perceived production goals as compatible with safety goals. Finally, no differences in attitudes to risk could be identified between accident and non-accident mployees.

Turning now to the nuclear industry (where the concept of safety culture originated) Lee (1995) assessed risk perceptions and attitudes to safety among 5,295 employees at a large British nuclear reprocessing plant using a questionnaire of 172 items. The study highlighted three factors of importance to risk and safety: risk-taking; a general assessment of the perceived risks involved in working at the plant; and the extent to which risks at the plant were perceived to be under personal control. Lee found major differences in the attitudes and perceptions of different occupational groups, according to supervisor status, type of shift worked (i.e., day or night workers), sex, age, and experience. Lee also found that these differences in risk perception and attitudes to safety were clearly linked with prior accident involvement.

In a study which moved away from a direct attitude survey, Guest, Peccei, and Thomas (1994) examined safety culture and safety performance in British Rail employees following the Clapham Junction disaster. The aim of the study was to determine whether there was any association between the safety culture and the accident rate among employees at both the level of the "gang" and the section. Four gangs of "permanent way" staff (who maintain the track and have one of the most dangerous jobs in the organization) were subjected to in-depth interviews using the Critical Incident Technique (CIT), The Repertory Grid, and general questions. The gangs were selected on the basis of their accident record, with two gangs having had few accidents in the past three years and two others having had a high accident record. CIT involved descriptions of accidents or near-accidents in an attempt to identify who (or what) staff "blamed" for the accidents, staff perceptions of how accidents could be prevented in future, and the factors which they saw as contributing to safe or unsafe working environments. The Repertory Grid was used to identify how staff construed and explained contrasts in safety performance (good to poor) and safety management within British Rail. In addition, the technique was used to develop a measure with which to rate local safety culture and safety behavior. Finally, the general questions were intended to gain insight into how staff viewed safety at their place of work. The in-depth nature of the interviews meant that sample size was restricted to a total of thirty-three interviews with a cross-section of operational management, supervision, and gang members. The conclusions were that it was possible to identify a safety culture among the "permanent way" staff that was part of the main culture of British Rail, characterized by:

- a belief in hierarchy and firm management;
- a belief in the value of technically sound and complex safety systems;
- a reluctance of those at lower levels in the organization to accept personal responsibility; and
- a sense of duty and commitment to running trains on time.

However, the study was only partly successful at linking local safety cultures and accident rates. This was because there were no differences in perceptions of safety performance or perception of risk in "safe" as opposed to "unsafe" gangs; however, gangs with a high accident rate were more likely to see accidents as the responsibility of others and not a consequence of their own behavior.

What can we conclude from this brief review of the literature on the definition and measurement of safety culture and safety climate? As in the organizational literature, there seems to be a degree of overlap between the definitions of the two concepts. Those researchers operating in the realms of "safety culture" tend to talk in terms of the attitudes, beliefs, perceptions, and values that employees share in relation to safety—a collective commitment to safety. Those operating in the safety climate domain describe a set of perceptions and beliefs held by an individual and/or a group about a particular entity. If one looks closely at the data collected on so-called "safety cultures," however, it is evident that only Cox and Cox (1991) have concerned themselves with what employees "share" or "have in common" with respect to safety and, even so, this only provided them with a partial description of safety culture. It would also appear that Guest et al. (1994) have used the best methodology to reveal the rich context in which members of an organization share and differ in their perceptions and beliefs about risk and safety.

In conclusion, the dimensions identified from studies of safety climate seem to be concerned with employees' perceptions of the prevailing conditions that impact upon safety. The dimensions identified from so-called studies of safety culture tend to be complex and diverse with a strong emphasis on *personal* issues. Is this, then, where distinctions between safety climate and culture come into their own? One could argue, perhaps, that safety can be assessed at two levels: 1) the more general level as predicted by norms, implied assumptions, and values (i.e., strategic/cultural); and 2) at the specific level as it relates to particular work tasks within the organization (tactical/ climatic). In order to fully understand the role of human and organizational factors in occupational and industrial safety one has to analyse perceptions and values at two levels within the system—the cultural and the climatic. It could be argued that, to some extent, the "cultural" elements of safety could reside in the societal culture in which the organization is located, which in turn influences how the safety climate within the organization develops. Figure 1 is adapted from Kopelman, Guzzo and Brief's (1990) model of the role of climate and culture in productivity (see also Cox, 1996). They suggest that societal differences may have a greater impact than organizational differences in determining the nature of a given organization's human resource management practices. These practices, in turn, influence organizational climate, which Kopelman et al. refer to as "meaningful interpretations of a work environment by the people in it" (1990). Changes in an organization's practices, for example, engaging in participative decision-making may cause changes in organizational climate, regarding both employee productivity and safety. Thus employee participation in planning and decision-making could affect climate dimensions, such as goal emphasis, means emphasis, task support, and socio-emotional support.

This relationship is also reflected in Schneider and Gunnarson's (1996) analysis of the psychology of the workplace through organizational climate and culture, as applied to safety. Using Zohar's measure of a *climate of safety* to illustrate their example, they point out that Zohar also made reference to a *culture of safety* that would be reflected in a management philosophy that is people-oriented as well as production-oriented. Schneider and Gunnarson also suggest some other values and assumptions that could make up a safety culture, including anticipating problems before they happen in the first place (i.e., being proactive rather than reactive); giving employees' well-being more priority than production issues; and stressing the importance of being cautious rather than being "macho" and taking risks. These basic assumptions, values, and philosophies could then support a climate for safety. On the other hand, some defensive strategies for establishing such a climate could be "let's not get sued" or "let's keep ourselves out of the press at all costs" (Schneider and Gunnarson, 1996). This raises the interesting question of whether it is possible to have a good safety climate but a poor safety culture. Thus, on the surface, an organization's safety record may be good (few accidents); management say they are committed to safety; there is plenty of safety training going on; and the organization has safety advisors and safety committees. However, the values on which these practices are based may be concerned more with covering management's backs and paying lip-service to safety than the well-being of all employees and a need to be proactive and creative in both identifying and solving problems.

MEASURING THE "STATE OF SAFETY" WITHIN ORGANIZATIONS

Given the above arguments, how do we set about measuring human and organizational factors in industrial safety? Reviews of the organizational literature indicate that whereas "perceptions" or "descriptive beliefs" form the basis of climate, "attitudes" or "normative beliefs" are taken as the cornerstones of culture. Although attitude surveys often form the basis for measurements of safety culture, there is more evidence to suggest that these so-called "attitudes" to risk and safety are "perceptions" or "descriptive beliefs" rather than "normative beliefs." This leads to the question of the validity of current methods for the measurement of safety culture and safety climate. Can safety culture within organizations actually be measured in any meaningful way by *quantitative* techniques? Or are *qualitative* methodologies investigating the operation of social systems and the interactions of units and sub-units within the organization more appropriate? This means moving away from the current belief that attitude surveys will disclose all that is required. Indeed, it could be argued that attitude surveys merely scratch the surface and what is needed are techniques such as Repertory Grid, Critical Incident, and in-depth interviews to uncover the more fundamental values, assumptions, and expectations underpinning safety within the organization. It may also be advisable for researchers to actually become part of the organization they are investigating for a period of time in order to get a feel for the culture, and also so that investigators can carry out behavioral observations to determine how people act and interact at all levels of the organization.

Other measures of safety performance could also be used to build up a comprehensive picture of an organization's state of safety? Recently, "leading indicators" have become of more interest in benchmarking organizational health and safety performance. The areas outlined below were used by the Norwegian state-owned oil company, Statoil, in an extensive benchmarking project carried out 1996 (both in-house and with companies with a proven record in health and safety). The project involved assessing how various departments and companies carried out the following activities:

- policy strategy, goals, and plans;
- health and safety expertise;
- visibility and involvement of managers, including meetings and inspections;
- motivation, attitudes/well-being, and job satisfaction;
- identification of hazards and risks;
- reporting and investigation of near-misses and accidents; and
- communicating results and use of statistics.

A number of safety performance indicators are currently being used by the offshore oil and gas industry (Blackmore, 1997). The industry has also recently launched "A step-change in safety" initiative, which has three main objectives: to achieve a 50 percent improvement in the industry's safety performance by the year 2000; to establish safety performance contracts demonstrating leadership's personal concern for safety as an equal to business performance; and to encourage industry members to work together to improve sharing of safety information and good practice. The identification of cross-industry health and safety performance measures has been a critical part of this process. Areas for measurement include:

- all injury frequency rates;
- dangerous occurrences;
- incident potential;
- senior management involvement and commitment;
- safety training provision; and
- number of days lost through injury or occupational illness.

These measures include both traditional "lagging" indicators, e.g., Lost Time Incidents, and proactive measures of safety activity, i.e. "leading" indicators.

The above would appear to be a comprehensive list of the type of factors which are known to contribute to the "safety culture" or "safety climate" of an organization and ties in with the types of measure which were found to be of relevance for offshore safety in a study of human and organizational factors in offshore safety (Mearns et al., 1997). The extent to which these factors are found to be "in tune" with each other may determine whether or not an organization has a positive safety culture. The "balanced scorecard" (Kaplan and Norton, 1992) may provide a tool for understanding the interaction of the many factors and processes which contributes a positive safety culture. The balanced scorecard includes financial measures that tells the results of actions already taken. It then complements these measures with operational measures on customer satisfaction, internal processes, and the organization's innovation and improvement activities—operational measures that are drivers of future financial performance. The use of the balanced scorecard to benchmark health and safety provides the basis of a research project currently being undertaken by Aberdeen University Industrial Psychology Group (Mearns et al., 1997). The exercise will allow organizations to look at the business of safety from four perspectives, providing the answer to four basic questions:

1. Customer perspective: Is the workforce satisfied with safety?
2. Internal business perspective: How is safety managed within the organization?
3. Financial perspective: What are the costs of safety?
4. Learning and growth perspective: What can be done to improve the process of safety?

More complex, multivariate analyses and modelling techniques (i.e., structural equation modelling that will reveal direct and indirect pathways) can also be used to examine the relationship between climatic and cultural measurements and performance indicators such as accidents, near-misses, work pace, and absenteeism. Since "safety culture" is not a thing that can be installed and managed directly, it is of crucial importance to understand the underlying dynamic processes that need to be supported in pursuit of a "good" culture and also to understand the subtle, symbolic, rhetorical matters that are so difficult to control (Turner and Pidgeon, 1997). It could be argued that measurement of the "safety climate" could at least give some indication as to how these covert processes express themselves at the work place, but it must be emphasised that much more digging behind the facade is required to determine an organization's true motives for developing norms and rules for dealing with risk and its capacity to reflect on safety practices.

REFERENCES

ACSNI. (1993). *Human factors study group third report: Organising for safety.* London: HMSO.

Alexander, M., Cox, S., and Cheyne, A. (1995). UK Offshore Safety Culture. Paper presented at the "Understanding Risk Perception" Conference. Aberdeen, February.

Ashforth, B. (1985) Climate formation—issues and extensions. *Academy of Management Review, 18*(4), 837–847.

Brown, R.L. and Holmes, H. (1986). The use of factor-analytic procedure for assessing the validity of an employee safety climate model. *Accident Analysis and Prevention, 18,* 289–297.

Blackmore, G.A. (1997). Leading performance indicators. Paper presented at the IADC North Sea Seminar, Performance Measures for Safety Management. Aberdeen, June.

Cooke, R.A. and Rousseau, D.M. (1988). Behavioural norms and expectations: A quantitative approach to the assessment of organizational culture. *Group and Organisational Studies, 13*(3), 245–273.

Cooper, M.D. (1998). *Improving safety culture.* A Practical Guide. Chichester: Wiley.

Cox, S. (1996). Maximising performance: The impact of positive safety culture. Paper presented at the 5th Offshore Installation Managers Conference, April, Aberdeen.

Cox, S. and Cox, T. (1991). The structure of employee attitudes to safety: a European example. *Work and Stress, 5,* 93–106.

Cox, S. and Cox, T. (1996). *Safety, systems and people.* Oxford: Butterworth-Heinemann.

Cox, S. and Flin, R. (1998). Safety culture: Philosopher's stone or man of straw? *Work and Stress* (special issue on safety culture), *12*(3), 189–201.

Denison, D. (1996). What is the difference between organisational culture and organisational climate? A native's point of view on a decade of paradigm wars. *Academy of Management Review, 21*(3), 619–654.

Glick, W. (1985). Conceptualising and measuring organisational and psychological climate: Pitfalls in multilevel research. *Academy of Management Review, 10,* 601–616.

Guest, D., Peccei, R., and Thomas, A. (1994). Safety culture and safety performance: British Rail in the aftermath of the Clapham Junction disaster. Unpublished paper.

International Nuclear Safety Advisory Group. (1991). *Safety culture.* Safety Series No 75–INSAG-4. Vienna: International Atomic Energy Agency (IAEA).

Kaplan, R.S. and Norton, D.P. (1996). *The balanced scorecard.* Boston: Harvard Business School.

Kopelman, R., Brief, A. and Guzzo, R. (1990). The role of climate and culture in productivity. In B. Schneider (ed.), *Organisational Climate and Culture.* Oxford: Jossey Bass.

Lee, T.R. (1995). The role of attitudes in the safety culture and how to change them. Paper presented at the Conference "Understanding Risk Perception." Aberdeen, February.

Lewin, K. (1951). *Field theory in social science.* New York: Harper and Row.

Mead, M. (1934). *Mind, self and society.* Chicago: University of Chicago Press.

Mearns, K., Flin, R., Fleming, M., and Gordon, R. (1997). *Human and Organisational Factors in Offshore Safety.* OTH 87 543. Suffolk: HSE Books.

Mearns, K., Flin, A., Gordon, R., and O'Connor, P. (1997). Factoring the human into safety: Translating research into practice. Research Paper. Department of Psychology, University of Aberdeen.

Moran, E. and Volkwein, J. (1992). The cultural approach to the formation of organisational climate. *Human Relations, 45* (1), 19–47.

OECD Nuclear Agency. (1987). *Chernobyl and the safety of nuclear reactors in OECD countries.* Paris: Organzation for Economic Co-operation and Development.

Pidgeon, N. (1991). Safety culture and risk management in organisations. *Journal of Cross-Cultural Psychology, 22,* 129–140.

Pidgeon, N. (1995). Risk construction and safety culture in managing high-risk technologies. Paper prepared for International Workshop on Institutional Vulnerabilities and Resilience in Public Administration, Crisis Research Centre. Leiden, The Netherlands.

Reason, J. (1997*). Managing the risks of organizational accidents*. Aldershot: Ashgate.

Rousseau, D. (1988). The construction of climate in organisational research. In: C. Cooper and I. Robertson (eds.) *International Review of Industrial and Organisational Psychology*. Chichester: Wiley.

Schein, E. (1984). Coming to a new awareness of organisational culture. *Sloan Management Review, 25*(2), 3–6.

Schneider, B. (1975). Organisational climate: Individual preferences and organisational realities revisited. *Journal of Applied Psychology, 60,* 459–465.

Schneider, B. (1990). *Organisational Climate and Culture*. Oxford: Jossey Bass.

Schneider, B. and Gunnarson, S. (1996). Organisational climate and culture: The psychology of the workplace. In: J. James, B. Steffy and D. Bray (eds.), *Applying Psychology in Business*. Mass: Lexington.

Turner, B., Pidgeon, N., Blockley, D., and Toft, B. (1989). Safety culture: Its importance in future risk management. Position paper for Second World Bank Workshop on Safety Control and Risk Management. Karlstad, Sweden.

Turner, B. and Pidgeon, N. (1997). *Man-made disasters* (2nd Ed.). London: Butterworth.

Williamson, A., Feyer, A-M., Cairns, D., and Biancotti, D. (1997). The development of a measure of safety climate: the role of safety perceptions and attitudes. *Safety Science, 25* (1–3), 15–27.

Zohar, D. (1980). Safety climate in industrial organisations: Theoretical and applied implications. *Journal of Applied Psychology, 65* (1), 96–102.

Why Did It Happen to Me? Social Cognition Processes in Adjustment and Recovery from Criminal Victimization and Illness

MALCOLM D. MACLEOD
University of St Andrews

This article reviews the theoretical framework and empirical evidence for the hypothesised relationship between self-blame attributions and psychological adjustment. In doing so, an argument is presented that poses an alternative interpretation to that which is widely accepted regarding the complex relationship between blame attributions, perceived control, self-esteem, and recovery. A number of fundamental issues concerning the assumptions underlying Janoff-Bulman's model are identified and explored. In particular, attention is given to the importance of distinguishing perceived control from likelihood of recurrence, and perceived control from outcome expectancy. Finally, the possibility that attributions may not play as fundamental a role in adjustment as first thought is considered, and future lines of enquiry are identified.

> *". . . . if we wish to conquer undesirable tendencies in ourselves, we must assiduously, and in the first instance cold bloodedly, go through the outward motions of those contrary dispositions we prefer to cultivate."*
> —William James (1884)

Having lost both his parents in the space of ten months during 1882, William James was well-placed to comment on the experience of the relationship between behavior and emotions. In particular, he believed that the way we feel can be altered by our extant behavior; if we act in a cheerful manner, then we are likely to replace our feelings of depression with cheerfulness. Conversely, if we act in a morose manner, we are likely to supplant our happy feelings with feelings of sadness and depression. In the intervening century of empirical research, psychology has largely neglected James' basic observation in favor of trying to establish how mood can affect behavior and well-being (Frasure-Smith et al., 1993). As a result, our social cognitions have been widely implicated in the process of adjustment and recovery from a wide range of traumatic events including bereavement (Downey et al., 1990; Kahler and MacLeod, 1996), rape (Frazier, 1990; Edward and MacLeod, 1996), burglary (Freedy et al., 1994; Winkel et al., 1994), accidents (Kiecolt-Glaser and Williams, 1987; Joseph et al., 1991), coronary heart disease (Gilutz et al., 1991), and cancer (Taylor et al., 1984; Timko and Janoff-Bulman, 1985).

Principal amongst these psychological factors are attributional processes: the reasons we construct for why we think people act in the way they do; the explanations we provide for our own behavior; and the basis for our predictions about our own and other people's future behavior. The ubiquity of attribution processes such as these has been demonstrated in domains as diverse as academic achievement (Dweck, 1975; Weiner, 1985a), marital satisfaction (Fincham et al., 1987; Horneffer and Fincham, 1996), juridic judgement (Macrae, 1989; Macrae and Shepherd, 1989a, 1989b), and memory for faces (Shepherd and Ellis, 1973; Shepherd et al., 1978). Increasingly, the application of ideas based on attribution theory has been a major focus of contemporary psychological research. It is unsurprising, therefore, that the link between attributions and people's recovery from traumatic life events should have received so much attention.

Much of this research indicates a possible mediating role for attributions in adjustment through the actions of perceived control, self-esteem, and/or the availability of coping strategies (Janoff-Bulman, 1979; Shaver, 1983; Tennen and Affleck, 1990). In the current paper, however, I would like to present a challenge to received wisdom by offering an alternative explanation as to why attributions *appear* to mediate psychological adjustment. In doing so, I will also consider some of the issues we should be focusing upon in future research.

OUTCOMES

The consequences of traumatic life events such as sexual assault, cancer, stroke, and heart disease are enormously varied and multi-levelled. At the most public level, these traumatic events may result in a loss of mobility, physical injury, or the loss or damage to one's property. At a less public level, they can result in behavioral effects ranging from anger and frustration to symptoms of psychological trauma such as intrusive ideation, emotional numbing, depression, and anxiety (Collins et al., 1990; MacLeod et al., 1996). These, in turn, can affect one's ability to cope with the stress and trauma associated with an incident (Frazier, 1990; Winkel et al., 1994). Some consequences, however, are more elusive in the sense that we are often unaware of how the trauma may have affected the way we organize and utilize existing and novel information. The challenge to previously cherished beliefs that typically accompany many criminal episodes such as rape may force a substantial re-organization of an individual's existing belief structures (Janoff-Bulman, 1985; McCann and Pearlman, 1990), often to the extent that recipients appear unusually preoccupied with the cause and effects of an incident (MacLeod et al., 1996).

Although some individuals may show an awareness of the need to come to terms with emotionally challenging event-related memories and ideation, most can only hazard a guess as to how this is actually accomplished in cognitive terms. Social psychological theory and research, however, has provided a plausible explanation as to how this assimilation is achieved, namely through the kinds of attributional processes in which we engage following a traumatic event. Specifically, attributions are considered important for psychological adjustment because they afford individuals a sense of "meaning, control and predictability" (Taylor, 1983; Taylor et al., 1984). and help us to place the negative events that happen to us within some kind of orderly and just framework (Lerner and Miller, 1978).

ATTRIBUTIONS AND ADJUSTMENT

Unfortunately, the mechanisms by which attributions are considered to bring about this reconciliation are not well-articulated. Rather, for the most part, it is *assumed* that attributions operate through perceived control and/or self-esteem. Janoff-Bulman's influential work

(1979, 1982). asserts that particular kinds of self-blame attributions (i.e., behavioral self-blame attributions). are related to better adjustment (Winkel et al., 1994). The basic thesis is that blaming the cause of a negative event on some aspect of one's behavior allows one to reassert control over the likelihood of a similar event occurring in the future. Identifying causes such as one's own behavior may allow one to regain a sense of control over one's life which, in turn, is associated with better psychological adjustment (Thompson et al., 1993). Thus, if one has just been burgled and entry was gained through an unlocked window, one should be better able to cope if one can identify that improved security (e.g., the addition of window bolts). could have avoided the burglary in the first place and also increase the likelihood of avoiding a similar incident in the future. Likewise, one's psychological adjustment to ill health may be enhanced through control beliefs that the changes one can make to one's diet or exercise routine may not only have prevented the illness, but also the likelihood of its recurrence.

Given this, we would expect to find that people who make characterological self-blame attributions (i.e., those concerning aspects of one's personality that are immutable) show poorer adjustment as these attributions do not afford a sense of control. Thus, in the case of burglary, someone who ascribes the reason for their victimisation as being due to their carelessness or forgetfulness may be more distressed because they feel they can do little about its possible recurrence. Similarly, other-blame can be considered dysfunctional because blame is ascribed to factors beyond one's control (i.e., to someone or something else). There is, however, the possibility that if one believes he can exert control over a situation and then fails, this may simply serve to exacerbate his level of distress (Thompson et al., 1988; Burger, 1989). although there are contra-indications to suggest that any sense of control may be beneficial, even when these control beliefs are subsequently disconfirmed (Thompson et al., 1993).

A parallel means by which attributions may be related to adjustment is through their action on self-esteem. Timko and Janoff-Bulman (1985). found that other-blame was associated with lower levels of self-esteem presumably because other-blame also implies that one had been unable to prevent the situation having occurred which, in turn, served to undermine beliefs about one's abilities and perceived invulnerability. This is consistent with the observation that participation in formal recovery interventions (e.g., debriefings). may be interpreted as an unfavorable source of information about one's own abilities and can threaten self-esteem (Gross et al., 1980; Coyne et al., 1990).

Additionally, Tennen and Affleck (1990). have argued that the act of blaming someone else is likely to restrict the range of available adaptive coping strategies. Those who appear to adapt best to stressful events are likely to have a range of available coping strategies which permits greater flexibility in dealing with the particular demands of the traumatic event (Silver and Wortman, 1980). The effects of attributional processes on self-esteem and the availability of coping strategies may be closely linked *via* self-efficacy beliefs in the sense that, if one does not feel sufficiently positive about oneself and one's abilities, there may be little motivation to enact behaviors that reduce psychological distress. The expectation that one has the capability to successfully implement a chosen course of action is generally considered a good predictor of behavior (Bandura, 1986, 1997).

There are, however, a number of qualifications to the general thesis regarding self-blame attributions and adjustment:

1). Where the consequences of a negative event are relatively low, loss of self-esteem through blaming oneself is likely to be negligible. On the other hand, where outcome severity is high, any form of self-blame may lead to increased feelings of vulnerability and lowered self-esteem. This seems to be borne out by findings in the literature. These indicate that for relatively minor outcomes, behavioral self-blame appears to have an adaptive role while, for serious outcomes, both behavioral and characterological self-blame tend to be related to poorer adjustment (MacLeod and Paton, in press).

2). Characterological and behavioral self-blame do not measure blame *per se*. In particular, Shaver and Drown (1986). argue that Janoff-Bulman's conception of behavioral self-blame actually constitutes a self-attribution of causality while characterological self-blame represents a self-attribution of responsibility (i.e., it lacks intentionality). The irony of these criticisms, however, is that even though these blame attributions may not actually measure blame, the associations predicted by Janoff-Bulman remain unaltered. Specifically, Shaver and Drown indicate that causal attributions should be highly related to the re-establishment of perceived control over future outcomes and that responsibility attributions should threaten self-esteem and increase perceived likelihood of future distress.

Thus, despite issues concerned with outcome severity and the constructs underlying self-blame, there has been no serious challenge to Janoff-Bulman's basic thesis regarding the relationship between blame attributions and adjustment. Consequently, Janoff-Bulman's model has dominated this field of research over the past twenty years—its predictions have been widely accepted as having import for the effective implementation of interventions for, and the counselling and treatment of those who have suffered accidents, crime, disasters, and ill health. Clearly, a model that encompasses such wide-ranging implications deserves careful critical consideration. In the remainder of this article, therefore, we will examine some of the assumptions that underlie Janoff-Bulman's model and their possible ramifications for our understanding of how people recover from traumatic events.

UTILITY AND APPLICATION

First of all, let us consider the relationship between attributions and outcome and the evidence that directly relates to Janoff-Bulman's model and its predictions. In particular, we will examine those studies that have failed to confirm the predicted relationship between behavioral self-blame and adjustment, and explore some of the possible reasons for these apparent failures.

According to Weiner (1985b), negative events are much more likely to give rise to attributions than are positive ones. To some extent, this basic assumption is implicit in Janoff-Bulman's model in that it is assumed that, on experiencing a traumatic event, we are likely to engage in attributional thinking in order to make sense of our experience. In reality, however, not everyone who finds themselves in such circumstances appears to engage in this kind of cognitive processing (Gotay, 1985; Lowery et al., 1987; Turnquist et al., 1988).

Thus, we have a naturally occurring experiment in the sense that, if attributions play a central role in our recovery from traumatic events, we could reasonably expect to find differences in psychological adjustment between those individuals who make attributions and those who do not. However, where such comparisons have been made, little difference in psychological adjustment has been evident (Taylor et al., 1984; Lowery et al., 1987). People who reported having made attributions appeared to fare no better or worse than those who reported they did not have attributional thoughts. Indeed, some studies have shown that anxiety levels were lower where no causal search had been initiated (Lowery et al., 1992). Benyamini, Leventhal, and Leventhal (1997). argue that these apparent inconsistencies may be due to the fact that different aspects of a disease are salient at different points in time. Soon after a traumatic episode, it may be the *absence* of causal search that is related to good psychological adjustment while, at later points in time, it is the *presence* of causal attributions that appears to confer benefits for well-being (Suls and Fletcher, 1985).

An alternative interpretation, however, is that the attributions we make following a traumatic episode may not actually play a central role in the recovery process. The difficulty with testing this hypothesis centers on the fact that some individuals who report not having engaged in attributional thinking may simply have had difficulties in recollecting whether they had or not and that, over time, the need to engage in making attributions diminishes. Additionally, the extent to which people offer information on their attributions for an event can depend on the particular methods employed by the investigator. If we assume, however, that there are no systematic differences in the likelihood of people being able to recall accurately whether they had engaged in attributional thought following a traumatic event, we would not expect to find substantial differences amongst those individuals who had experienced similar classes of events. This, of course, assumes that event outcome drives our need to make attributions. In a carefully designed set of studies, Kanazawa (1992). found that expectancy had the only independent effect on spontaneous causal attributions and that any effect of outcome could be eliminated once expectancy had been adequately controlled. Thus, it would appear that there is no good theoretical reason to believe that negative outcomes should produce more spontaneous causal attributions than would positive outcomes except that, of course, most negative events in real life are unexpected. At the very least, we cannot assume that people will engage in attributional thinking on the basis of the valence of outcome alone.

What this means in practical terms is that if spontaneous causal attributions are not dependent on outcome, then we have no reason to expect that individuals who have suffered a traumatic event will be predisposed to make an adaptive form of attribution (i.e., behavioral self-blame). which according to Shaver and Drown (1986). is actually a self-attribution of causality. Thus, the fact that some individuals have been found to make behavioral self-blame attributions following a traumatic event may be entirely unrelated to psychological adjustment.

Indeed, some studies have indicated that self-blame attributions (both behavioral and characterological). may actually be related to poor psychological adjustment (Meyer and Taylor, 1986; Frazier, 1990; Edward and MacLeod, 1996) and that other-blame attributions are related to better adjustment. These findings are consistent with predictions based on Abramson, Seligman, and Teasdale's (1978). reformulated model of learned helplessness where external attributions for bad outcomes should buffer self-esteem and therefore be associated with better recovery. Specifically, they argue that individuals are likely to experience depression when a maladaptive attributional style is adopted in which internal, stable, and global causes are provided for noncontingent negative events. Thus, in contrast to Janoff-Bulman's predictions, self-esteem is likely to be substantially lowered by blaming oneself for the occurrence of a traumatic event such as rape. Similarly, Shaver (1985). has argued that attributing the cause of a negative event to external factors such as chance or fate will enhance or protect an individual's self-esteem.

More recently, Janoff-Bulman (1992). has argued that behavioral self-blame attributions are unlikely to be related to adjustment when an individual has also made characterological self-blame attributions. In other words, any benefit of blaming one's behavior for a traumatic event is likely to be undone if some aspect of one's personality is also implicated. The problem for this qualification is that people often experience difficulties in distinguishing between the two kinds of self-blame (Meyer and Taylor, 1986). Indeed, it may be very difficult to blame one's behavior without implicating some aspect of one's personality (Downey et al., 1990). For example, a victim of stranger rape may have difficulty deciding whether the reason she believes she was to blame for the incident having happened was behavioral (i.e., she went out walking late at night on her own). or characterological (i.e., she is not a safety-conscious type person). Frazier (1990). and Frazier and Schauben (1994). have also indicated that behavioral and characterological self-blame are significantly correlated with each other. Thus, people are likely to make both characterological and behavioral self-blame attributions in their explanations for a negative event because they typically fail to distinguish between them. This is hardly surprising given that our personality drives a great deal of our behavior. Consequently, the value of a model which predicts better psychological adjustment on the basis of behavioral self-blame attributions only is questionable.

Also, we should not necessarily expect that other-blame will be dysfunctional across all domains as would be predicted from Tennen and Affleck's model (1990). Carson and MacLeod (1997), for example, make the point that unlike illness (which is seldom the consequence of human agency), crime always has a perpetrator. Indeed, they point out in their study that many crime victims who had apparently coped well with their experiences blamed the offenders. Thus, when examining the relationship between attributions and recovery, we need to be sensitive to the possibility that the form of psychological entailment will vary depending upon the kinds of explanations provided within particular social contexts.

PERCEIVED CONTROL AND LIKELIHOOD OF RECURRENCE

Second, we need to consider the relationship between perceived control and adjustment, which is central to Janoff-Bulman's argument. In reality, the evidence for this relationship is equivocal. Many studies have indicated support for the notion that enhanced perceived control is associated with good psychological adjustment (Taylor et al., 1984; Thompson and Spacapan, 1991), but others have failed to find this predicted relationship (Reich and Zautra, 1990). Tennen, Affleck, and Gershman (1986). have suggested that such discrepancies may be due to confusion concerning the way in which attributions are related to perceptions of control over *outcome* and over *recurrence*. Specifically, they suggest that behavioral self-blame may have little influence on an individual's feeling of control over the progression or outcome of a chronic illness such as cancer, but may afford a sense of control over the recurrence of the disease. A recent study by Malcarne, Compas, Epping-Jordan, and Howell (1995). provides evidence consistent with this interpretation. Cancer patients' attributions of self-blame were found to be related to adjustment via their effects on perceived control over future recurrence rather than on perceived control over current symptoms.

In addition, Frazier and Schauben (1994). have suggested that perceived control might be better conceptualised as being focused in three different ways: on past events, on the effects of the event (i.e., present control); and on future events. Assuming this to be the case, one could expect to find that individuals who typically focus on past and present control would be more likely to show poorer recovery from stress and trauma than those who focus on future events. Similarly, it could be expected that those who perceive a high level of control over past events and a low level of control over future events would show poorer recovery than those who perceive a low level of control over past events and a high level of control over future events. Anecdotal accounts of recovery are consistent with such predictions in that enhanced perceived control over future events appears to confer benefits on recovery and well-being (Duckworth, 1986; Paton et al., 1989; Alexander and Wells, 1991). It has also been suggested that strategies that assist emergency workers to focus on using past experiences in order to identify ways of enhancing future performance may be particularly effective in promoting adjustment (MacLeod and Paton, in press).

Edward and MacLeod (1996), however, have pointed out that the empirical evidence for this reappraisal of the relationship between perceived control and recovery remains inadequate. Specifically, they argue that Frazier and Schauben equated, and therefore confounded, perceived likelihood of the target event recurring with perceived control over future events. One could imagine, for example, incidents likely to recur over which one believes one has a high degree of control and others which afford no sense of control whatsoever. Thus to equate perceived likelihood of recurrence with perceived control is, at best, tenuous. Indeed, Frazier and Schauben's actual measures of perceived control failed to show any relationship with psychological adjustment. Instead, they found that lower levels of distress were most likely when likelihood of recurrence for rape or relationship loss was also perceived as being low. Thus, not only did Frazier and Schauben fail to find evidence of the relationships predicted by Janoff-Bulman, they also failed to find evidence for their hypothesised relationship between perceived control over future events and adjustment.

PERCEIVED CONTROL AND EXPECTANCY

Third, we need to consider whether the inconsistencies in the literature are due to unidentified variables that moderate the effects of perceived control or whether there are other factors that may prove better predictors of psychological adjustment.

One of the possible reasons for Frazier and Schauben's failure to find evidence for the predicted relationship between perceived control and adjustment may be due to the fact that they examined relatively low control incidents (i.e., relationship breakdown and bereavement). While participants in their studies perceived relationship breakdown as being significantly more controllable than bereavement, against this kind of contrast, almost anything would. In fact, mean ratings for perceived control (taken on a five-point scale). for the bereavement episode in question was 1.63 and only 2.69 for relationship breakdown. Clearly, people are less likely to feel they have control over bereavement than over relationship breakdown, but it does not imply that the latter constitutes a high control event. Many individuals may feel incapable of reestablishing a relationship, particularly where the partner has instigated the break-up.

In low control incidents, perceived likelihood of recurrence rather than perceived control *per se* may be the vital factor. In a qualitative analysis of ethnic minority and white victims' crime experiences, Carson and MacLeod (1997). found that a greater perceived intentional element on the part of offender(s). to harm victims or their property was associated with higher levels of reported psychological distress in the victim. The perception of an intentional element on the part of the offender appeared to be closely linked to perceived likelihood of recurrence (as in cases of racial harassment). The greater the perception of intention, the greater the perceived likelihood of recurrence, and the greater the associated psychological distress. In contrast, where an incident was perceived to be due to bad luck or chance, the victim was less likely to expect a recurrence which, in turn, was associated with lower levels of reported distress. It is possible, therefore, that perceived control over future traumatic events may only play a limited role in the recovery process, at least for those who have experienced low control incidents, thereby explaining Frazier and Schauben's data.

Importantly, this interpretation is consistent with Carver and Scheier's (1990, 1994). argument that the expectations we hold about an event occurring at some point in the future may be more important for our understanding of the underlying processes involved in recovery than are our perceptions of personal control. They argue that while people may consider the effects of external factors and their feelings of personal control in arriving at an expected outcome, it is the issue of whether the outcome is *expected* that predicts our emotional reactions. Thus, there is the possibility that the way in which an outcome is achieved may be less important than whether the outcome actually occurs. More recently, Carver (1997). has raised the issue that locus of control measures have been typically confounded with outcome probability, and specifically our expectancies about the occurrence of future events. Consequently, he warns about the danger of making the assumption that perceived control plays a fundamental role in psychological adjustment and that there may be other factors, closely related to control beliefs, which may prove to have greater predictive value (Wallston, 1992).

CONCLUSIONS

Taken together, these arguments raise serious doubts about the relationship between attributions, perceived control, and psychological adjustment, and whether this relationship can be considered causal. For the most part, it has been assumed that attributions affect psychological well-being but the issues raised in the present article point to the possibility that our attributions following a traumatic episode may actually be driven by the level of our psychological distress, and that our attributional thoughts may tell us little about how psychological adjustment is actually achieved. At the very least, we have to entertain the idea that our current levels of distress can influence our attributional processes. Malcarne et al. (1995). have recently provided empirical evidence in support of this view. They found that some cancer patients appeared to engage in a cycle of cognitions whereby self-blame attributions and distress mutually contributed to each other. Initial psychological distress was found to account for approximately four times the amount of variance in subsequent characterological self-blame (i.e., four months later). than did initial self-blame for subsequent distress.

In addition to the perennial issue of causality, there has been a tendency to treat attributions as a means of providing a "window" on our cognitive processes, despite the warnings by Nisbett and Wilson (1977). of the inherent dangers of doing so. Sometimes our attributions may match our cognitive processes, while at other times they are clearly influenced by our current goals (such as impression management). and the context in which we engage in attributional activity.

We cannot assume that the rationalisations we make about our own behavior are likely to be any more enlightening than what other people's inferential processes tell them about our behavior. Indeed, we have to accept that we may adopt exactly the same kinds of inferential procedures when trying to understand our own behavior that we employ when attempting to understand other people's behavior. A cross-cultural perspective indicates that the kind of attributions one makes for one's behavior may also be dependent upon cultural factors (Miller, 1984). In this knowledge, it would appear unsatisfactory to treat attributions as fundamental cognitive processes when, in fact, their content is heavily shaped by our motivations and the social world in which we live.

The arguments raised in the present article also indicate the possibility that we may have been investigating a chance set of associations whose existence is dependent upon the presence of other (so far undetected). variables. If this is the case, we could expect that, under some circumstances, attributions and perceived control will appear to be closely related to adjustment while, for others, we will fail to find the predicted relationship because of the absence of those factors that are actually predictive of psychological adjustment. This pattern of results closely matches what currently pertains in the psychological literature.

So what might these other factors be? Current theory has advanced the idea that there may be automatic processes at work in addition to the rational processes of attribution making. Indeed, perhaps the most interesting aspect from the point of view of understanding psychological adjustment has been Wegner's (1992). innovative work on the suppression or control of these automatic processes. The act of trying to suppress the memory for a traumatic episode may lead to a search for the very thing that the person is trying to forget. Wegner (1994), for example, has demonstrated that suppressed thoughts are not only difficult to keep out of mind, but when people are asked to think about a target thought after initially trying to suppress that thought, they are more likely to think about the suppressed thought than people who never suppressed the thought in the first place. Thus, the irony would appear to be that the act of trying not to think about a traumatic event may actually have the opposite effect of what could be expected (Gold and Wegner, 1995), i.e., it may result in hyperaccessibility which, in turn, may lead to repeated and uncontrollable intrusions of unwanted thoughts and ideas. As Gold and Wegner observe, the harder we try to push away unwanted thoughts, the more likely it seems that we are to think about them.

While thought suppression is clearly an avenue of research that merits our attention, we cannot entirely eliminate the possibility that blame attributions are related to adjustment. The fact that we have failed to provide conclusive evidence of this relationship may be due to an over-reliance on cross-sectional rather than prospective methodology. Similarly, the fact that little account appears to have been taken of outcome severity and outcome expectancy (as discussed above). has added to the general opacity of this area of research. In addition, there are difficulties with how attributions, perceived control, and self-esteem are best measured. In particular, there is considerable confusion over the definition of constructs, especially in the case of perceived control and a lack of standardised methods of assessment. These have all added to the difficulty in interpreting and drawing meaningful comparisons across studies (Lefcourt, 1991; Katz et al., 1995; Thompson and Collins, 1995).

Perhaps the strongest argument in support of the vast amount of work that has been carried out on attributions and adjustment is that, irrespective of their reality, they can provide us with the illusion of control and ability (Taylor, 1983). Indeed, illusory control beliefs may be more important to an individual's recovery from trauma than the reality of control. Illusion and self-aggrandisement can confer significant benefits on an individual's emotional well-being (Taylor et al., 1991). However, if we acknowledge that attributions are, for at least part of the time, illusory and contingency-based, then we also need to consider whether we can hope to gain a full understanding of how psychological adjustment is achieved by continuing to examine those variables that only reflect underlying cognitive processes to a limited extent. Indeed, in our search for the psychological mechanisms by which we adjust to and recover from traumatic events, future research may be better served by revisiting James's observation that "everything real must be experienceable somewhere, and every kind of thing experienced must somewhere be real" (1912). In doing so, we may come to rely less upon self-report measures of adjustment and attempt to investigate those factors that underlie attributional thoughts.

REFERENCES

Abramson, L.Y., Seligman, M.E.P., and Teasdale, J.D. (1978). Learned helplessness in humans: Critique and reformulation. *Journal of Abnormal Psychology, 87,* 49–74.
Alexander, D.A. and Wells, A. (1991). Reactions of police officers to body handling after a major disaster: A before and after comparison. *British Journal of Psychiatry 159,* 517–555.
Bandura, A. (1986). *Social foundations of thought and action: A social cognitive theory.* Englewood Cliffs, NJ: Prentice Hall.
Bandura, A. (1997). *Self-efficacy: The exercise of control.* New York: Freeman.
Benyamini, Y., Leventhal, E.A., and Leventhal, H. (1997). Attributions and health. In A. Baum, S. Newman, J. Weinman, R. West, and C. McManus (eds.), *Cambridge Handbook of Psychology, Health and Medicine.* Cambridge: Cambridge University Press.
Burger, J.M. (1989). Negative reactions to increases in perceived personal control. *Journal of Personality and Social Psychology, 56,* 246–256.
Carson, L. and MacLeod, M.D. (1997). Explanations about crime and psychological distress in ethnic minority and white victims of crime: A qualitative exploration. *Journal of Community and Applied Social Psychology, 7,* 361–375.
Carver, C.S. (1997). The internal-external scale confounds internal locus of control with expectancies of positive outcomes. *Personality and Social Psychology Bulletin, 23,* 580–585.
Carver, C.S. and Scheier, M.F. (1990). Principles of self-regulation: Action and emotion. In E.T. Higgins and R.M. Sorrentino (eds.), *Handbook of motivation and cognition: Foundations of social behavior.* New York: Guilford.
Carver, C.S. and Scheier, M.F. (1994). Optimism and health-related cognition: What variables actually matter? *Psychology and Health, 9,* 191–195.
Collins, R.L., Taylor, S.E., and Skogan, L.A. (1990). A better world or shattered vision? Changes in life perspectives following victimization. *Social Cognition, 8,* 263–285.
Coyne, J.C., Ellard, J.H., and Smith, D.A.F. (1990). Social support, interdependence, and the dilemmas of helping. In B.R. Sarason, I.G. Sarason & C.R. Pierce (Eds.), *Social Support: An Interactional View.* New York: Wiley.
Downey, G., Silver, R.C., and Wortman, C.B. (1990). Reconsidering the attribution-adjustment relation following a major negative event: Coping with the loss of a child. *Journal of Personality and Social Psychology, 59,* 925–940.
Duckworth, D. (1986). Psychological problems arising from disaster work. *Stress Medicine, 2,* 315–323.
Dweck, C.S. (1975). The role of expectations and attributions in the alleviation of learned helplessness. *Journal of Personality and Social Psychology, 31,* 674–685.
Edward, K.E. and MacLeod, M.D. (1996). *Blame, beliefs and recovery: An examination of factors affecting victim recovery from sexual and non-sexual crimes.* Paper presented at the VI European Conference on Psychology and Law, Siena.
Fincham, F., Beach, S., and Baucom, D. (1987). Attributional processes in distressed and non-distressed couples. *Journal of Personality and Social Psychology, 52,* 739–748.
Frasure-Smith, N., Lesperance, F., and Taljic, M. (1993). Depression following myocardial infarction: Impact on 6-month survival. *Journal American Medical Association, 270,* 1819–1825.
Frazier, P.A. (1990). Victim attributions and post-rape trauma. *Journal of Personality and Social Psychology, 59,* 298–304.
Frazier, P.A. and Schauben, L. (1994). Causal attributions and recovery from rape and other stressful life events. *Journal of Social and Clinical Psychology, 13,* 1–14
Freedy, J.R., Resnick, H.S., Kilpatrick, D.G., Dansky, B.S., and Tidwell, R.P. (1994). The psychological adjustment of recent crime victims in the criminal justice system. *Journal of Interpersonal Violence, 9,* 450–468.
Gilutz, H., Bar-On, D., Billing, E., Rehnquist, N., and Cristal, N. (1991). The relationship between causal attribution and rehabilitation in patients after their first myocardial infarction: A cross cultural study. *European Heart Journal, 12,* 883–888.

Gold, D.B. and Wegner, D.M. (1995). Origins of ruminative thought: Trauma, incompleteness, nondisclosure, and suppression. *Journal of Applied Social Psychology 25*, 1245–1261.

Gotay, C. (1985). Why me? Attributions and adjustment by cancer patients and their mates at two stages of the disease process. *Social Science and Medicine, 20*, 825–831.

Gross, A.E., Wallston, B.S., and Pilliavin, I.M. (1980). The help recipient's perspective, In D.H. Smith and J. McCalay (Eds.), *Participation in Social and Political Activities.* San Francisco: Josey Bass.

Horneffer, K. and Fincham, F. (1996). Attributional modes of depression and marital distress. *Personality and Social Psychology Bulletin, 22*, 678–689.

James, W. (1884). What is an emotion? *Mind, 9.*

James, W. (1912). Essays *in Radical Empiricism.* London: Longmans, Green.

Janoff-Bulman, R. (1979). Characterological versus behavioural self-blame: Inquiries into depression and rape. *Journal of Personality and Social Psychology, 37*, 1798–1809.

Janoff-Bulman, R. (1982). Esteem and control bases of blame: 'Adaptive' strategies for victims versus observers. *Journal of Personality, 50*, 180–192,

Janoff-Bulman, R. (1985). The aftermath of victimization: Rebuilding shattered assumptions. In C. R. Figley (Ed.), *Trauma and its wake.* New York: Brunner/Mazel.

Janoff-Bulman, R. (1992). *Shattered assumptions: Towards a new psychology of trauma.* New York: Free Press.

Joseph, S.A. Brewin, C.R., Yule, W., and Williams, R. (1991). Causal attributions and psychiatric symptoms in survivors of the Herald of Free Enterprise disaster. *British Journal of Psychiatry, 159*, 542–546.

Kahler, A.S. and MacLeod, M.D. (1996). Blame, revenge and the bereavement process. Paper presented at the XXVI International Congress of Psychology, Ottawa. *International Journal of Psychology, 31* (3–4), 3174.

Kanazawa, S. (1992). Outcome or expectancy? Antecedent of spontaneous causal attribution. *Personality and Social Psychology Bulletin, 18*, 659–668.

Katz, M.R., Rodin, G., and Devins, G.M. (1995). Self-esteem and cancer: Theory and research. *Canadian Journal of Psychiatry, 40*, 608–615.

Kiecolt-Glaser, J.K., and Williams, D.A. (1987). Self-blame, compliance, and distress among burn patients. *Journal of Personality and Social Psychology, 53*, 187–193.

Lefcourt, H.M. (1991). Locus of control. In J.P. Robinson, P.R. Shaver, and L.S. Wrightsman (eds.), *Measures of personality and social psychological attitudes.* San Diego: Academic Press.

Lerner, M.J. and Miller, D.T. (1978). Just world research and the attribution process. Looking back and ahead. *Psychological Bulletin, 85*, 1030–1051.

Lowery, B.J., Jacobsen, B.S., Cera, M.A., McIndoe, D., Kleman, M., and Menapace, F. (1992). Attention versus avoidance: Attributional search and denial after myocardial infarction. *Heart and Lung, 21*, 523–528.

Lowery, B.J., Jacobsen, B.S., and McCauley, K. (1987). On the prevalence of causal search in illness situations. *Nursing Research, 36*, 88–93.

MacLeod, M.D., Carson, L., and Prescott, R.G.W. (1996). *Listening to victims: Victimisation episodes and the criminal justice system in Scotland.* Edinburgh: HMSO.

MacLeod, M.D. and Paton, D. (in press). Police officers and violent crime: Social psychological perspectives on impact and recovery. In J. Violante and D. Paton (eds.), *Police trauma: Psychological aftermath of civilian combat.* Springfield, Illinois: Charles C. Thomas.

Macrae, C.N. (1989). The good, the bad, and the ugly: Facial stereotyping and juridic judgements. *The Police Journal, 62*, 194–199.

Macrae, C.N. and Shepherd, J.W (1989a). Do criminal stereotypes mediate juridic judgements? *British Journal of Social Psychology, 28*, 189–191.

Macrae, C.N. and Shepherd, J.W. (1989b). Stereotypes and social judgements. *British Journal of Social Psychology, 28*, 319–325.

Malcarne, V.L., Compas, B.E., Epping-Jordan, J.E., and Howell, D.C. (1995). Cognitive factors in adjustment to cancer: Attributions of self-blame and perceptions of control. *Journal of Behavioural Medicine, 18,* 401–417

McCann, I. and Pearlman, L. (1990). *Psychological trauma and the adult survivor.* New York: Brunner/Mazel,

Meyer, C.B. and Taylor, S.E., (1986). Adjustment to rape. *Journal of Personality and Social Psychology, 50,* 1226–1234.

Miller, J. (1984). Culture and the development of everyday social explanation. *Journal of Personality and Social Psychology, 24,* 1063–1075.

Nisbett, R.E. and Wilson, T.D. (1977). Telling more than we can know: Verbal reports on mental processes. *Psychological Review, 84,* 231–259.

Paton, D., Cox, D.E.H., and Andrew, C. (1989). *A preliminary investigation into stress in rescue workers.* R.G.I.T Applied Social Science Report, No. 1.

Reich, J.W. and Zautra, A.J. (1991). Experimental and measurement approaches to internal control in at-risk older adults. *Journal of Social Issues, 47,* 143–158.

Shaver, H.G. (1985). *The attribution of blame: Causality, responsibility, and blameworthiness.* New York: Springer-Verlag.

Shaver, K.G. and Drown, D. (1986). On causality, responsibility, and self-blame: A theoretical note. *Journal of Personality and Social Psychology, 50,* 697–702.

Shepherd, J.W. and Ellis, H.D. (1973). The effect of attractiveness on recognition memory for faces. *American Journal of Psychology, 86,* 627–633.

Shepherd, J.W., Ellis, H.D., McMurran, M., and Davies, G.M. (1978). Effect of character attribution on photofit reconstruction of a face. *European Journal of Social Psychology, 8,* 263–268.

Silver, R. and Wortman, C. (1980). Coping with undesirable life events. In J. Garber and M. Seligmam (Eds.), *Human helplessness* (pp. 279–340). New York: Academic Press.

Suls, J. and Fletcher, B. (1985). The relative efficacy of avoidant and non-avoidant coping strategies: A meta analysis. *Health Psychology, 4,* 249–288.

Taylor, S.E. (1983). Adjustment to threatening events: A theory of cognitive adaptation. *American Psychologist, 38,* 1161–1173.

Taylor, S.E., Helgeson, V.S., Reed, G.M., and Skogan, L.A. (1991). Self-generated feelings of control and adjustment to physical illness. *Journal of Social Issues, 47,* 91–109,

Taylor, S.E., Lichtman, R.R., and Wood, J.V. (1984). Attributions, beliefs about control and adjustment to breast cancer. *Journal of Personality and Social Psychology, 46,* 489–502.

Tennen, H. and Affleck, G. (1990). Blaming others for threatening events. Psychological *Bulletin, 108,* 209–232.

Tennen, H., Affleck, G., and Gershman, K. (1986). Self-blame among parents of infants with perinatal complications: The role of self-protective motives. *Journal of Personality and Social Psychology, 50,* 690–696.

Thompson, S.C., Cheek, P.R., and Graham, M.A. (1988). The other side of perceived control: Disadvantages and negative effects. In S. Spacapan and S. Oskamp (eds.), *The social psychology of health.* Beverly Hills, CA: Sage.

Thompson, S.C. and Collins, M.A. (1995). Applications of perceived control to cancer: An overview of theory and measurement. *Journal of Psychosocial Oncology, 13,* 11–26.

Thompson, S.C., Sobolew-Shubin, A., Galbraith, M., Schwankovsky, L., and Cruzen, D. (1993). Maintaining perceptions of control: Finding perceived control in low-control circumstances. *Journal of Personality, and Social Psychology 64,* 293–304.

Thompson, S.C. and Spacapan, S. (1991). Perceptions of control in vulnerable populations. *Journal of Social Issues, 47,* 1–21.

Timko, C. and Janoff-Bulman, R. (1985). Attribution, vulnerability and psychological adjustment: The case of breast cancer. *Health Psychology, 4,* 521–546.

Turnquist, D., Harvey, J., and Andersen, B. (1988). Attributions and adjustment to life-threatening illness. *British Journal of Clinical Psychology, 27,* 55–65.

Wallston, K.A. (1992). Hocus-pocus, the focus isn't strictly on locus: Rotter's social learning theory modified for health. *Cognitive Therapy and Research, 16,* 183–199.

Wegner, D.M. (1992). You can't always think what you want: Problems in the suppression of unwanted thoughts. In M. Zanna (Ed.), *Advances in experimental social psychology, vol. 25.* San Diego: Academic Press.

Wegner, D.M. (1994). *White bears and other unwanted thoughts.* New York: Guilford.

Weinberg, N. (1994). Self-blame, other-blame and desire for revenge: Factors in recovery from bereavement. *Death Studies, 18,* 583–593.

Weiner, B. (1985a). An attributional theory of achievement motivation and emotion. *Psychological Review, 92,* 548–573.

Weiner, B. (1985b). "Spontaneous" causal thinking. *Psychological Bulletin, 97,* 74–84.

Winkel, F.W., Denkers, A., and Vrij, A. (1994). The effects of attributions on crime victims' psychological readjustment. *Genetic, Social and General Psychology Monographs, 120,* 147–168.

What's in a Name, What's in a Place? The Role of Verbal Labels in Distinct Cognitive Tasks

**J.B. DERĘGOWSKI, D.M. PARKER, and
P. MCGEORGE**
University of Aberdeen

The effects of congruent and incongruent labelling on two simple cognitive tasks, sequence learning and place learning, were investigated. The results of both studies indicate the greater cognitive importance of information derived from the object compared to information derived from the verbal label.

Stroop (1935) observed that when a spoken response is requested to a stimulus containing perceptually incongruent cues, that response requires a longer processing time than does an identical response when the cues are congruent. Thus a response "red" to the word "green" written in red ink takes longer than the response "red" to a row of five red Xs. This kind of interference (the Stroop effect) occurs in a variety of stimuli. McLeod (1991) in his extensive review of the Stroop effect lists several studies concerned with picture-word interference, which showed that when words are presented within outline figures, naming of the incongruently labelled depicted objects is much slower than naming of congruently labelled depicted objects and of unlabelled pictures. Gerhand, Deręgowski, and McAllister (1995) found that the Stroop effect also occurs when real objects are used. Subjects, it was found, take significantly longer to name objects that are incorrectly labelled (so that the resultant stimuli are incongruent) than they take to name correctly labelled objects (i.e., congruent stimuli). Thus the phenomenon occurs not only when symbolic entities, such as pictures, are contrasted with their descriptors but also when real objects extended in space are used. In all these cases linguistic labelling appears to dominate the responses. It may do so because the responses are linguistic, but it may also be a general characteristic of the cognitive system which, whatever the task, is dominated by language. This possibility is augmented by Levinson's (1995) reports of the spatial skills of the Guugu-Yimithirr whose spatial descriptors, which are related to geographical coordinates, appear to correlate with their unusually well-developed spatial skills. Davies and Corbett's (1997) study on the effect of language on color categorisation by the Tswana supports such contention.

There is, however, also a body of contradictory evidence. Paivio and his co-workers (Paivio, 1991) have argued that the representation and processing of information in human cognition is based on two symbolic systems. Each of these separate but interconnected systems deals with a distinct type of information. One system, the verbal system, is specialized for dealing with language. The second system is specialized for dealing with non-verbal, image-based information. There are important differences in the nature of the functional organization of the two coding systems; the verbal system can be described in terms of symbolic structures that are organized in a sequential fashion, while those of the non-verbal system are organized in a hierarchical fashion. Thus, the verbal system is suited to storing and retrieving sequential information but not spatial information, while the non-verbal (imaginal) system shows the opposite pattern of specializations. An effect of these different specializations was demonstrated by Paivio and Csapo (1971). They presented subjects with a series of words or pictures, fast or slowly, and subjects were then required to arrange a series of small blocks bearing the stimulus items in the order in which the items had been presented. The aim of fast presentation was, in the case of picture stimuli, to reduce the availability of the verbal code. The results indicated that subjects' ability to recall the order of presentation was poorest when pictures were presented fast. There were no differences in the recall accuracy of words presented at two presentation rates, or for words and pictures presented slowly. The results indicate that sequence learning is facilitated by each stimulus having a verbal tag. In summary, and based on dual coding theory, the evidence suggests that tasks that require the learning of information about sequential structure should be accomplished optimally using verbal coding, while tasks that require the learning of spatial relationships should be accomplished optimally using non-verbal coding.

Although Paivio and Csapo used pictures of objects, their results can be extrapolated to objects. The extrapolation is justified by the very assumption of dual coding, since the same verbal code must apply to pictures and the depicted objects. However, empirical findings have shown that in similar circumstances objects evoke analogous but stronger responses than do their portrayals. It could be argued that objects, unlike words and pictures, do not represent concepts but exemplify them. Evidence for the relatively greater perceptual cogency of objects in a variety of settings has been reported by several investigators. For example, children find it easier to categorize objects than pictures (Deręgowski and Serpell, 1971; Sigel, 1978). When children are asked to show how a tool is used, they mime the action more vigorously when shown the tool itself than when shown a picture (Klapper and Birch, 1969). Deręgowski and Jahoda (1975) used objects, pictures, and words in an experiment in which the subjects were required to learn to associate stimuli with places marked on a table. It was found that the difficulty of the task was least when objects themselves were used, greater when pictures of these objects were used, and greatest when labels bearing names of objects were used. Since both an object and its depiction share the same verbal code, the advantage of objects over pictures must lie in their ability to generate a more robust non-verbal code.

The present investigation is concerned with the importance of information derived from objects in comparison with information derived from verbal labels. It assesses the extent to which labelling of objects affects subjects' performance on two types of task: (i) a sequence learning task in which the subject has to learn the order of stimuli presented one after the other in the same place, and (ii) a place learning task in which the subject has to learn places arbitrarily allocated to stimuli. The above speculations suggest that learning of a *sequence* of stimuli should be accomplished optimally using verbal coding, whilst learning of a spatial arrangement should be accomplished optimally using a non-verbal code.

Four principal types of stimulus are possible: unlabelled objects, labelled objects (such labelling can either be correct, leading to congruent stimuli, or incorrect, leading to incongruent stimuli), and labels only. A familiar unlabelled object will generate both an imaginal code and an associated verbal code. A correctly labelled object will also generate an imaginal and verbal code (there may be some advantage in having the verbal code activated both by the object and the attached label). In the case of an incorrectly labelled object, the object will generate both an imaginal and verbal code but the label will generate a competing verbal code. It seems plausible that competition between these two verbal codes will reduce the efficiency of the verbal system and increase reliance on the imaginal code. A mere label will result in the formation of a verbal code alone.

EXPERIMENT 1: THE ROLE OF LABELS IN A SEQUENCE LEARNING TASK

According to Paivio (1991), the verbal system can be described in terms of symbolic structures that are naturally organised in a sequential fashion. As such, the verbal system has an advantage over the imaginal system when the task requires the learning of sequential structure. Using unlabelled objects (Ob), congruent stimuli (Cs); objects with congruent labels—incongruent stimuli (Is); objects with incongruent labels—labels alone (La), the following predictions can be made concerning performance on the sequence learning task. Performance should be best under conditions where both the verbal code and the imaginal code are available. Therefore, sequences involving unlabelled objects and congruent stimuli should be learned most easily. It might be expected that there would be some advantage for congruent stimuli over objects without labels. The verbal code associated with congruent stimuli is activated twice, once by the object and once by the accompanying label. In the case of an unlabelled object, it is activated only once. Sequences of unlabelled objects should be learned more readily than labels alone, since objects generate both codes, and labels only one. Sequences involving the presentation of labels alone should be learned more readily than those of sequences involving incongruent stimuli. Labels generate a verbal code (optimal for sequence learning) whilst, in incongruent stimuli, the competing effects of the verbal code generated by seeing the object and the verbal code generated by the label should reduce the efficacy of the verbal code relative to the imaginal code and so impair sequence learning. The expected sequence would therefore be Cs>Ob>La>Is.

It should be noted that this predicted sequence differs from that derived from the reading speed of the label. In this case, both Fraisse's (1968) observations that it takes longer to name a picture than to read its name, and the results of Gerhand's (1995) experiment suggest that the condition in which only labels are used should prove easiest, since the information from these is most rapidly acquired, the order of the remaining three conditions being unchanged. The expected sequence would therefore be La>Cs>Ob>Is. In view of the discrepancy between the two predicted sequences, it was decided to obtain a sequence empirically.

Method

Subjects. Forty-eight paid subjects (twenty-four men and twenty-four women; mean age: 20 years; s.d. = 4 years) drawn from the Aberdeen University student subject panel were used. Men and women were randomly allocated to four groups of twelve subjects, each of which contained six men. Each group responded to one type of stimulus only.

Procedure. The apparatus was constructed using three identical arrays of each of the two types of items namely:

(i) twelve common household objects, and
(ii) A set of twelve labels displaying the names of the objects.

Four sets of stimuli were constructed using these elements:

(a) a set of objects on their own;
(b) a set of labels on their own;
(c) a set of congruently labelled objects; and
(d) a set of incongruently labelled objects.

The subject sat at a table facing the experimenter, and told that they were to participate in a sequence learning task in which an object/label would be shown, and they would have to give the name of the next object/label in a series, but first the entire set of objects/labels would be displayed to them. They were then shown, for about thirty seconds, all twelve stimuli displayed on a table. The display was covered, and the stimuli were presented in the sequence in which they were to be learned. Four random sequences of stimuli were used, each subject being allocated randomly to one of these. Following the introductory presentation, the subject was presented with the first object/label of the sequence and asked to name the second; when the subject had done so, whether correctly or not, the second stimulus of the sequence was presented, and the subject requested to name the third, and so on. The sequence was presented repeatedly either until the subject gave eleven correct responses (the largest number possible) on two consecutive runs, or until the subject had completed ten runs. The sequential number of the trial preceding the two criterial trials was taken as the subject's score. When the criterion was not reached, the score was taken to be ten.

Results

The trials to criterion scores obtained were subjected to an Analysis of Variance which yielded a significant effect of stimulus type: $F(3,44) = 5.1$, $p < 0.005$. The mean scores obtained with the four types of stimuli were: (i) Objects: 2.3 (s.d. = 1.7), (ii) Congruent Stimuli: 3.7 (s.d. = 2.0), (iii) Incongruent Stimuli: 4.7 (s.d. = 1.4), (iv) Labels: 5.7 (s.d. = 3. 1).

These means were compared using Newman-Keuls test and it was found that the responses to objects and those to congruent stimuli did not differ significantly nor did the responses to congruent stimuli, incongruent stimuli, and labels. All other differences were significant at the 5 percent level.

Discussion

The data clearly do not agree with expectations derived from Fraisse's (1968) findings. Absence of a significant discrepancy between responses to congruent and incongruent stimuli is contrary to such expectations, although the direction of the difference is as predicted, as is the evident absence of superiority of Congruent stimuli over Objects. In addition and more significantly, responses obtained with Labels are worst, whereas they were expected to be the best.

The order of scores obtained with the various groups of stimuli does not appear to agree with the predicted sequence derived on the basis of dual coding theory. As predicted, sequences of unlabelled objects and sequences of congruent stimuli are learned most readily. However, contrary to expectations, there is a small numeric (but not significant) advantage for unlabelled objects over congruent stimuli as opposed to the opposite pattern. It would appear that the addition of a second and faster route to the generation of a verbal code for the stimulus conveys no additional advantage. Again, contrary to predictions, sequences of labels are learned no more readily than sequences of incongruent stimuli. Indeed, there is no significant difference in the ease with which sequences are learned whether the stimuli are labels, incongruent stimuli, or congruent stimuli.

It may be that the Stroop-type interference, which was observed by Gerhand et al. (1995) when subjects were asked to name objects with incongruent labels, explains these results. When a label is present, the associated verbal code becomes available more quickly than the verbal code associated with the object. So, for congruent stimuli, incongruent stimuli, and labels on their own, the verbal code associated with the label becomes available quickly. (In the case of the incongruent stimuli this would conflict with the verbal code generated by the object.) The speed with which this verbal code becomes available may present subjects with the opportunity to focus on this code to the possible exclusion of the codes (verbal and imagined) generated by the object. The possibility that subjects may adopt this strategy is increased when, as in this experiment, subjects are free to adopt any strategy when learning the sequence. From this perspective, congruent stimuli, incongruent stimuli, and labels on their own result in equivalent verbal codes, and sequences composed of these stimuli are learned with approximately equal ease. The object only stimuli lack the fast label route to a verbal code, and so subjects generate and make use of both the imaginal and verbal codes. Since the object only stimuli are learned with greatest ease, the availability of the imaginal code does enhance performance. This is also apparent in the case of the congruent and incongruent stimuli, where there is a small but non-significant advantage for stimuli including the object (congruent and incongruent stimuli) over labels alone.

This experiment has demonstrated that, while sequence learning can be achieved using a verbal code, it is enhanced by the availability of an imaginal code and it indicates that the strategy adopted by subjects may play an important role in the ease with which learning occurs. In the second experiment, the role of verbal and imaginal codes in a spatial learning task was investigated, and variations in the instructions given to subjects used to examine the effect of focusing attention on the verbal or object component of the compound stimuli.

EXPERIMENT 2: THE EFFECT OF VERBAL LABELS ON A
PLACE LEARNING TASK

The first experiment examined the relative importance of verbal and imaginal codes in a sequence learning task, a task which should have been achieved optimally using a verbal code. This experiment examines the relative contributions of imaginal and verbal codes in a spatial learning task. According to dual coding theory, spatial learning is achieved optimally using an imaginal code. This suggests that performance should be about equal for the unlabelled objects and congruent stimuli—both are equivalent in terms of the availability of an imaginal code. Performance with incongruent stimuli should be better than with labels alone, as labels on their own would not normally be expected to lead to a robust imaginal code. The expected sequence would therefore be: Cs=Ob>=Is>La.

In addition, and because of the possibility that strategic influences may have contributed to the results obtained in the first experiment, it was decided to regulate the strategies adopted by subjects in respect of the different elements of the stimuli by using two variants of instructions. In one of these variants subjects' attention was drawn to the objects and in another to the labels. Such stressing is expected to augment the influence of the stressed element on the subjects' learning, and thus show the extent to which the non-stressed element can be disregarded. The results obtained under Stroop conditions (McLeod, 1991) show that such disregard of the irrelevant element does not occur when the irrelevant element is the verbal label.

Method

Subjects. One hundred and twenty students (sixty men, sixty women, mean age: twenty-two years; s.d. = seven years) drawn from the Aberdeen University student subject panel took part in the study. They were randomly allocated to groups of twelve persons, six men and six women each.

Design and Procedure. Two of the groups were selected at random for determination of the datum levels of performance. These groups participated only in the first phase of the experiment consisting of eight trials during which they learned the locations of the stimuli. The stimuli used with these groups were unlabelled objects and labels on their own, respectively. These groups are referred to as "solo" groups.

The remaining eight groups responded to composite stimuli. These groups participated in a two-stage procedure and are referred to as "consecutive" groups. In the first stage (the training stage), consisting of eight trials, the subjects learned the allocations of composite stimuli to locations, and in the second stage (the verification stage) the effects of this learning were assessed. Four of the "consecutive" groups, chosen at random, learned the allocation of the congruent and four the incongruent stimuli. The procedure used in the first phase of the experiment was essentially identical to that used with the "solo" groups, but for the fact that the experimenter in his instructions to the subjects stressed either the "object" (four groups) or the "label" (four groups) characteristics of the stimuli. To this end, one set of instructions (Object) referred to the stimulus as "this object" and stressed that the subject had to learn the placing of objects. Another set (Label) drew the subject's attention to the label and instructed the subject to learn the placing of the labels, implying strongly that the objects to which the labels were attached were irrelevant. For all eight "consecutive" groups, this training phase was followed by a verification phase. Subjects were told that the task had changed; they were to continue with the previous procedure by learning the appropriate place for each stimulus (with the same stimulus as previously), but that either the stimulus labels would be removed (four groups) or they were now to learn the appropriate place for each label presented. Thus, the verification phase endeavoured to assess how well subjects had learned to associate particular locations with the two features of the stimulus, the object and the label.

All the subjects were tested individually: the subject and the experimenter sat opposite each other at a table that bore four green squares (of 20 cm side) placed in a line perpendicular to the subject's median plane and with 2 cm gaps between them.

At the beginning of the training phase, subjects of all groups were told that three of the stimuli belonged to each green square and that they would be required to learn to which square each stimulus belonged. They were also told that on the first trial they would have to guess. Following instructions, the experimenter produced the first stimulus and the subject indicated one of the squares. The stimulus was placed in this square, and the subject told whether the choice made was right or wrong. The stimulus was then removed and the next stimulus presented. The correctness of the choice was judged by reference to a schedule created for each subject before the experiment. In this schedule the stimuli were randomly allocated to four groups of three, one group to each square. The stimuli were randomised before each presentation. Each subject was presented with eight different random sequences of the stimulus set, and on each of the eight runs the number of stimuli correctly placed by the subject was recorded. The procedure used in the second stage of the experiment was identical as far as the subjects' task was concerned. It differed from the procedure of the first stage in that only two varieties of stimuli were used: objects on their own and labels on their own. (Table 1)

RESULTS

The results obtained from the two "solo" groups (Groups 1 and 2) are presented graphically in Figure 1, the graph shows mean number of correct responses at each trial. Subjects in Group 1 responded to objects only, subjects in Group 2 to labels only. It is apparent from the graph that the mean number of correct responses when objects were used was consistently higher than the number of correct responses when labels were used. This difference is not, however, statistically significant, as Analysis of Variance comparing individual total scores shows $(F(1, 20) = 1.93, p = 0.18)$.

The data obtained from subjects in the "consecutive" groups were analysed by considering separately responses made in the first eight training trials, and the eight verification trials. Each subject's performance was therefore defined in terms of *two measures*, each measure being simply the total of correct responses made during a run of eight trials. These measures are referred to as training scores, and verification scores.

1. *Training trials data.* Analysis of variance of the data obtained from the "consecutive" groups yielded no significant main effect of congruence or instruction bias, but a significant interaction between congruence and instruction $(F(1,92) = 3.9, p = 0.05)$. Analysis of these data for simple effects indicates that there is one significant difference; subjects instructed to attend to labels perform significantly worse than do subjects instructed to attend to objects when incongruent stimuli are used $(p = 0.02)$.

TABLE 1
Experiment 2: Summary of group characteristics as a function of population sampled, training and test procedures.

Nature of the stimulus	Feature of stimulus stressed in training trials	Type of stimulus used in verification trials	Group number
OBJECT	"OBJECT"	OBJECT (12)	1
LABEL	"LABEL"	LABEL (12)	2
CONGRUENT	"OBJECT"	OBJECT (12)	3
		LABEL (12)	4
INCONGRUENT	"OBJECT"	OBJECT (12)	5
		LABEL (12)	6
CONGRUENT	"LABEL"	OBJECT (12)	7
		LABEL (12)	8
INCONGRUENT	"LABEL"	OBJECT (12)	9
		LABEL (12)	10

2. *Verification scores.* Figure 2a shows the mean accuracy scores from groups where subjects' attention was directed towards the objects. Figure 2b shows the mean accuracy scores obtained from the groups where subjects' attention was directed to the labels.

The data obtained from the eight verification trials were analysed using a three-way analysis of variance with the type of training stimuli (congruent/incongruent), type of training instruction (attend to objects/ attend to labels), and the type of verification stimuli employed (objects/labels) as the three factors. The analysis yielded two significant main effects; type of training stimuli ($F(1,88) = 22.6$, $p < 0.001$), and the effect of the type of verification stimuli (objects or labels), ($F(1,88) < 5.61$, $p = 0.03$). Significant interactions were also obtained. These were: Type of training instruction x Type of verification stimulus ($F(1,88) = 2.14$ $p < 0.001$); Type of training stimuli x Type of verification stimulus ($F(1,88) = 5.6$, $p < 0.03$); and Type of training instruction x Type of training stimuli x Type of verification stimulus ($F(1,88) = 9.1$, $p < 0.003$). Mean values for the experimental conditions are given in Table 2.

FIGURE 1
**Experiment 2: Mean number of correct responses as a function of
trial and stimulus type.**

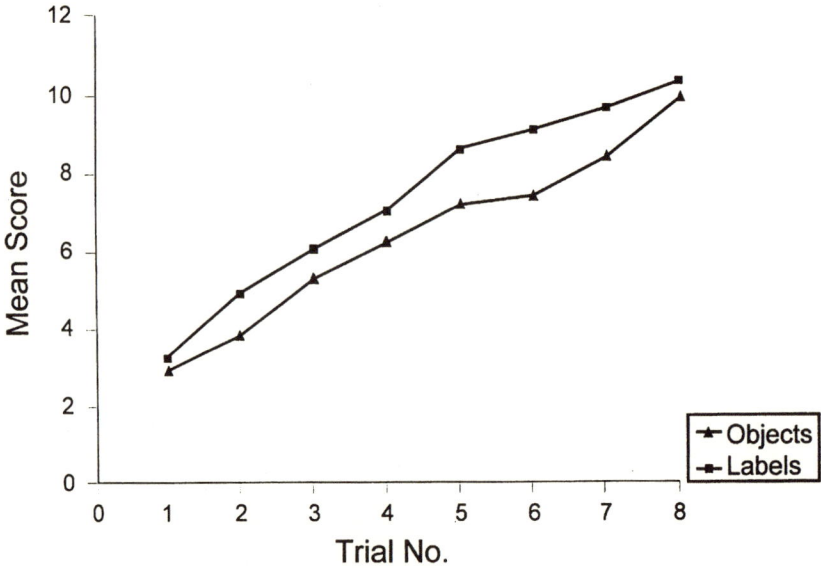

Mean responses of the "solo" groups to Labels and Objects.

Because of the three-way interaction, the responses associated with the congruent and incongruent training stimuli were analyzed separately. For subjects trained using congruent stimuli, analysis of variance of the scores showed no significant effects; both labels and objects were about equally well learned by these subjects. In contrast, scores of subjects trained on the incongruent stimuli showed a highly significant difference associated with the type of verification stimuli $(F(1,44) = 9.4, p < 0.005)$ and a highly significant interaction of the type of verification stimulus and the initial instruction $(F(1,44) = 24.4, p < 0.0001)$. Simple effects analysis showed that there were highly significant differences between scores within the following pairs of variables: (i) the nature of instruction (object/label) when objects were used in the verification trials, $(F(1,44) = 13.7, p = 0.0001;$ Mean values: Object 91.3, Label 70.6), (ii) the nature of instruction (object/label) when labels are used in the verification trials, $(F(1,44) = 10.8, p < 0.003;$ Mean values: Object 59.7, Label 78.0), and (iii) the effect of objects and labels in the verification trials following

FIGURE 2
Experiment 2: Mean number of correct responses as a function of trial
and congruency of object and label for (a) attention initially directed
to objects, (b) attention initially directed to labels.

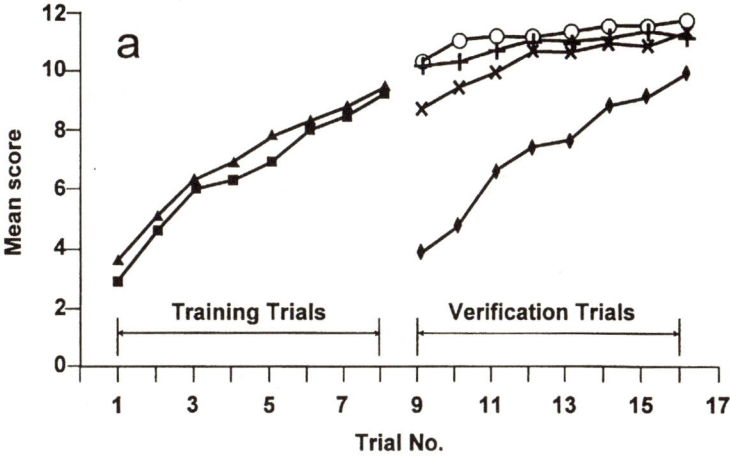

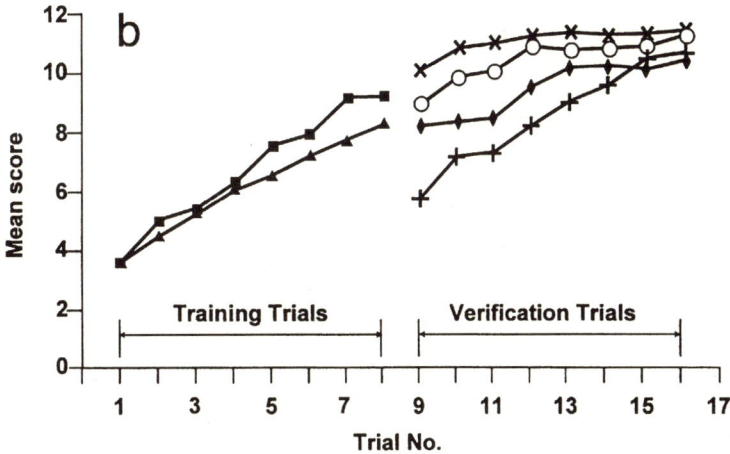

(a) Mean responses of subjects instructed to attend to objects.
(b) Mean responses of subjects instructed to attend to labels.

TABLE 2
Experiment 2: Mean number of correct responses as a function of training conditions.

Stage I: Type of stimulus used for training/Instructions given to subject				
	Congruent		Incongruent	
Type of verification stimulus	"Attend to Object"	"Attend to Label"	"Attend to Object"	"Attend to Label"
Object	88.1 (a)	85.9(a)	9 1.3 (b)	70.6(d)
Label	84.0(a)	90.0(a)	59.7(c)	78.0 (d)

Note: N.B. Means indexed with same letter do not differ significantly.

instructions that objects should be attended to (F(1,44) = 32.1, $p <$ 0.001; Mean values: Object 91.3, Label 59.7).

DISCUSSION

In summary, consistency matters; the scores tend to be higher when the verification stimuli are consistent with the initial instructions used than when these are inconsistent. They also are higher when subjects are enjoined to attend to objects. The use of labels on verification trials appears to affect scores much more than use of objects on verification trials after the injunction to attend to labels.

The training trials yield a significant interaction between the types of stimuli (congruent and incongruent) and the nature of the instructions given to the subjects (attend to the object or the label). For incongruent stimuli, an instruction that subjects should attend to objects yields significantly higher scores than an instruction that they should attend to labels. In the case of congruent stimuli, locations are learned about equally well irrespective of whether subjects are asked to attend to objects or labels.

In the case of incongruent stimuli, the label should result in the generation of a verbal code, while the object should result in the generation of both a conflicting, verbal code *and* an associated imaginal code. Stroop findings indicate that the verbal code generated by a label becomes available very quickly, and this then interferes with subjects' ability to name the object in incongruent stimuli. The second experiment appears to represent the opposite effect to this traditional Stroop interference. The interference observed in the second experiment is greatest under conditions in which subjects are instructed to attend to the label. It therefore appears that the imaginal code is of particular importance when subjects are learning spatial positions.

The results obtained in the course of the verification trials show no significant effects for congruent stimuli. It appears that, after learning to associate congruent stimuli with specific spatial locations, transfer to objects alone or labels alone is equally easy.

In the case of incongruent stimuli, instruction as to what characteristic of the stimulus should be attended to in the training trials affects the responses when either objects or labels are used in the verification trials in the expected manner. When subjects learning the locations of the incongruent stimuli are instructed to attend to objects, their performance on the verification trials differs depending on whether objects (mean score: 91.3) or labels (mean score: 59.7) are used; performance with labels is markedly worse. Furthermore, performance on the first verification trials (see Figure 2) suggests that transfer of incidental learning (with incongruent stimuli) is markedly worse when, after attending to objects, subjects are required to learn the positions of labels than it is when, after being instructed to attend to labels, subjects are tested with objects; in the former case, the result does not differ from chance. It would appear that the object attributes rather than the verbal attributes (as enshrined in the labels) of the stimuli are associated with the locations. The results of these verification trials confirm those of the training trials. Objects dominate the process. Labels affect the outcome only when drawn to subjects' attention by specific overt instructions. It is noteworthy, however, that even when this is done, there is no significant difference between response scores to objects and labels on verification trials.

In order to check whether these results generalize to a broader population, the experiment was partially replicated on a sample of subjects drawn from the general public (mean age forty-three years, s.d. = fourteen years). The procedure used was identical with that already described, but only the effect of drawing subjects' attention to the object was explored. Comparison of the scores of corresponding samples from the general public panel and the student panel showed that the former scored less on the training trials ($F(1,44) = 5.9$, $p < 0.02$), but there were no other significant differences. This implies that, as one would expect, the general public panel subjects learn less speedily than do students, there was no evidence of a differential effect of the two types of stimulus (object/label) on learning in the two populations (the relevant mean scores were: students; object, 59.3, label, 51.5; general public; object, 55.1, label, 47.0). Analysis of variance of the scores obtained from the two populations on the verification trials yielded no significant effects whatsoever. There appears, therefore, to be no evidence against the tentative generalisation from the results obtained to a wider population.

GENERAL DISCUSSION

Published findings and the results obtained suggest that there are marked differences in the extent to which verbal and non-verbal parameters of stimuli affect performance. On Stroop-like tasks, where speed of processing is dominated by the verbal labels, this is shown by the fact that labelled objects are responded to more quickly than unlabelled objects and that congruity of labelling is more advantageous than incongruity (Gerhand et al., 1995). The role of labels is less when subjects are required to learn a sequence of stimuli (Experiment 1) even though subjects are compelled to use the names of the stimuli in the course of learning. Congruency, the data show, offers no advantage over unlabelled objects and labels on their own are treated no differently from labelled stimuli (both congruent and incongruent) and yield the lowest score. The role of labels is clearly secondary when subjects are required to learn the spatial locations of stimuli (Experiment 2). This is cogently demonstrated by considering the irrelevant feature of a stimulus as a distractor. The efficacy of a distractor depends on both the initial instructions and the verification task. When the initial instructions and the verification procedure are consistent (e.g., "attend to objects" on initial trials; "learn location of objects" on verification trials) then the distractor efficacy of the irrelevant attribute (in this case label) is low; when they are inconsistent (e.g. "attend to labels"; "learn locations of objects") then it is high. Taking into account the two variables: the nature of the distractor (object or label) and its strength (high or low), the verification scores obtained from students trained on incongruent stimuli were subjected to analysis of variance. The analysis yielded two main effects: that of the nature of the distractor ($F(1,44) = 9.39$, $p < 0.005$); and the strength of the distractor ($F(1,44) = 24.5$, $p < 0.001$). The object appears to be a significantly stronger distractor than the label, the scores forming the following sequence: Os (60), Ls (71), Ow (78), Lw (91) wherein O = object, L = label, s = strong, w = weak, and the bracketed numbers are the approximate mean scores.

This analysis suggests that it is hazardous to extrapolate from a particular cognitive task to cognition in general when considering the relative importance of objects and their labels for cognitive operations. Indeed, careful consideration of Paivio's dual- coding theory demonstrates the dangers.

It is clear from the pattern of the results reported here that verbal processes do not significantly affect the learning of a sequence or the spatial location of objects when teamed with object-based instructions. Irrelevant labels, despite evidence that they are processed, do not disrupt learning, but subjects seem able to transfer from object to label with ease. When trained with label-based instructions, irrelevant objects cause a serious disruption of learning. Furthermore, this occurs even when learning sequences objects are superior to names. It seems unlikely then that Paivio's (1991) proposal that verbal coding is required for reasonable performance of sequential presentation tasks is true.

The results are concordant with those of Kearins' (1981, 1986) extensive studies of recall of the spatial arrangements of objects. Australian children of both Aborigine and European origin served as subjects, and two sets of objects were used. In one set, the objects were from different categories (they were either man-made, e.g., a knife, an eraser, or a thimble, or natural objects, e.g., a feather, a leaf, or a flower). The other set was composed of objects from the same category (different kinds of bottles or different pieces of rock). The "different category" objects enjoy well established linguistic support, since there are distinct names for various objects in this set, but there are no distinct names (at least not in common parlance) for variously shaped bottles or pieces of rock. Kearins found that the Aborigine subjects consistently made fewer errors than did the white Australians on all the tasks, and that in the case of the Aborigine subjects there was no significant difference between the scores obtained using "natural" stimuli (with which they are likely to have been familiar and for which they probably had distinctive names) and the artefactual stimuli (which are likely to have been unfamiliar to them and the names of which they are unlikely to have known). Thus, Aborigine responses do not appear to be greatly affected by the existence or not of linguistic categories. Nor can such an influence be readily detected in the responses of the white subjects. These subjects responded correctly to "different artefactual" items more often than to the "different natural" items, but they were likely to have had names for items in both categories. When responding to items that fell in the "same" category, i.e., bottles or rocks, they were correct significantly more often on artefactual items, yet again it seems unlikely that their vocabulary pertaining to bottles was richer than their vocabulary pertaining to rocks. The influence of vocabulary on accuracy of spatial recall, therefore, appears to be questionable.

The relative perceptual weakness of linguistic labels demonstrated by these studies implicitly questions the validity of procedures in which linguistic labelling is used as an index of perceptual process. It demonstrates, for example, that it is probably illegitimate to regard as equivalent pictures of objects and objects (an assumption commonly made in face studies), just because subjects' spoken response to both of them is identical. This caveat agrees with that derivable from earlier studies (Deręgowski and Jahoda, 1975; Sigel, 1978) reviewed in the introduction.

ACKNOWLEDGMENTS

Our thanks to Dr. Norman Wetherick for his most helpful comments on an earlier version of this paper.

REFERENCES

Davies, I.R.L. and Corbett, G.C. (1997). A cross-cultural study of colour grouping: evidence for weak linguistic relativity. *British Journal of Psychology, 88,* 493–517.

Deręgowski, J.B. (1971). Responses mediating pictorial recognition. *Journal of Social Psychology, 84,* 27–33.

Deręgowski, J.B. and Jahoda G. (1971). Efficacy of objects, pictures and words in a simple learning task. *International Journal of Psychology, 10,* 19–25.

Deręgowski, J.B. and Serpell, R. (1971). Performance on a sorting task: A cross-cultural experiment. *International Journal of Psychology, 4,* 273–281.

Fraisse, P. (1968). Motor and verbal reaction times to words and drawings. *Psychonomic Science, 12,* 235–6.

Gerhand, S.J., Deręgowski, J.B., and McAllister, H. (1995). Stroop phenomenon as a measure of cognitive functioning of bilingual (Gaelic/English) subjects. *British Journal of Psychology, 86,* 89–92.

Kearins, J. (1981). Visual spatial memory of Australian Aboriginal children of desert regions. *Cognitive Psychology, 13,* 434–460.

Kearins, J. (1986). Visual spatial memory in Aboriginal and White Australian children. *Australian Journal of Psychiatry, 38,* 203–214.

Klapper, Z.S. and Birch, H.G., (1969). Perceptual and action equivalence of photographs in children. *Perceptual and Motor Skills, 29,* 763–771.

Levinson, S.C. (1995). Language and space. *Annual Review of Anthropology, 25,* 353–382.

McLeod, C.M. (1991). Half a century of research on Stroop effect: An integrative review. *Psychological Bulletin, 109,* 163–203.

Paivio, A. (1991). *Images in Mind: The Evolution of a Theory,* New York: Harvester Wheatsheaf.

Paivio, A. and Csapo, K. (1971). Short-term sequential memory for pictures and words. *Psychonomic Science, 24,* 50–51.

Sigel, I.A. (1978). The development of pictorial comprehension. In B.S. Randhawa and W.E. Coffman (Eds), *Visual Learning, Thinking, and Communication.* New York: Academic Press.

Stroop, J.R. (1935). Studies of interference in serial verbal reactions. *Journal of Experimental Psychology, 18,* 643–662.

On Disregarding Deviants: Exemplar Typicality and Person Perception

C. NEIL MACRAE
University of Bristol

GALEN V. BODENHAUSEN
Northwestern University

ALAN B. MILNE
University of Aberdeen

LUIGI CASTELLI
University of Bologna

A pervasive problem in mental life is that of exemplar selectivity or how one isolates specific category members from other instances of a class. This problem is particularly pronounced in person perception, where perceivers may routinely want to personalize selected individuals while continuing to respond towards other members of the category in a stereotype-based manner. To realize these flexible effects, we hypothesized that, when perceivers encounter a group member, they inevitably encode an exemplar-based representation of the individual in mind. Part of this representation, moreover, is information signaling the person's goodness-of-fit with respect to his or her salient group memberships. When the representation is activated on a subsequent occasion, these inferences of category fit moderate the extent of stereotypical thinking. The results of two studies provided converging evidence for this analysis of stereotype function. Exemplar typicality moderated both the accessibility of stereotypic knowledge (Study 1) anxd the extent to which perceivers used a stereotype to organize information about a target (Study 2). We consider the theoretical and practical implications of these findings for our understanding of the role of stereotypes in person perception.

Upon encountering an unfamiliar person, the social perceiver faces the potentially daunting task of constructing a meaningful and coherent impression of the individual. Rather than start this process from scratch, the wily perceiver is likely to make use of whatever cues are most readily available, such as the person's gender, ethnicity, or apparent occupation. By identifying the social categories to which the target belongs, the perceiver can then rely upon pre-existing beliefs about these groups to solve the task rather effortlessly (Lippmann, 1922; Allport, 1954). If our beliefs about groups were uniformly accurate, this process of stereotyping would be an ideal strategy for social perception. Alas, social realities are not so accommodating. For example, on meeting a scantily clad woman with blonde hair, perceivers may feel that they already know a great deal about her (i.e., a "bimbo" stereotype may be activated). However, a quick glance at the book she is reading may shake them out of their sexist complacency: rather than a Harlequin romance novel, the book is *Principles of Neuroscience*. Clearly it would be fruitless to continue relying upon the bimbo stereotype in construing this particular target. Given that some percentage of blondes fit the bimbo stereotype very badly, how can perceivers deal with these exceptions while still making use of the stereotype in those instances where it does appear to fit the target? This question of selective stereotyping lies at the heart of the present investigation.

DEALING WITH DISCONFIRMATION

Conventional wisdom deals with the above problem in a relatively straightforward manner. When category disconfirmation occurs, perceivers are believed to search long-term memory for alternative knowledge structures that can successfully accommodate the attributes of deviant group members (Brewer, 1988; Fiske and Neuberg, 1990). For example, if one's initial classification of Malcolm as a "traditional male" were challenged by the discovery that he enjoys cooking, knitting, and child rearing (i.e., low goodness-of-category fit), then one would implement a process of "recategorization" in an attempt to preserve a stereotype-based conception of him. This renewed attempt to find an adequate categorical solution can prompt a variety of outcomes. As Fiske and Neuberg note:

> Recategorization is an attempt to find a different category that can be interpreted as adequately organizing the bulk of current informa-

tion. It may entail accessing a subcategory . . . an exemplar . . . a self schema . . . or recategorization may entail accessing an entirely new category. . . . If the perceiver can successfully recategorize the target, then the perceiver's affect, cognitions, and behavioural tendencies in relation to the target are likely to be those relevant to the new category. (1990)

The message emerging here is an instructive one: if at first you don't succeed, try again until you locate an alternative knowledge structure that can capture a target's idiosyncratic constellation of attributes. Once activated, it is business as usual as this cognitive representation guides one's impressions, recollections, and evaluations of the target.

The flexibility of categorization and stereotype activation processes that we have just described is a compelling notion in the abstract, but the underlying cognitive mechanisms that provide this adaptive flexibility are currently not well specified. Consider, for instance. the previous example of Malcolm, the ostensibly non-traditional male. Given his poor fit to the general category stereotype (after all, real men don't knit; they repair cars and play football), perceivers are believed to search memory for alternative knowledge structures that can accommodate his deviant characteristics. Thus knowledge of his atypical attributes may prompt perceivers to re-classify Malcolm as a "modern" man (i.e., a category subtype); as someone who resembles Uncle Bob (i.e., an exemplar-based representation); or else in terms of an entirely different social category, such as "hippie." Despite the flexibility of the recategorization process, however, it cannot alter a simple fact of life: Malcolm remains a man, albeit a relatively atypical member of the category. One may reasonably speculate, therefore, on what would happen if perceivers were to re-encounter Malcolm in a situation where his gender categorization was the entirely appropriate classification to make, as would surely be the case in a variety of social settings (e.g., when looking for a male tennis partner). Under these conditions, how would one's previous experience of Malcolm (as an atypical male) shape the course and products of the categorization process? In particular, what would be the fate of the ill-fitting initial categorization?

The issue of category disconfirmation, of course, raises another thorny issue. When perceivers encounter individual exemplars who seem to be atypical of their social group, they clearly face something of a dilemma. Obviously, they must modify any stereotypic impression of the atypical target that has formed, but do they also need to revise their stereotypic preconceptions about the target's social group as a whole? After all, a central premise of contemporary models of category representation is that, among other things, social perceivers store information about specific group exemplars in memory (Elio and Anderson, 1981; Smith and Medin, 1981; Lingle, Altom and Medin, 1984; Medin et al., 1984; Brewer, 1988; Judd and Park, 1988; Smith and Zárate, 1992; Bodenhausen et al., 1995). If these exemplars constitute an important basis for category representation, what then is the impact of atypical exemplars on people's general categorical beliefs? An inspection of the available literature on this topic confirms that people are quite facile at finding reasons for viewing disconfirming instances as exceptions to a generally valid rule. Accordingly, they see little reason to generalize the attributes of deviant exemplars to the wider social group (Allport, 1954; Brewer et al., 1981; Weber and Crocker, 1983; Wilder, 1984; Rothbart and John, 1985; Kunda and Oleson, 1995). Herein, however, lie several important theoretical puzzles. For example, exactly how is it that perceivers can construe some exemplars in a non-stereotypic manner while continuing to respond towards other members of the group in a predominantly stereotype-based fashion? What are the underlying cognitive processes that make these disparate information-processing outcomes possible? Moreover, at a wider representational level, what sort of cognitive architecture can sustain the flexible stereotyping of group members? Our intuition is that an episodic retrieval model of person perception may provide some useful initial insights into these as yet unresolved theoretical issues.

AN EPISODIC RETRIEVAL MODEL OF PERSON PERCEPTION

Episodic retrieval (i.e., exemplar-based) models of mind posit that information is stored in memory in an instance-based manner. Thus, each experience with a stimulus, be it a hamburger, a bicycle, or a loved one, is located in mind as an independent exemplar-based representation (i.e., episodic trace). Within this cognitive architecture, attention plays a central role in the memorial processes of encoding and retrieval (Hintzman, 1976; Jacoby and Brooks, 1984; Logan, 1988; Smith and Zárate, 1992). As Logan puts it:

Encoding into memory is an obligatory, unavoidable consequence of attention. Attending to a stimulus is sufficient to commit it to memory. It may be remembered well or poorly, depending upon the conditions of attention, but it will be encoded. Retrieval from memory is [also] an obligatory, unavoidable consequence of attention. Attending to a stimulus is sufficient to retrieve from memory whatever has been associated with it in the past. Retrieval may not always be successful, but it occurs nonetheless. Encoding and retrieval are linked through attention; the same act of attention that causes encoding also causes retrieval. (1988)

Models based on these structural and processing assumptions have provided impressive explanatory power in cognitive psychology, leading to new insights into topics as diverse as object categorization (Medin and Schaffer, 1978; Jacoby and Brooks, 1984; Hintzman, 1986; Nosofsky, 1986); episodic memory (Hintzman, 1976; Jacoby and Brooks, 1984); and automaticity and skill acquisition (Logan, 1988). It comes as no real surprise, therefore, to learn that comparable accounts of mental life have also illuminated a variety of issues in social cognition, most notably how perceivers categorize and construe others (Gilovitch, 1981; Lewicki, 1986; Baldwin and Holmes, 1987; Andersen and Cole, 1990; Smith, 1990; Zárate and Smith, 1990; Smith and Zárate, 1992; Bodenhausen, Schwarz et al., 1995). Extending some of these ideas to the stereotyping domain, we propose that the application of an episodic retrieval model of person representation may also unlock one of the more perplexing mysteries of social perception—namely, how it is that perceivers can realize the selective stereotyping of others?

The essence of an episodic retrieval model of person memory is that mere exposure to a target is sufficient to locate an exemplar-based representation of the individual in mind (Smith and Zárate, 1992). These representations, of course, vary considerably in specificity. While some are detailed, content-rich entities (e.g., friends, lovers, relatives), others are more minimalist in stature, emphasizing only a few attributes or characteristics of the person in question (e.g., the women one passes each Friday while walking to work). Of particular relevance, however, is the form that these stored person-based representations are believed to take. As Smith and Zárate note, "Exemplars in memory are records of the stimulus as interpreted or as processed on the previous occasion, rather than a veridical record of the stimulus information that was present" (1992). Thus, it is not an exact copy of the person that enters memory, rather it is the person-as-interpreted by the perceiver that forms the basis of an exemplar-based representation (Fazio, 1986; Logan, 1988; Smith, 1989; Zárate and Smith, 1990).

Given the constructive nature of the person perception process (Bruner, 1957), it is easy to appreciate how factors such as current concerns, temporary task objectives, and prevailing prejudices may shape the contents of people's exemplar-based representations. Often we may not represent people in mind as they really are, but rather as we want them or expect them to be. This facet of memory function provides valuable insight into how exemplars may affect the person perception process. If, upon meeting a new neighbor, one infers that he is pretty rude, then this attribute-related information will be encoded in memory as part of the cognitive representation of him (Logan, 1988; Smith and Zárate, 1992). When, therefore, the representation is retrieved on a subsequent occasion, as indeed would be the case if one were to re-encounter the neighbor (or alternatively just to think about him), knowledge of his rudeness would be highly accessible and hence potentially applicable in any evaluation of the neighbor or his behavior (Smith and Zárate, 1992; Higgins, 1996). This phenomenon is a basic feature of episodic retrieval models—target-based inferences undertaken at stimulus encoding are furnished to perceivers as an obligatory consequence of the exemplar retrieval process (Logan, 1988; Smith and Zárate, 1992).

In this respect, potentially one of the most influential inferences that perceivers make about others concerns the degree to which they are representative of the social groups to which they belong (Bruner, 1957; Brewer, 1988; Fiske and Neuberg, 1990). According to Medin and his colleagues (Medin and Schaffer, 1978; Medin and Smith, 1981; Medin, Dewey and Murphy, 1983), part of each exemplar-based representation in memory is information signaling the categorical typicality of the exemplar. Thus, upon witnessing an honest politician, part of the perceiver's resulting cognitive representation would be information indicating the politician's low-goodness-of-category fit. This estimate of group representativeness, in turn, would have a critical bearing on his or her subsequent evaluations and treatment of the target. In particular, if the generic stereotype (i.e., politician) is deemed to be an inappropriate basis for characterizing the target, then perceivers are unlikely to apply it in their dealings with the politician. After all, if the shoe doesn't fit, why wear it? As a result, impressions and recollections of the politician are likely to be decidedly nonstereotypic in flavor (Brewer, 1988; Fiske and Neuberg, 1990). At the same time, however, as goodness-of-category-fit has only been challenged for this particular group member, impressions of other politicians should still reflect the discriminatory elements of stereotypical thinking. Effects such as these (i.e., flexible stereotyping), importantly, sit comfortably within an episodic retrieval account of person representation (Smith and Zárate, 1992). Having encoded an exemplar as an atypical member of the group, perceivers will inevitably retrieve this information when the representation is activated on a subsequent occasion. Moreover, given that atypicality is tied to a *specific* exemplar, perceivers can continue to respond towards other members of the group (i.e., other exemplars) in a predominantly stereotype-based manner.

Our episodic retrieval model of person perception makes three basic assumptions. First, the allocation of attention to a group member is sufficient to locate an exemplar-based representation of the individual in mind (Logan, 1988; Smith and Zárate, 1992). Second, a fundamental component of the resulting representation is information signaling the target's goodness-of-fit with respect to his or her salient group memberships (Bruner, 1957; Brewer, 1988). Third, subsequent allocation of attention to the individual is sufficient to retrieve the exemplar-based representation and its associated inferences from memory (Logan, 1988; Smith and Zárate, 1992). Ultimately, it is the categorical typicality of the person that determines the extent to which a stereotype is activated and applied when perceivers think about him or her. When goodness of fit is high, construals of the target will likely be highly stereotypic in implication. This is because goodness-of-category fit moderates the relative accessibility of stereotype-related material in semantic memory. If little information is available regarding a target's goodness of category fit, then good fit is likely to be assumed by default, and stereotype activation and application will ensue (Fiske and Neuberg, 1990). Moreover, when the available information is ambiguous with respect to goodness of fit, biased assimilation processes may lead to the perception of a relatively high degree of fit, also resulting in stereotype use. However, when goodness-of-category fit it is unambiguously low (i.e., the stereotype provides poor predictive accuracy), then the accessibility of stereotype-related information should be correspondingly impaired.

Interestingly, functionally comparable effects have been observed when researchers assess the relative accessibility of category exemplars in memory. It is well known, for example, that in response to a category label (e.g., bird), perceivers find it easier to bring typical (e.g., sparrow) rather than atypical (e.g., ostrich) exemplars to mind (Rosch, 1978; Rothbart and Lewis, 1988; Rothbart et al., 1996). In this context, goodness-of-category fit moderates the ease of retrieval (i.e., accessibility) of exemplars from mind. Our contention is that similar effects may exist in person perception, with a target's goodness-of-category fit determining the relative accessibility of generic stereotype-based material in memory. When category-fit is high, stereotypic information should be highly accessible; when category fit is low, it should be relatively inaccessible (Rothbart and John, 1985). In other words, construct applicability should gate the accessibility of stereotypic material in semantic memory (Collins and Loftus, 1975; Higgins, 1996; Neely, 1991).

Driving this analysis of person perception is our belief that stereotypes frequently function as mental tools (Gilbert and Hixon, 1991; Macrae, Milne and Bodenhausen, 1994; Macrae et al., 1997). Like any other tool, however, a stereotype will only be useful if it is applied in the right place at the right time. It would after all be futile to utilize generic stereotype-based knowledge to inform one's understanding of a highly atypical group exemplar. By regulating the mental accessibility of social stereotypes, goodness-of-category fit can prevent perceivers from employing potentially inappropriate mental contents in their dealings with others.

THE PRESENT RESEARCH

When perceivers encounter a particular group member, we suspect that they will inevitably encode an exemplar-based representation of the individual in mind (Hintzman, 1986; Logan, 1988; Smith and Zárate, 1992). Part of this representation, moreover, will be information signaling the person's goodness-of-fit with respect to his or her salient group memberships. If, for example, one witnesses a woman welding, then the resulting cognitive representation will inevitably signal her categorical atypicality. When, therefore, the representation is activated on a subsequent occasion, stereotypic knowledge will be relatively inaccessible. This effect, however, will be restricted to only the previously encountered exemplar. When any other woman is encountered, as long as her goodness-of-category fit has not been challenged, stereotype-based material will remain highly accessible in memory. With a category system that operates at this level of cognitive specificity, it is easy to see how perceivers can realize the flexible stereotyping of others. In our first study, with a paradigm that closely resembles the previous example, we investigated the effects of exemplar typicality on the accessibility of stereotypic information. In our second study, we widened the scope of our inquiry and considered the effects of exemplar typicality on the memorability of stereotype-related material.

STUDY I

Method

Participants and Overview. Thirty-six female undergraduates were paid £2 for their participation in the experiment. The students were asked to form an impression of a female target who was either described in counterstereotypic or stereotype-neutral terms. In a control condition, participants read about an unrelated topic. In a second phase, all participants watched a video of the same target who had been presented in the first phase of the experiment (in relevant conditions) as well as one featuring a new female exemplar. Accessibility of typical female stereotypes was assessed during this second phase. Thus, the study had a 3 (initial female profile: atypical or neutral or none) × 2 (exemplar: old or new) × 2 (item type: stereotypic or irrelevant) mixed design with repeated measures on the second and third factors.

Procedure and Stimulus Materials. Participants arrived at the laboratory individually, were greeted by a female experimenter, and randomly assigned to one of the treatment conditions. The experimenter then explained that she required the participant's assistance in piloting some studies for future departmental research projects. Participants in the two experimental conditions (i.e., atypical and neutral) were then instructed to form an impression of a target (i.e., a woman) based on a photograph of the person, together with material that was presented in the form of a "self-descriptive information sheet." It was explained that later in the experimental session, participants' impressions would be assessed. The information sheet comprised factual background information about the target (e.g., name, age, address, date of birth), together with details of her hobbies and lifestyle. What differed for participants was the self-descriptive material pertaining to the woman's hobbies and activities. Whereas in the atypical condition (i.e., bad-category fit) this material consisted of five items of counterstereotypic information (e.g., does her own car maintenance, enjoys attending soccer matches), in the neutral condition it consisted of five items of information that were irrelevant with respect to the target's group membership (e.g., enjoys jazz music; has a pet canary). Prior to the experiment proper, an independent group of participants (N=28) were given either the atypical or neutral profile and were asked to rate the categorical representativeness of the target (nine-point rating scale: 1 = "not at all representative" to 9 = "highly representative"). Participants' responses confirmed that the target was considered to be less representative when described by the atypical than the neutral profile (respective Ms: 3.76 versus 5.91, $p < .01$).

We anticipated that, in the atypical condition, the unrepresentativeness of the target would prompt participants to encode her in memory as an atypical group exemplar. That is, the stored representation would signal the target's poor fit to the general category stereotype. In the neutral condition, however, as the details in the profile did not challenge the applicable sex stereotype in any way, we expected participants to encode the target as a typical group exemplar. Participants in the control condition were presented with no information whatsoever about a person during this stage of the study. Instead, they were asked to form an impression of a Mediterranean holiday resort, based on an information sheet and a photograph of a hotel. The information sheet contained the same number of items as the comparable sheet in the two experimental conditions.

Next, all participants performed some ostensibly unrelated tasks. After being seated facing a television monitor, the experimenter explained that the Psychology Department was compiling videotaped materials for future research projects. The participant's task was simply to check the edit quality of a videotape. Participants in the experimental conditions were shown a taped extract of a woman sitting in a chair, reading a book. Previous research has demonstrated that an orientation to check the edit-quality of a videotape featuring a person is sufficient to activate a stereotype-based construal of the individual (Pendry and Macrae, 1996). Participants in the control condition were shown an extract from a holiday show depicting hotels and coastal scenery. Importantly, in the experimental conditions, the woman in the tape was either the person participants had seen before (i.e., old exemplar), or else she was a previously unseen individual (i.e., new exemplar). Participants in the control condition were shown an extract from a holiday show featuring either the hotel they had seen before, or a previously unseen hotel. Prior to performing the edit-quality task, the experimenter explained that she had an interest in how well people could perform simultaneous activities. As such, while watching the videotape, participants were required to perform an additional auditory word-identification task. The experimenter explained that, periodically, a computer in the room would utter a letter string. The participant's task was simply to indicate, by means of a button press, as quickly and accurately as possible, whether the letter string was a word or nonword. The list of to-be-identified letter strings (Set A) comprised ten words and ten nonwords, and each letter string was spoken in a female voice. Of the ten words, five were traits that are stereotypic of women (i.e., tender, nurturing, loving, caring, gentle) and five were traits that are stereotype- irrelevant with respect to the category woman (i.e., sporty, optimistic, daring, healthy, astute). These words were selected on the basis of a previous pilot study wherein participants (N=30) were asked to rate the extent to which a large number of personality traits were descriptive of various social categories, including women. Ratings were made on a nine-point scale (where –4 = counterstereotypic, 0 = stereotype-irrelevant, and 4 = stereotypic). The stimulus items were digitized using a Macintosh PowerBook 160. The recording format was monophonic and the sampling rate was 22kHz. The envelope of each sample was shaped using a sound editor program so that the onset and offset of each item were well defined. Care was taken to ensure that intelligibility was not compromised and that artifacts were not introduced. The envelopes of the word sets were stretched or compressed before editing to ensure a standard mean presentation time (i.e., 720ms). If necessary, the transformed samples were frequency shifted to maintain a constant pitch. The trait sets were matched for valence, length, and frequency.

Upon the termination of the videotape, the experimenter explained, rather apologetically, that there had been an equipment malfunction and that the computer had not recorded the participant's responses to the letter strings. As such, the participant was requested to perform the task again. The experimenter indicated that, given this turn of events, the participant might as well take the opportunity to check the edit quality of a different video. Thus, for those in the experimental conditions, if the woman on the first tape had been the initially encountered target (i.e.. old exemplar), on the second tape, she was a previously unseen exemplar (i.e., new exemplar), and vice-versa. Participants in the control condition were shown a different excerpt from a holiday show. Again, the participant's task was to check the edit quality of the tape while simultaneously performing a word-identification task. To avoid repetition priming effects, different letter strings accompanied the second videotape. Of the twenty to-be-identified letter strings (Set B), five were traits that pretested as stereotypic of women (i.e., warm, emotional, kind, sympathetic, patient); five were traits that are stereotype-irrelevant with respect to the category woman (i.e., loud, realistic, safe, complicated, nervous); and ten were nonwords. Presentation of the letter strings during both videotapes was randomized by an Apple Macintosh computer (Mac IIvi) and a variable interstimulus interval was employed. The computer recorded participants' lexical decisions and decision times (in ms). Timing commenced upon the articulation of each letter string by the computer (i.e., onset RTs). Accordingly, participants' response times reflected both the time taken to register the stimulus and the time taken to make a lexical decision. The identity of the target, the order of presentation of the target and exemplar, the order of presentation of the letter strings (Set A and B), and the labeling of the response buttons (i.e., word or nonword) were counterbalanced across the sample. On completion of the task, participants were debriefed, paid, and dismissed.

RESULTS AND DISCUSSION

Participants' lexical decision times provide an index of the relative accessibility of female stereotypes during the video-presentation task (Macrae et al., 1995). To evaluate our predictions, we therefore calculated the mean time taken by participants to characterize the stereotypic and irrelevant traits as words. Given the presence of outlying responses in the data set, lexical-decision times that were slower than three standard deviations from the mean were excluded from the analysis, as were trials where participants classified the words incorrectly. This resulted in 1.7 percent of the data being excluded from the statistical analysis. Because of the skew of the response latencies, a normalizing log transformation was performed on the data prior to analysis (Fazio, 1990).

Participants' responses were submitted to a 3 (profile: atypical or neutral or none) × 2 (exemplar: old or new) × 2 (item type: stereotypic or irrelevant) mixed model analysis of variance (ANOVA) with repeated measures on the second and third factors. This revealed a significant Profile × Exemplar × Item Type interaction on participants' lexical decision times, $F(2, 33) = 3.74$, $p < .05$ (see Table 1 for treatment means). Additional analysis of this interaction confirmed the theoretically important Profile × Exemplar interaction on participants' responses to the stereotypic traits, $F(2, 33) = 3.33$, $p < .05$. Simple effects analysis confirmed an effect of Profile for the old exemplar, $F(2, 61) = 3.25$, $p < .05$. Post hoc Tukey tests revealed that, relative to the control condition (i.e., no profile), whereas the provision of a neutral profile facilitated participants' lexical-decision times, the provision of an atypical profile impaired performance on this task (both $ps < .05$). These effects are consistent with our prediction that stereotype accessibility is moderated by a target's goodness-of-fit to the applicable superordinate category. While the treatment means fall in the anticipated direction, the simple main effect of Profile for the new exemplar was only marginally significant, $F(2, 61) = 3.12$, $p < .10$. Post hoc Tukey tests revealed that, relative to the control condition, the provision of an atypical profile facilitated participants' lexical decision times ($p < .05$). The provision of a neutral profile had a marginally significant facilitatory effect on participants' responses ($p < .09$). Simple effects analysis also revealed that the provision of an atypical profile impaired lexical performance when the stereotypic traits accompanied the old rather than the new exemplar, $F(1,33) = 7.57$, $p < .01$. There were no comparable effects on participants' responses to the irrelevant traits.

These findings provide some preliminary evidence for the operation of an episodic retrieval model in person perception. When participants encountered a woman who was described in a counterstereotypic manner, it appears that they stored an exemplar-based representation of her in mind. Part of this representation, moreover, consisted of information signaling her categorical atypicality (Logan, 1988; Smith and Zárate, 1992). When the exemplar-based representation was activated on a subsequent occasion (i.e., during the video presentation task), the

TABLE 1
Participants' Lexical Decision Times (log RTs) as a Function of Profile,
Exemplar, and Item Type (Study 1)

Item Type	Neutral	Profile Atypical	None
Stereotypic Traits			
old exemplar	6.89	7.08	7.00
new exemplar	6.91	6.90	7.01
Irrelevant Traits			
old exemplar	7.01	7.02	7.04
new exemplar	7.02	6.98	6.99

accessibility of stereotypic material was impaired, an effect that one would expect if categorical representativeness (i.e., goodness-of-category fit) moderates the accessibility of generic stereotype-based knowledge (Rosch, 1978; Rothbart et al., 1996).

The impaired accessibility of stereotype contents for an atypical exemplar can be attributed to attentional competition during the lexical decision task (Neely, 1991). When the exemplar-based representation of the atypical group member was activated, attention would have been directed to the stereotype-discrepant material that comprises part of the representation. As such, this counterstereotypic material would have competed for attention with the stereotypic traits in the lexical decision task, thereby impairing participants' lexical performance on these items (Logan, 1988). When a different group exemplar was encountered, stereotypic information was highly accessible, thereby suggesting that participants construed this new exemplar in a stereotype-based manner (i.e., high goodness-of-category fit). Importantly, a quite different pattern of effects emerged when the target was initially described in a stereotype-neutral manner. Under these conditions, enhanced lexical performance was observed on stereotypic traits when participants encountered both the old exemplar and a previously unseen group member. The failure of the neutral information to eliminate stereotype activation is inconsistent with the view that stereotypes are easily diluted by irrelevant information (Nisbett et al., 1981) and suggests that in the absence of explicitly disconfirmatory information, perceivers encode exemplars as generally representative members of the group in question, thereby potentially providing access to a repository of stereotype-related material in memory.

These findings, then, confirm our prediction that stereotyping can operate on internal representations at the level of individual exemplars (Smith and Zárate, 1992). This specificity obviously serves perceivers well in their quest to stereotype group members in a flexible and adaptive manner (Allport, 1954). By diminishing the accessibility of stereotypic material for atypical exemplars, but atypical exemplars only, perceivers can regulate the incidence of stereotypical thinking and its resultant judgmental effects.

STUDY 2

As mental tools, stereotypes serve a variety of functions in the person perception process. As observed in Study 1, once activated, they can provide perceivers with enhanced access to material in semantic memory (Dovidio et al., 1986; Devine, 1989; Perdue and Gurtman, 1990; Macrae et al., 1994; Macrae et al., 1995; Blair and Banaji, 1996; Macrae et al., 1997; Wittenbrink et al., 1997). This "information provision" function is likely to be employed when perceivers want to learn something about a target, but have neither the energy nor inclination to bother assembling the necessary individuating material (Brewer, 1988; Fiske and Neuberg, 1990). Knowing that John is an accountant, for example, may be sufficient to inform one that he is possibly boring, dependable, and wealthy. Thus, a picture of John can be constructed without the burdensome necessity of social interaction, all one needs to do is inspect the contents of memory to acquire some information about him—although, of course, this information may be wholly inaccurate. Under these conditions, stereotypes function as enriching or elaborating mental devices, furnishing perceivers with target-related information at very little cognitive cost (Allport, 1954; Gilbert and Hixon, 1991; Macrae, Milne, and Bodenhausen, 1994).

Inspection of the available literature confirms that stereotypes also serve a complementary function in person perception—namely, that of target simplification. This generally takes place when target-related information is freely available, and perceivers use stereotypes to organize their impressions of others (Bodenhausen and Wyer, 1985; Bodenhausen and Lichtenstein, 1987; Macrae, Hewstone and Griffiths, 1993; Pendry and Macrae, 1994; Dijksterhuis and van Knippenberg, 1996). Under these conditions, a reliable effect emerges—when both stereotype-relevant and irrelevant information are available, perceivers generally demonstrate a memorial preference for the stereotypic material (Bodenhausen and Wyer, 1985; Macrae et al., 1993). As simplifying or organizing mental structures, stereotypes appear to favor the representation of relevant rather than irrelevant information in mind. Thus, we are more likely to remember that our red-headed cousin has a fiery temper than that she enjoys eating anchovies. Given the robustness of this effect, perceivers' preferences for stereotype-relevant material in recognition and recall is commonly taken as a structural signature that target-based information has been processed in the context of an activated social stereotype (Hamilton and Sherman, 1994).

To widen the scope of the present inquiry and extend the results of Study 1, in our second experiment we investigated the effects of target typicality on the memorability of stereotype-related information. Our belief is that target typicality should not only moderate the accessibility of stereotypic knowledge in memory (as was demonstrated in Study 1), but should also determine the extent to which a stereotype is applied when perceivers organize their impressions of a target. Functionally speaking, if stereotypes remain inaccessible for atypical group members (i.e., Study 1), then one would not expect perceivers to use them when organizing their impressions of these exemplars. For other group members (i.e., typical ones), however, one would expect perceivers to employ stereotypes to help streamline the person perception process. In our second study, we investigated these predictions.

Method

Participants and Overview. Forty-two female undergraduates were paid £2 for their participation in the experiment. The students were asked to form an impression of a female target who was either described in counterstereotypic or stereotype-neutral terms. In a control condition, participants read about an unrelated topic. In a second phase, all participants were given additional information about the target who had been presented in the first phase of the experiment (in relevant conditions) as well as information describing a new female exemplar. The memorability of this information was then assessed in a cued-recognition memory task. Thus, the study had a 3 (initial female profile: atypical or neutral or none) × 2 (exemplar: old or new) × 2 (item type: stereotypic or irrelevant) mixed design with repeated measures on the second and third factors.

Procedure and Stimulus Materials. Each participant arrived at the laboratory individually, was greeted by a female experimenter, and randomly assigned to one of the treatment conditions. The experimenter explained that she required the participant's assistance in piloting some studies for future departmental research projects. As in Study 1, participants in the two experimental conditions (i.e., atypical and neutral) were then instructed to form an impression of a target (i.e., a woman) based on a photograph of the person, together with material that was presented in the form of a "self-descriptive information sheet." As before, what differed for participants was the self-descriptive material pertaining to woman's hobbies and activities. Whereas in the atypical condition (i.e., bad-category fit) this material comprised five items of counterstereotypic information; in the neutral condition (i.e., good-category fit), it comprised five items of information that were irrelevant with respect to the target's group membership. In the atypical condition, we anticipated that the unrepresentativeness of the target would prompt participants to encode her in memory as an atypical group exemplar. In the neutral condition, however, as the details in the profile did not challenge the applicable sex stereotype in any way, we expected participants to encode the target as a typical group exemplar (Fiske and Neuberg, 1990). As in Study 1, during this phase of the study, participants in the control condition were presented with no information whatsoever about a person. Instead, they were asked to form an impression of a Mediterranean holiday resort, based on an information sheet and a photograph of a hotel.

Next, all participants performed either a continuation of the impression-formation task (i.e., experimental conditions) or a completely new impression-formation task (i.e., control condition). After being seated facing the monitor of an Apple Macintosh computer, the experimenter explained that she would like the participants to form impressions of two individuals. In the experimental conditions, it was explained that the study was a continuation of the previous task and that the individuals were two women, one of whom the participants had encountered before (i.e., the old exemplar) and one of whom they had not (i.e., a new exemplar). In the control condition, participants were not told that the impression targets were women; instead, the targets were simply identified by their first initial (i.e., S and B). The experimenter then explained that the participant's task was simply to form an impression of each target, as afterwards these impressions would be assessed. Two sets of person descriptors were used to describe the targets (see Study 1). Each set (i.e., Set A and Set B) comprised five traits that were stereotypic of women and five traits that were stereotype-irrelevant with respect to women. On the computer screen, participants were presented with the target's forename (or initial) and a personality trait. These items were presented simultaneously in the center of the screen with the forename (or initial) appearing just above the trait. As each target was described in terms of relatively few traits, the presentation duration of each stimulus-pair (i.e., name and trait) was relatively brief (i.e., 105 ms). Presentation of the targets and traits was completely randomized for each participant and a variable interstimulus interval was employed. The presentation of the trait lists (Set A or Set B) for each respective target was counterbalanced across the sample.

Upon completion of the trait presentation phase, participants spent about forty-five minutes performing a variety of filler tasks. They then sat down at the computer and completed a cued-recognition task. The experimenter explained that she was interested in the participant's ability to remember the trait information that had been presented in the earlier phase of the impression-formation task. It was explained that, in the center of the screen, participants would be presented with a stimulus-pair comprising the target's forename (or initial) and a personality trait. The task was simply to indicate, by means of a key press, whether this trait had described the target in the previous phase of the study. That is, was the trait "old" or "new"? Participants were requested to make their responses as quickly and accurately as possible by pressing the appropriately-labeled key on the computer keyboard. In the course of this cued-recognition task, participants were presented with twenty items for each target (i.e., ten original traits and ten matched foils). Two trait-foil sets were constructed (Set A: vain, shy, desirable, reliable, romantic, artistic, clean, honest, gloomy, blunt; and Set B: mature, compliant, tidy, poised, understanding, urbane, secure, pompous, poetic, grim). Traits for the foil sets were selected on the basis of a previous pilot study (see Study 1). Each stimulus-pair remained on the screen until participants made a response. Presentation of the targets and traits was completely randomized for each participant. The labels on the response keys and the presentation of the foils (i.e., Foil-Set A and Foil-Set B) were counterbalanced across the

TABLE 2
Participants' Recognition Sensitivity (A´) as a Function of Profile,
Exemplar, and Item Type (Study 2)

		Profile	
Exemplar	Neutral	Atypical	None
Old Exemplar			
stereotypic traits	.981	.784	.852
irrelevant traits	.842	.830	.826
New Exemplar			
stereotypic traits	.992	.984	.810
irrelevant traits	.827	.816	.838

sample. On completion of the task, participants were debriefed, paid, and dismissed.

Results and Discussion

To control for guessing and response biases, a non-parametric measure of recognition sensitivity (A´) was computed for each participant. These data were then submitted to a 3 (profile: atypical or neutral or none) × 2 (exemplar: old or new) × 2 (item type: stereotypic or irrelevant) mixed model analysis of variance (ANOVA) with repeated measures on the second and third factors. This analysis revealed a range of significant main effects and two-way interactions. All of these effects, however, were qualified by the anticipated Profile × Exemplar × Item Type interaction, $F(2, 39)$ 14.65, $p < .0001$ (see Table 2 for treatment means). Additional analysis of this interaction confirmed the theoretically important Profile × Exemplar interactions on participants' recollections of both the old $[F(2,39) = 12.34, p < .001]$ and new $[F(2,39) = 5.66, p <.007]$ exemplars. For the old exemplar, simple effects analysis confirmed an effect of Profile on recognition performance for the stereotypic traits, $F(2,68) = 43.91, p < .001$. Post hoc Tukey tests revealed that, relative to performance the control (i.e., no profile) and atypical conditions, the provision of a neutral profile facilitated recognition performance (atypical/neutral, $p < .01$; none/neutral, $p < .05$). Simple effects analysis also revealed an effect of Item Type when the old exemplar was described by a neutral profile, $F(1,39) = 30.77, p < .001$. That is, when the exemplar's goodness-of-category fit was high, recognition performance was better on the stereotypic than the irrelevant traits. Taken together, then, these findings confirm that the effects of stereotype application on recognition performance are determined by an exemplar's goodness of category fit. When category fit is high, the memorability of stereotypic information is enhanced. When, however, category fit is low, there is no evidence to suggest that a stereotype has been used to guide participants' impressions of the exemplar.

As expected, quite different effects emerged on participants' recollections of the new exemplar. Simple effects analysis revealed an effect of Profile on the memorability of stereotypic traits, $F(2,76)$ 8.11, $p < .001$. Post hoc Tukey tests confirmed that, relative to performance in the control condition, the provision of either a neutral or an atypical profile enhanced recognition performance (both $ps < .01$). The analysis also confirmed effects of Item Type when the old exemplar was characterized in terms of either a neutral [$F(1,39) = 11.77, p < .001$] or an atypical [$F(1,39) = 12.72, p < .001$] profile. In both cases, recognition performance for the new exemplar was better on stereotypic than irrelevant traits. Thus, how the old exemplar was characterized had no impact whatsoever on participants' recollections of the new woman. In each of the experimental conditions, participants used a stereotype to guide their impressions of the woman, as is apparent from· their enhanced performance on the stereotypic traits in the cued-recognition task.

These results, then, extend the findings of Study 1 and provide further evidence for the role of exemplar typicality in the moderation of social stereotyping. Whereas for typical group members participants demonstrated the conventional effect of recognizing more stereotypic than irrelevant items (Bodenhausen and Wyer, 1985; Bodenhausen and Lichtenstein, 1987; Stangor and Duan, 1991; Macrae et al., 1993; Pendry and Macrae, 1994; Dijksterhuis and van Knippenberg, 1996), for an atypical exemplar this effect was eliminated. This latter finding is particularly noteworthy as it suggests that for an atypical exemplar, perceivers do not use an available (but ill-fitting) stereotype to guide their construals of the target. It is possible, of course, that when an atypical group member is described by stereotype-congruent material perceivers may continue to demonstrate a memorial preference for this information. This is because in the context of an atypical group exemplar, stereotypic material may appear unusual (i.e., why did an atypical exemplar perform a stereotype-congruent action?), hence relevant to the target's stereotype. Interestingly, however, we obtained no evidence for the operation of this effect in the present research. Instead, when the target was a poor fit to the category stereotype, participants simply appeared to abandon the stereotype as a basis for organizing information about the target. One important task for future research will be to identify the boundary conditions of this effect.

GENERAL DISCUSSION

The flexibility of categorical perception undoubtedly resides in its ability to admit exceptions. Female airline pilots, athletic grandparents, and slender sumo-wrestlers would all be considered violations of the rules that determine their respective category memberships. Nonetheless, not only are these exceptional instances readily acknowledged by perceivers, but they also occupy a position of prominence in most influential treatments of category representation (Allport, 1954; Brewer et al., 1981; Weber and Crocker, 1983; Rothbart and John, 1985; Devine and Baker, 1991; Kunda and Oleson, 1995; Maurer et al., 1995). This state of affairs gives rise to an important question. By admitting the existence of category deviants, how is it that perceivers can maintain their generalized beliefs about groups as a whole? After all, if one svelte supermodel enjoys a mid-afternoon carton of pistachio ice cream, maybe they all do.

As it turns out, the solution to the previous puzzle is relatively straightforward. To circumvent the revision of stereotype-based beliefs each time an exceptional (i.e., atypical) exemplar is encountered, perceivers need only engage in some rather elementary mental housekeeping. By encoding a category deviant in memory as an atypical group exemplar, perceivers can avoid stereotyping this individual whenever his or her exemplar-based representation is activated. As the representation signals the exemplar's categorical atypicality, the associated stereotype is not deemed to he an appropriate basis for evaluating or thinking about the person. Moreover, because atypicality is tied to a particular exemplar, and a particular exemplar only, perceivers' generic stereotype-based beliefs (i.e., semantic knowledge) remain undisturbed. The present findings provide preliminary support for this analysis of the stereotyping process. In each of the reported studies, stereotypical thinking was eliminated when perceivers encountered an atypical group exemplar. However, when they considered other members of the group, stereotypical thinking prevailed. These effects generalized to different measures of stereotype application. Whether we assessed the accessibility of stereotype contents (i.e., Study 1) or the extent to which a stereotype was used to organize target-related information (i.e., Study 2), the results were the same—stereotype application was moderated by an exemplar's goodness-of-category fit.

Our favored explanation for the elimination of stereotyping for atypical exemplars emphasized the role of memory-based processes in person perception. According to this account, the presentation of a familiar target evokes the retrieval of recent episodes involving that target from memory. Each retrieved episode, moreover, includes information about the target as processed by the perceiver, such as his or her categorical typicality (Medin et al., 1983; Logan, 1988; Smith and Zárate, 1992). It is this information that determines the applicability of schematic knowledge (Higgins, 1996), hence the accessibility of stereotypic material in mind. Just as perceivers find it troublesome to bring unrepresentative members of a category to mind (Rosch, 1978; Rothbart et al., 1996), then so, too, they find it difficult to access stereotypic material for these atypical exemplars. Indeed, when a target is deemed to be atypical, stereotypic material is less accessible than if a stereotype had never been activated at all.

The inaccessibility of stereotypes for atypical exemplars is interesting as it resembles an effect that has previously been reported in the literature on person perception. Macrae, Bodenhausen, and Milne (1995) have suggested that, to simplify person perception, inhibitory processes (i.e., cognitive inhibition) are employed to minimize the impact of unwanted social stereotypes. Thus, when confronted with a target for whom multiple competing construals are possible (e.g., an Asian female engineer), inhibitory processes are implemented to block the accessibility of unwanted (i.e., potentially competing, contextually inappropriate) mental constructs (Bodenhausen and Macrae, 1998). As already noted, a similar effect emerged in the present research (i.e., Study 1) with stereotypic material remaining inaccessible for an atypical group member. How, then, might these two lines of research be related? If cognitive inhibition and episodic retrieval produce identical effects (i.e., inaccessible stereotype contents), can we predict when each process will operate in person perception? Recent work on this topic suggests that we can and asserts that the accessibility of mental contents can be determined either by episodic retrieval or cognitive inhibition. What matters are the characteristics of the task environment (Kane et al., 1997). The general contention appears to be that unwanted mental contents (e.g., stereotypes) are rendered inaccessible via inhibitory processes except in circumstances where episodic retrieval is induced by features of the task context; most notably, the multiple presentation of a stimulus item. Given the repeated presentation of an exemplar to participants in the research reported herein (Macrae et al., 1995), the present findings, therefore, appear congenial to an explanation based on episodic retrieval rather than cognitive inhibition (Kane et al., 1997). Clearly, however, additional research is required to clarify the exact role that episodic retrieval and cognitive inhibition play in person perception.

FLEXIBLE STEREOTYPING

By conceptualizing stereotypes as mental tools, researchers have provided some valuable insights into how social perceivers organize their impressions and recollections of others (Bodenhausen and Wyer, 1985; Bodenhausen and Lichtenstein, 1987; Gilbert and Hixon, 1991; Macrae, Milne and Bodenhausen, 1994; Bodenhausen et al., 1998; Macrae et al., 1998). As simplifying mental devices, stereotypes provide order and structure to an otherwise chaotic social world (Allport, 1954). Interestingly, the rise of this functional perspective in social cognition has prompted a timely re-appraisal of exactly how stereotypes operate in mental life. Until quite recently, the "inevitability of stereotyping" viewpoint tended to dominate research and theorizing on the topic. From this standpoint, stereotype activation (hence application) was deemed to he an obligatory component of the person perception process (Dovidio et al., 1986; Fiske and Neuberg, 1990; Perdue and Gurtman, 1990). Just as night follows day, stereotype activation was believed to follow the perception and registration of a triggering stimulus, be it a Moroccan, a geriatric juggler, or a hirsute optometrist. For social perceivers, stereotyping was inescapable and uncontrollable—something of a blunt cognitive instrument.

Happily, more recent treatments of the topic paint a considerably less pessimistic picture of the social perceiver, with stereotyping characterized as a flexible (and potentially adaptive) mental process. For a modest attentional outlay, suitably motivated perceivers can readily overcome the pitfalls of stereotypical thinking (Devine, 1989; Fiske and Neuberg, 1990; Devine et al., 1991; Monteith, 1993; Monteith et al., 1993; Pendry and Macrae, 1994; Macrae et al., 1997; Bodenhausen and Macrae, 1998; Macrae et al., 1998). In addition, the actual activation of stereotypes in memory is no longer deemed to he an unconditionally automatic mental process (Bargh, 1989, 1994). Recent research has demonstrated that stereotype activation is moderated by a variety of factors, ranging from resource availability (Gilbert and Hixon, 1991) and temporary goal states (Blair and Banaji, 1996; Macrae et al., 1997) to chronic prejudices and motivations (Locke ct al., 1994; Lepore and Brown, 1997; Wittenbrink et al., 1997). These findings are theoretically noteworthy as they dispel the myth that stereotypes inevitably taint the person perception process. While there are undeniably neural mechanisms that promote categorical thinking, it is not inevitable that the outputs of these systems will dominate perceivers' conceptions of others—social perception is better characterized by its flexibility than its rigidity.

What could be more flexible in person perception than a mental system that operates on representations at the level of individual exemplars (Medin and Shaffer, 1978; Hinztman, 1986; Nosofsky, 1986; Logan, 1988; Smith and Zárate, 1992)? Locked away in semantic memory are the libraries of the mind, vast repositories of schematic knowledge just waiting to be pulled from the shelf and applied in person perception. It is in semantic memory that our stereotype-based beliefs reside, along of course with just about every other thing we know or suspect to be true (e.g., Germans are hardworking, Rome is the capital of Italy, and Nessie is a prehistoric creature living in a deep Scottish loch). The secret of success in mental life is to access these knowledge structures at just the right time, in just the right place, for just the right purpose, otherwise uncertainty and confusion will prevail. When walking round the streets of Paris trying to locate the Eiffel Tower, for instance, it would be hopeless to access one's recollections of London—such a strategy would be profitless, as one's knowledge of the English capital is inapplicable in this particular context. Social perception, by necessity, must also operate according to the principle of applicability (Higgins, 1996). If stereotype-based knowledge structures are to inform people's understanding of others, then they must in some sense be applicable or relevant to the target(s) in question. If they are not, then their potential utility is surely diminished and the costs of inappropriate application may be considerable. One need only misemploy one's American stereotype in Canada for a graphic illustration of the case in point. For stereotypes to be beneficial, they must be applied in the appropriate information-processing context.

As we have argued (and indeed demonstrated), the extent to which a stereotype is applied in person perception depends in no small part upon a target's goodness-of-category-fit. Of fundamental importance, therefore, is the question of how perceivers compute categorical representativeness. As one might expect, this is no simple matter, with a variety of endogenous and exogenous factors moderating inferences of category fit (Rothbart et al., 1996). Turning first to endogenous factors: temporary processing objectives, mood states, and chronic prejudices are all likely determinants of goodness-of-category fit (Fiske and Neuberg, 1990). Take levels of prejudice toward ethnic minority groups, for example. One fundamental difference between bigots and humanitarians may reside in the manner in which they compute category representativeness (Devine, 1989). Whereas hapless bigots may ignore the presence of category-discrepent material and, thereby, consider all group members to be highly typical; thoughtful humanitarians may acknowledge this information and use it to guide their inferences of category fit. This, then, would explain why these groups differ so radically in the extent to which they apply stereotypes when confronted with members of an outgroup. While bigots have privileged access to stereotype-based knowledge structures in memory, humanitarians do not (Locke et al., 1994; Wittenbrink et al., 1997).

The most significant exogenous factor in the moderation of stereotyping is probably the task context or environment in which a target is encountered, as situational cues inevitably shape inferences of category fit (Taylor et al., 1978). Consider, for example, two women who are encountered in different work environments: one changing a wheel in an auto-repair shop; and another typing a letter in a busy office. All other things being equal, these women will probably elicit quite different information-processing outcomes, with the secretary (i.e., high goodness-of-category fit) triggering considerably more stereotypical thinking than the mechanic (i.e., low goodness-of-category fit). As the roles occupied by men and woman in society are believed to be an important causal determinant of sex stereotyping (Eagly and Steffen, 1984), the present research provides a potentially useful insight into the cognitive processes through which societal effects of this sort may operate. As inferences of category fit are not fixed in stone, but instead are responsive to perceivers' psychological states, the information-processing context, and the presence of target-related individuating information, it is probable that any given target will routinely elicit a range of information-processing outcomes, varying considerably in stereotypicality.

THE ORIGIN OF CATEGORY SUBTYPES

A common tendency in person perception is to view some individuals, not as members of generic social groups, but rather as instances of more constrained representational structures, termed category subtypes (Allport, 1954; Brewer et al., 1981; Weber and Crocker, 1983; Rothbart and John, 1985; Devine and Baker, 1991; Kunda and Oleson, 1995). Subtyping, in the eyes of many, is a process whereby disconfirming exemplars are identified, clustered together, and represented in mind in a subordinate categorical structure. When, for example, a particular combination of identities is repeatedly encountered, social perceivers may develop a new set of stereotypes pertaining specifically to the combination, or subtype, in question (e.g., "female entrepreneurs"). The obvious benefit of subtyping is that it enables perceivers to preserve their stereotype-based beliefs in the face of potential disconfirmation. As Kunda and Oleson assert, "Consigning deviants to a subtype believed to be atypical and unrepresentative of the group as a whole may enable people to maintain their pre-existing global stereotypes even though they are aware that deviants exist" (1995). Thus, if atypical exemplars are subtyped on the basis of their exceptional characteristics (i.e., stereotype-disconfirming attributes), perceivers can obviate the need to attribute these properties to the group as a whole. As a result, generalized stereotype-based beliefs can be preserved in the face of potential disconfirmation.

Given the widely acknowledged utility of subtyping, it is somewhat surprising to learn that critical aspects of its operation remain largely unspecified. In particular, relatively little is known about the cognitive processes through which subtypes originate. One question of notable interest, for example, centers on the issue of how the categorization process unfolds when perceivers encounter a class of targets for whom a global stereotype-based classification is no longer appropriate and a subordinate subtype is preferred. Take, for example, a situation in which a number of wealthy women are subtyped as "female entrepreneurs." What is it that prevents perceivers from stereotyping these individuals as women, while simultaneously enabling them to construe any other woman who may be encountered in this manner? Moreover, how does the category subtype develop and how is it represented in mind? Although not the primary purpose of the present research, we believe an application of the episodic retrieval model advanced herein may inform our understanding of these issues.

When perceivers encounter a class of targets who clearly do not fit a global stereotype (e.g., ambitious women), it is probable that each critical exemplar-based representation will contain some common details, most notably information signaling the target's representativeness with respect to the two categories of interest—woman (i.e., low goodness-of-category fit) and entrepreneur (i.e., high goodness-of-category fit). As goodness-of-category fit gates the accessibility of stereotypic knowledge in memory, it is easy to see why each of these exemplars will elicit comparable stereotypical outcomes. That is, whereas access to female stereotypes (e.g., emotional, unambitious) will be impaired for each exemplar, access to stereotypic knowledge pertaining to entrepreneurs (e.g., wealthy, aggressive) will be enhanced. In this account, then, subtypes have no privileged or independent existence in mental life—they are not separate cognitive representations (Brewer et al., 1981; Brewer, 1988). Instead, they are simply a collection of exemplars who happen to share common category memberships and associated inferences of structural fit.

This account of subtyping is consistent with recent developments in the social cognition literature emphasizing the multiplicity of social identity (Macrae et al., 1995; Bodenhausen and Macrae, 1998). Every individual we encounter belongs to multiple social groups (e.g., age, sex, ethnicity, occupation). Part of the problem in person perception research, therefore, is to explicate the conditions under which specific stereotypes (e.g., sex stereotypes) will dominate perceivers' impressions and recollections of others. In this respect, our intuition is that exemplar-based representations probably contain information signaling a target's categorical representativeness with respect to a range of salient social group memberships. Thus, Uncle Peter's exemplar-based representation may signal that he is an excellent example of a plumber, a moderate example of an Australian, but a lousy example of a Catholic. When, therefore, any of these classifications dominate the categorization process (Bodenhausen and Macrae, 1998), relative goodness-of-category fit will determine the incidence and impact of stereotypical thinking.

CONCLUSIONS

The flexibility of social stereotyping is revealed on a daily basis. While some group members regularly feel the full force of stereotypical thinking, others are only lightly touched by schematic processes. Some contexts and task environments reliably facilitate stereotyping, whereas others do the opposite and seemingly inhibit discriminatory practices. Finally, some individuals routinely employ stereotypes in their dealings with outgroup members, while others never seem to use stereotypes at all. In what way, then, might these scenarios be linked? How do target, situation, and perceiver factors moderate the incidence and extent of social stereotyping? In the present article, we have advanced an episodic retrieval model of person perception that we believe provides some preliminary answers to these questions (Smith and Zárate, 1992). Our findings confirmed that goodness-of-category fit moderates the extent to which perceivers stereotype others. This implies, of course, that there is a fundamental dissociation between categorization (i.e., assigning a person to a particular social group) and stereotyping (i.e., accessing and applying stereotype-based knowledge structures) in person perception (Brewer, 1988; Macrae et al., 1997). Equivalent categorizations (e.g., bimbo) can prompt radically different stereotypical outcomes—what matters is the target's categorical representativeness, with contextual, perceiver, and target-related factors all contributing to the computation of this critical inference. Just as atypical confectionery need not be pleasant on the tongue, atypical folk singers need not be unpleasant on the ear.

REFERENCES

Allport, G.W. (1954). *The nature of prejudice.* Reading, MA: Addison-Wesley.

Andersen, S.M. and Cole, S.W. (1990). "Do I know you?" The role of significant others in general social perception. *Journal of Personality and Social Psychology, 59,* 384–399.

Baldwin, M.W. and Holmes, J.G. (1987). Salient private audiences and awareness of the self. *Journal of Personality and Social Psychology, 53,* 1087–1098.

Bargh, J.A. (1989) Conditional automaticity: Varieties of automatic influence in social perception and cognition. In J.S. Uleman and J.A. Bargh (eds.), *Unintended thought* (pp. 3–51). New York: Guilford.

Bargh, J.A. (1994). The four horsemen of automaticity: Awareness, intention, efficiency, and control in social cognition. In R.S. Wyer, Jr., and T.K. Srull (eds.), *Handbook of social cognition* (2nd Ed., Vol. 1, pp. 1–40). Hillsdale, NJ: Erlbaum.

Blair, I. and Banaji, M. (1996). Automatic and controlled processes in stereotype priming. *Journal of Personality and Social Psychology, 70,* 1142–1163.

Bodenhausen, G.V. and Lichtenstein, M. (1987). Social stereotypes and information processing strategies: The impact of task complexity. *Journal of Personality and Social Psychology, 52,* 871–880.

Bodenhausen, G.V. and Macrae, C.N. (1998). Stereotype activation and inhibition. In R.S. Wyer, Jr. (Ed.), *Stereotype activation and inhibition: Advances in social cognition* (Vol. 11, pp. 1–52). Mahwah, NJ: Erlbaum.

Bodenhausen, G.V., Macrae, C.N., and Garst, J. (1998). Stereotypes in thought and deed: Social-cognitive origins of intergroup discrimination. In C. Sedikides, J. Schopler, and C.A. Insko (eds.), *Intergroup cognition and intergroup behavior* (pp. 311–335). Mahwah, NJ: Erlbaum.

Bodenhausen, G.V., Macrae, C.N., and Milne, A.B. (1998). Disregarding social stereotypes: Implications for memory, judgment, and behavior. In J.M. Golding and C.M. MacLeod (eds.), *Intentional forgetting: Interdisciplinary approaches* (pp. 349–368). Mahwah, NJ: Erlbaum.

Bodenhausen, G.V., Schwarz, N., Bless, H., and Wänke, M. (1995). Effects of atypical exemplars on racial beliefs: Enlightened racism or generalized appraisals? *Journal of Experimental Social Psychology, 31,* 48–63.

Bodenhausen, G.V. and Wyer, R.S., Jr. (1985). Effects of stereotypes on decision making and information processing strategies. *Journal of Personality and Social Psychology, 48,* 267–282.

Brewer, M.B. (1988). A dual process model of impression formation. In R.S. Wyer, Jr. and T.K. Srull (eds.), *A dual process model of impression formation: Advances in social cognition* (Vol. 1, pp. 1–36). Hillsdale, NJ: Erlbaum.

Brewer, M.B., Dull, V., and Lui, L. (1981). Perceptions of the elderly: Stereotypes as prototypes. *Journal of Personality and Social Psychology, 41,* 656–670.

Bruner, J. (1957). On perceptual readiness. *Psychological Review, 64,* 123–152.

Collins, A.M. and Loftus, E.F. (1975). A spreading activation theory of semantic processing, *Psychological Review, 82,* 407–428.

Devine, P.G. (1989). Stereotypes and prejudice: Their automatic and controlled components. *Journal of Personality and Social Psychology, 56,* 5–18.

Devine, P.G. and Baker, S.M. (1991). Measurement of racial stereotype subtyping. *Personality and Social Psychology Bulletin, 17,* 44–50.

Devine, P.G., Monteith, M.J., Zuwerink, J.R., and Elliot, A.J. (1991). Prejudice with and without compunction. *Journal of Personality and Social Psychology, 60,* 817–830.

Dijksterhuis, A., and van Knippenberg, A. (1996). The knife that cuts both ways: Facilitated and inhibited access to traits as a function of stereotype activation. *Journal of Experimental Social Psychology, 32,* 271–288.

Dovidio, J.F., Evans, N., and Tyler, R.B. (1986). Racial stereotypes: The contents of their cognitive representations. *Journal of Experimental Social Psychology, 22,* 22–37.

Eagly, A.H. and Steffen, V.J. (1984). Gender stereotypes stem from the distribution of women and men into social roles. *Journal of Personality and Social Psychology, 46,* 735–754.

Elio, R. and Anderson, J.R. (1981). The effects of category generalization and instance similarity on schema abstraction. *Journal of Experimental Psychology: Human Learning and Memory. 7,* 397–417.

Fazio, R.H. (1986). How do attitudes guide behavior? In R.M. Sorrentino and E.T. Higgins (eds.), *Handbook of motivation and cognition* (pp. 204–243). New York: Guilford Press.

Fazio, R.H. (1990). A practical guide to the use of response latency in social psychological research. In C. Hendrick and M.S. Clark (Eds.), *Review of personality and social psychology: Research methods in personality and social psychology* (Vol. 11, pp. 74–97). Newbury Park, CA: Sage Publications.

Fiske, S.T. and Neuberg, S.L. (1990). A continuum model of impression formation from category-based to individuating processes: Influences of information and motivation on attention and interpretation. In M.P. Zanna (ed.), *Advances in experimental social psychology* (Vol. 3, pp. 1–74). San Diego: Academic Press.

Gilbert, D.T. and Hixon, J.G. (1991). The trouble of thinking: Activation and application of stereotypic beliefs. *Journal of Personality and Social Psychology, 60,* 509–517.

Gilovitch, T. (1981). Seeing the past in the present: The effect of associations to familiar events on judgments and decisions. *Journal of Personality and Social Psychology, 40,* 797–808.

Hamilton, D.L. and Sherman, J.W. (1994). Stereotypes. In R.S. Wyer, Jr. and T.K. Srull (Eds.), *Handbook of social cognition: Vol. 2. Applications* (pp. 1–68). Hillsdale, NJ: Erlbaum.

Higgins, E.T. (1996). Knowledge activation: Accessibility, applicability, and salience. In E.T. Higgins and A.W. Kruglanski (eds.), *Social psychology: Handbook of basic principles* (pp. 133–168). New York: Guilford Press.

Hintzman, D.L. (1976). Repetition and memory. In G.H. Bower (ed.), *The psychology of learning and motivation* (pp. 47–91). New York: Academic Press.

Hintzman, D.L. (1986). "Schema abstraction" in a multiple trace model. *Psychological Review, 93,* 411–428.

Jacoby, L.L. and Brooks, L.R. (1984). Nonanalytic cognition: Memory, perception, and concept learning. In G.H. Bower (ed.), *The psychology of learning and motivation* (pp. 1–47). New York: Academic Press.

Judd, C.M. and Park, B. (1988). Out-group homogeneity: Judgments of variability at the individual and group levels. *Journal of Personality and Social Psychology, 54,* 778–788.

Kane, M.J., May, C.P., Hasher, L., Rahhal, T., and Stoltzfus, E. (1997). Dual mechanisms of negative priming. *Journal of Experimental Psychology: Human Perception and Performance, 23,* 632–650.

Kunda, Z. and Oleson, K.C. (1995). Maintaining stereotypes in the face of disconfirmation: Constructing grounds for subtyping deviants. *Journal of Personality and Social Psychology, 68,* 565–579.

Lepore, L. and Brown, R. (1997). Category and stereotype activation: Is prejudice inevitable? *Journal of Personality and Social Psychology, 72,* 275–287.

Lewicki, P. (1986). *Nonconscious social information processing.* San Diego, CA: Academic Press.

Lingle, J.H., Altom, M.W., and Medin, D.L. (1984). Of cabbages and kings: Assessing the extensibility of natural object concept models to social things. In R.S. Wyer, Jr. and T.K. Srull (eds.). *Handbook of social cognition* (Vol. 1, pp. 71–117). Hillsdale, NJ: Erlbaum.

Lippmann, W. (1922). *Public opinion.* New York: Harcourt, Brace, Jovanovich.

Locke, V., MacLeod, C., and Walker, I. (1994). Automatic and controlled activation of stereotypes: Individual differences associated with prejudice. *British Journal of Social Psychology, 33,* 29–45.

Logan, G.D. (1988). Toward an instance theory of automatization. *Psychological Review, 95,* 492–527.

Macrae, C.N., Bodenhausen, G.V., and Milne, A.B. (1995). The dissection of selection in person perception. Inhibitory processes in social stereotyping. *Journal of Personality and Social Psychology, 69,* 397–407.

Macrae, C.N., Bodenhausen, G.V., and Milne, A.B. (1998). Saying no to unwanted thoughts: Self focus and the regulation of mental life. *Journal of Personality and Social Psychology, 74,* 578–589,

Macrae, C.N., Bodenhausen, G.V., Milne, A.B., and Ford, R. (1997). On the regulation of recollection: The intentional forgetting of stereotypical memories. *Journal of Personality and Social Psychology, 72,* 709–719.

Macrae, C.N., Bodenhausen, G.V., Milne, A.B., Thorn, T.M.J., and Castelli, L. (1997). On the activation of social stereotypes: The moderating role of processing objectives. *Journal of Experimental Social Psychology, 33,* 471–489.

Macrae, C.N., Hewstone, M., and Griffiths, R.J. (1993). Processing load and memory for stereotype-based information. *European Journal of Social Psychology, 23,* 76–87.

Macrae, C.N., Milne, A.B., and Bodenhausen, G.V. (1994). Stereotypes as energy-saving devices: A peek inside the cognitive toolbox. *Journal of Personality and Social Psychology, 66,* 37–47.

Macrae, C.N., Stangor, C., and Milne, A.B. (1994). Activating social stereotypes: A functional analysis. *Journal of Experimental Social Psychology, 30,* 370–389.

Maurer, K.L., Park, B., and Rothbart, M. (1995). Subtyping versus subgrouping processes in stereotype representation. *Journal of Personality and Social Psychology, 69,* 812–824.

Medin, D.L., Altom, M.W., and Murphy, T.D. (1984). Given versus induced category representations: Use of prototype and exemplar information in classification. *Journal of Experimental Psychology: Learning, Memory, and Cognition, 10,* 333–352.

Medin, D.L., Dewey, G.I., and Murphy, T.D. (1983). Relationships between item and category learning: Evidence that abstraction is not automatic. *Journal of Experimental Psychology: Learning, Memory, and Cognition, 9,* 607–625.

Medin, D.L. and Schaffer, M.M. (1978). Context theory of classification. *Psychological Review, 85,* 207–238.

Medin, D.L. and Smith, E.E. (1981). Strategies and classification learning. *Journal of Experimental Psychology: Human Learning and Memory, 7,* 241–253.

Monteith, M.J. (1993). Self-regulation of prejudiced responses: Implications for progress in prejudice-reduction efforts. *Journal of Personality and Social Psychology, 65,* 469–485.

Monteith, M.J., Devine., P.G., and Zuwerink, J.R. (1993). Self-directed versus other-directed affect as a consequence of prejudice-related discrepancies. *Journal of Personality and Social Psychology, 64,* 198–210.

Neely, J.H. (1991). Semantic priming effects in visual word recognition: A selective review of current findings and theories. In D. Besner and G. Humphreys (eds.), *Basic processes in reading: Visual word recognition* (pp. 264–336). Hillsdale, NJ: Erlbaum.

Nisbett, R.E., Zukier, H., and Lemley, R.E. (1981). The dilution effect: Nondiagnostic information weakens the implications of diagnostic information. *Cognitive Psychology, 13,* 248–277.

Nosofsky, R.M. (1986). Attention, similarity, and the identification-categorization relationship. *Journal of Experimental Psychology: General, 115,* 39–57.

Pendry, L.F. and Macrae, C.N. (1994). Stereotypes and mental life: The case of the motivated but thwarted tactician. *Journal of Experimental Social Psychology, 30,* 303–325.

Pendry, L.F. and Macrae, C.N. (1996). What the disinterested perceiver overlooks: Goal-directed social categorization. *Personality and Social Psychology Bulletin, 22,* 249–256.

Perdue, C.W. and Gurtman, M.B. (1990). Evidence for the automaticity of ageism. *Journal of Experimental Social Psychology, 26,* 199–216.

Rosch, E. (1978). Principles of categorization. In E. Rosch and B.B. Lloyd (Eds.), *Cognition and categorization (pp. 27–48).* Hillsdale, NJ: Erlbaum.

Rothbart, M. and John, O.P. (1985). Social categorization and behavioral episodes: A cognitive analysis of the effects of intergroup contact. *Journal of Social Issues, 41*(3), 81–104.

Rothbart, M. and Lewis, S. (1988). Inferring category attributes from exemplar attributes: Geometric shapes and social categories. *Journal of Personality and Social Psychology, 55,* 861–872.

Rothbart, M. Sriram, N., and Davis-Stitt, C. (1996). The retrieval of typical and atypical category members. *Journal of Experimental Social Psychology, 32,* 309–336.

Smith, E.E. and Medin, D.L. (1981). *Categories and concepts.* Cambridge, MA: Harvard University Press.

Smith, E.R. (1989). Procedural efficiency: General and specific components and effects on social judgment. *Journal of Experimental Social Psychology, 25,* 500–523,

Smith, E.R. (1990). Content and process specificity in the effects of prior experiences. In T.K. Srull and R.S. Wyer, Jr. (eds.), *Advances in social cognition* (Vol. 3, pp. 1–59). Hillsdale, NJ: Erlbaum.

Smith, E.R. and Zárate, M.A. (1992). Exemplar-based model of social judgment. *Psychological Review, 99,* 3–21.

Tajfel, H. (1969). Cognitive aspects of prejudice. *Journal of Social Issues, 25,* 79–97.

Taylor, S.E., Fiske, S.T., Etcoff, N.L., and Ruderman, A. (1978). Categorical bases of person memory and stereotyping. *Journal of Personality and Social Psychology, 36,* 778–793.

Von Hippel, W., Sekaquaptewa, D., and Vargas, P. (1995). On the role of encoding processes in stereotype maintenance. In M.P. Zanna (ed.), *Advances in experimental social psychology* (Vol. 27, pp. 177–254). New York: Academic Press.

Weber, R. and Crocker, J. (1983). Cognitive processes in the revision of stereotypic beliefs. *Journal of Personality and Social Psychology, 45,* 961–977.

Wilder, D.A. (1984). Intergroup contact: The typical member and the exception to the rule. *Journal of Experimental Social Psychology, 20,* 177–194.

Wittenbrink, B., Judd, C.M., and Park, B. (1997). Evidence for racial prejudice at the implicit level and its relationship with questionnaire measures. *Journal of Personality and Social Psychology, 72,* 262–274.

Zárate, M.A. and Smith, E.R. (1990). Person categorization and stereotyping. *Social Cognition, 8,* 161–185.

Mood in Chronic Disease: Questioning the Answers

MARIE JOHNSTON
University of St. Andrews

The main research questions concerning mood and chronic disease are about the extent, sources, and consequences of emotional distress. Answers to these questions are informative both to psychological theory and to the design of interventions aimed at improving outcomes for patients. However, as a result of practical and ethical limitations in research designs, the answers obtained are rarely definitive and typically need to be interpreted carefully. This article illustrates some of the problems using studies of patients with cancer, myocardial infarction, stroke, and other disabling conditions. The first group of studies illustrates problems in the timing of mood measurement including both timing within an interview, and issues concerned with identifying equivalent timing in the stages of disease and its treatment. The remaining studies are used to illustrate the limits of non-experimental longitudinal, and of experimental designs. It is concluded that research in this area requires the use of more than one research paradigm to achieve dependable answers.

The impact of chronic disease on mood, stress, emotional states, and emotional disorders has been studied extensively and diversely for decades without a resulting coherent body of knowledge being established. There is no overarching dominant theoretical approach to provide an organising structure, and so, like other areas of research with large quantities of poorly-ordered empirical studies, it becomes comparable in value to "a three-car garage filled to the rafters with junk" (Taylor, 1990). There is implicit agreement about the major research questions, but the quality of the evidence is limited largely owing to the restrictions inherent in this research field. Experimental studies are ethically problematic, and even predictive studies are difficult to mount due to the burden on people who are ill and disabled, as well as the costs involved. As a result, there is a proliferation of studies with varying degrees of imperfection and which therefore provide disputable answers to the questions.

By contrast, the effects of mood on disease onset have achieved a considerable degree of coherence (Steptoe, in press). Progress has been made in this field by the combination of longitudinal, predictive studies such as the early studies on Type A behavior or later studies of people living with chronic stress combined with experimental studies of animals subjected to chronic stressors. Developments in endocrinology and immunology with the resulting advances in psychoneuroimmunology have led to a more effective framework for the investigation of the impact of mood related factors on disease onset.

This article examines the main research questions concerning the impact of disease on mood and explores methodological problems which make the interpretation of the findings difficult. The aim of the article is to illustrate both the potential and the drawbacks of the main research approaches in answering the key research questions using evidence from the author's program of research in chronic disease.

RESEARCH QUESTIONS

In considering the impact of chronic disease on mood, four major questions guide research efforts:

- How distressed do people become as a result of chronic disease?
- What factors influence how distressed they become?
- Do more distressed individuals have a poorer disease outcome?
- Can psychological interventions reduce the distress and its consequences?

It seems intuitively plausible that chronic disease should have a detrimental effect on mood. Theoretical frameworks, especially within a stress and coping or a mental health approach, would predict that the chronic stress associated with such diseases should result in not only lowered mood, but more chronic effects including emotional disorder. A simple stress model might suggest that the effects depend on the severity of the disease and should increase over time either because individuals become progressively more affected or because there is an increased probability of each individual becoming affected.

Coping models would propose that the effects should be moderated by individual coping responses. More recent models of the mental representations of illness (Petrie and Weinman, 1997) would suggest that the effects would be moderated by the individual's beliefs about the condition, especially beliefs in the identity of the condition, its expected pattern over time, its causes, its consequences, and means of management or control.

Both coping and mental representation approaches propose factors which may reduce or exacerbate the effects of the chronic illness on the individual's mood. Coping models propose that people attempt to reduce the effects of stressors in many different ways and that some of these methods serve to minimise the impact whereas others may maximise the effects. These coping strategies or procedures can be behavioural (e.g., seeking alternative therapies) or cognitive (e.g., reconstruing the illness), and may be avoidant (e.g., distraction methods) or may direct attention toward the threat (e.g., seeking information). Mental representation approaches suggest that the mood will depend on what the individual believes about the condition, whether or not these representations influence coping responses; thus it mirrors the models underlying current cognitive behavioral therapies for mood disorders (Clark and Fairbairn, 1996). Pre-existing cognitive styles may determine the kind of mental representation developed, e.g., individuals high in negative affectivity will probably have a more negative view of their condition than someone low in negative affectivity.

The third question concerns the consequences of emotional states for the *progression* of disease. Unlike the work on *onset* of disease, the theoretical basis of this question is very limited although it has acquired more validity from recent psychoneuroimmunology work suggesting that mood may affect endocrine and immune responses, which may in turn influence disease outcomes. Instead, research on disease progression derives from a mixture of intuition and clinical anecdote, such as the observation that a patient dies as a result of "turning his face to the wall."

Finally, there is a drive to find remedy for distress in people with physical illness, largely to reduce distress per se, but also to minimize disease effects such as disability or even survival, which may be consequent on mood.

HOW DISTRESSED DO PEOPLE BECOME AS A RESULT
OF CHRONIC DISEASE?

Cross-sectional studies can be useful in assessing levels of distress and in comparing patients with different diseases. For example, it can be informative to assess levels of distress in a sample of patients with chronic disease, using a standard test and compare these results with appropriate norms for the test. One might expect people with serious diseases to show high levels of distress.

Numerous studies report the levels of distress of people with chronic disease. These studies usually use one of the measures of mood, such as the Hospital Anxiety and Depression Scale (HADS); Zigmond and Snaith, 1983), which avoid somatic items such as fatigue or sleep problems to ensure that estimates of mood disorder are not inflated by symptoms of the disease. In general, these studies demonstrate that people with chronic disease have high levels of anxiety and depression. However, there are problems in interpreting the findings owing to both the variability in the stage in the disease and its treatment, and the timing and location of the assessments.

Care needs to be taken in sampling respondents and in administering the tests. Cross-sectional prevalence samples may be unrepresentative of people with the disease. In diseases that reduce life expectancy, convenience samples are likely to over-represent those with long survival times. They are also likely to have an excess of people in touch with agencies used to recruit, such as support agencies or health services. The latter are likely to be particularly problematic as they are more likely to have contact with individuals currently complaining of exacerbation of symptoms or receiving treatments, both factors associated with increased distress. There is ample evidence that medical consultations and procedures are associated with increased anxiety (Johnston and Wallace, 1989). Indeed, many measures of anxiety have been validated using surgical patients as a criterion group of people with high anxiety. For diseases with an ambiguous onset and a variable course, diagnosis and later consultations will occur at the time of symptom exacerbation and so mood is likely to be lower than at other times. These issues are particularly important in comparing distress in patients with different diseases

Assessments are frequently done in patients' homes, especially where the condition is disabling and the person is restricted as a result. Such measures are less likely to be confounded with stage of illness or current treatment than clinic based assessments, and it is not clear whether they produce different results as a result of the more reassuring setting. On the other hand, there may be negative effects of interviewing the individual about their thoughts and feelings about their disease. Current psychological explanations of mood disorders focus on the effect of cognitions on mood. Interviews that review patients' problems typically rehearse a series of negative cognitions and one might therefore expect a detrimental effect on mood. Even the completion of mood measures may be anxiety provoking and this may be more of a problem on the first occasion that the measure is completed.

The following three studies address issues in assessing distress in people with chronic disease. Study 1 examines levels of distress in patients with three clinical conditions and compares them with a nonpatient group to control for the effects of having the disease and associated medical treatments. Study 2 examines the effects of (a) interviewing at home versus in a clinical setting and (b) first versus later assessments. Study 3 investigates the effect on mood of placing the measure before or after other interview material.

Study 1: Comparison of Mood in Patients with Different Diseases and with a Non-Patient Control Group

The first study compares mood in three samples of patients with motor neurone disease (MND), myocardial infarction (MI), and stroke. In all of these conditions life expectancy is reduced, so that a prevalence sample will be biased with respect to disease severity. This is particularly true of MND where survival times are shortest. The point of diagnosis involves medical investigations and possibly therapeutic procedures for all three conditions and is therefore likely to be a time of high anxiety. This comparison uses assessments between one and two months of the diagnosis and to control for the confounding of sampling bias and concurrent medical treatment, uses a cohort of patients for each condition. All the assessments were done in the individuals' homes, in the initial stages of the interview, before enquiring about other aspects of their current state and all patients had completed the questionnaire on a previous occasion.

Methods. Consecutive cohorts of patients completed the HADS between one and two months after discharge from the hospital stay,

FIGURE 1
Mean Distress by Group

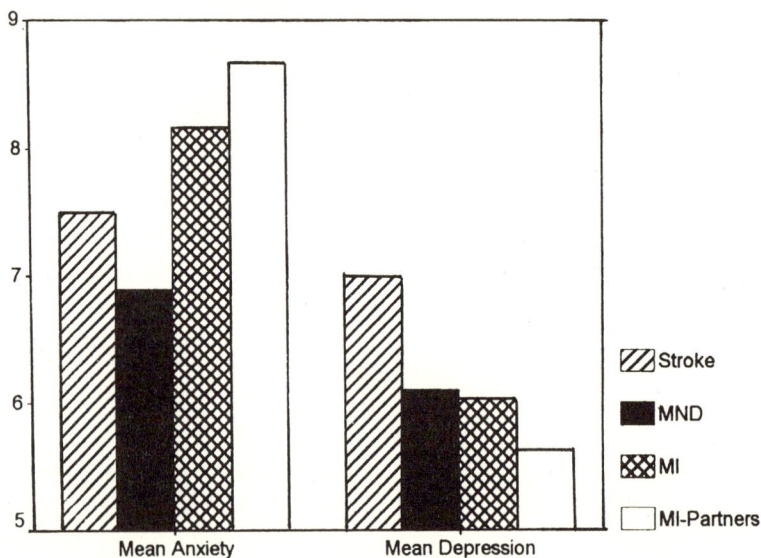

following acute onset or during which their condition was diagnosed. These samples were therefore at a similar stage of the condition and its treatment and not biased with respect to patients' self-selection for interview. The clinical conditions were acute stroke, including all patients who passed a cognitive and communication screening test, (N = 78) (Johnston et al., 1999; Momson et al., in submission); MI (N = 32) (Johnston et al., in press); and MND (N = 29) (Johnston et al., 1996). In addition, data are available at the same timepoint for twenty-four partners of the MI patients (Johnston et al., in press).

Results. As shown in Figure 1, Anxiety levels were highest for the MI Partners, but there were no significant differences between the groups ($F(3, 162) < 1$). Similarly, there were no significant differences between groups on Depression ($F(3, 162) < 1$). For both anxiety and depression, the means for each group are higher than those reported for other clinical groups below, and higher than available means for a large group of cancer patients. Moorey et al. (1991) reported means of 5.44 (s.d. 4.07) for anxiety and 3.02 (s.d. 2.98) for depression for a group of 573 cancer patients at the time of the initial diagnosis or first recurrence.

Discussion. These results show that using the same standard test and patients identified at the same point in the disease and its treatment, there were no differences in emotional distress. Further, these groups were not more distressed than a control group of MI partners, indicating that suffering from a disease *per se* does not result in higher levels of distress. The high levels of Anxiety in MI Partners suggests that the threats associated with having a sick partner are as great as the threats of being ill oneself, even with disease such as MI which is universally considered to be serious. For both patients and partners, the mean level of anxiety falls within the range for "possible" disorder for the norms of the test. These results are compatible with a life events approach whereby the level of adjustment required determines the stressfulness of the event. Thus the mood impact of chronic disease is not restricted to the sufferer alone, as others are also making adjustments to their lives.

These data do not address comparisons at earlier or later stages in the diseases. Earlier comparisons are difficult owing to the patients' state in acute stroke, to the ambiguity of the timing of onset in patients with MND, and to the very different medical treatment of the three conditions. As a result, finding a point of comparison would be problematic. Later comparisons face problems of the poor survival rates of patients with MND, resulting in comparisons with a restricted sample. The comparison presented identifies a narrow window of time in which the current medical treatment is relatively similar for all groups, when they have recovered from the acute phase of illness and when few of the cohort have declined to a point where they could not participate.

The study controls for place and timing of assessment, but these are investigated in the following studies.

Study 2: Effects of Place of Administration and Repeated Test Administration

In cross-sectional studies, one may be choosing between test administration in different places, especially between home and health service premises. Since hospitals and clinics are usually associated both with increased symptoms and with stressful investigations and procedures, one might expect that higher levels of anxiety would be recorded than in home settings.

In longitudinal designs, some assessments may be undertaken in clinical settings and some in home settings, and the clinic versus home comparison would also inform these studies. Additionally, these studies involve increased confounding due to the effects of repeated measurement. If patients have higher scores in the clinic than they do in a subsequent home measure, this may be due to a clinic-home difference or to familiarisation with the measure.

These measures are frequently repeated to assess changes with time with the patient's condition, or with treatment. The questionnaires and assessment procedures are unfamiliar on the first occasion, a situation that may by itself give rise to anxiety. Ludwick-Rosenthal and Neufeld (1988), reviewing studies of medical procedures, concluded that lack of familiarity with the procedure led to higher levels of anxiety and this might apply to psychological assessments as a procedure within a medical context. If so, then one might observe apparent reductions in anxiety which are due entirely to familiarisation with the assessment procedures rather than time, stage of disease, or place of assessment.

Two research questions were addressed concerning mood measurement—is mood affected by:

1. place of measurement—are patients less distressed when assessed at home compared with in a hospital clinic?
2. repetition of measurement—are patients less distressed when assessed for the second time compared with the first?

Methods. Sixty-five women (age range 25–88) attending a breast clinic were asked to complete the HADS plus one other questionnaire which dealt with quality of life. They were randomly allocated to a "home only" group who completed the questionnaires at home on the day following the clinic visit only, or to a "clinic + home" group who completed the questionnaires both during the clinic visit and on the following day at home.

Results. For both anxiety and depression, the "clinic + home" group gave lower ratings at home (see Table 1). Comparing the group answering for the first time with those answering for the second time, home scores were significantly lower for the "clinic + home" group for anxiety and tended to be lower for depression also. There were no differences between scores obtained on the first assessment in the clinic or at home

Discussion. These results suggest that the differences observed are due not to the home versus hospital comparison, but to completing the

TABLE 1
HADS Anxiety and Depression comparing home versus hospital
and first versus second administrations

Group	N	Mean Anxiety		Mean Depression	
		Hospital	Home	Hospital	Home
Home only	31		7.41		3.26
Clinic + Home	34	6.12	4.47	2.94	2.12
Between groups for home scores		$t = 3.21, p < .002$		$t = 1.77, p < .09$	
Within 'clinic + home' group		$t = 3.37, p < .002$		$t = 2.57, p < .02$	
Between groups for first scores		$t = 1.30$, n.s.		$t = 0.47$, n.s.	

questionnaire for the first compared with the second time. There is no evidence that patients are less distressed at home, and these results would appear to justify the common practice of making comparisons over time or across stages of the disease where some assessments are done in clinics and some in the patients' homes. However, they seriously question comparisons of first versus second assessments. For example, studies which assess patients before and after surgery may obtain higher anxiety levels before surgery simply because this is the first measure and where repeated assessments have been made prior to surgery, there has been no clear difference between before and after measures (Johnston, 1980). These data do not give information about the effects of repetitions beyond two administrations, but informal comments by participants suggest that it is the initial experience of these questionnaires which are most worrying as they have no idea what to expect.

The implications for interpreting and planning studies are that one should be suspicious of high initial values and that critical assessments should either not be the first or should be the first for all respondents. Finding that the place of assessment was not critical would appear to allow variability in the location of interviews, but this finding could usefully be replicated.

Study 3: The Effects of Other Interview Material on Mood Measurement

There may even be confounding within the psychological interview. In addition to assessing mood, these interviews typically make some assessment of the patients' perceptions of their clinical condition. Thus it is likely that they will be rehearsing health problems. Since selective focussing on negative cognitions results in more negative moods, one might expect that these interviews would result in lower moods. The following investigation examined whether mood ratings were influenced by making the assessment before or after other interview material.

Method. Forty-nine women (mean age 57 years, s.d. 10.15) with breast disease attending a breast clinic were asked to complete the HADS plus questions concerning demographic and clinical factors, social support, and attitudes to attending a support group for women with breast disease. They were randomly allocated to a group of twenty-five who answered the HADS before any other measure and a group of twenty-four answering the HADS after answering the other questionnaires.

Results. Women answering the HADS following other questionnaires were significantly more anxious than those answering the HADS first (Table 2). There were no significant effects on Depression.

Discussion. Engaging in the research interviews increased women's anxiety levels. Given that these interviews addressed problems of their clinical condition, this is hardly surprising and is borne out by a further experimental study reported below (Study 7). However, these results do have implications for the assessment for mood. Mood measures inserted in a complex interview are likely to be affected by that interview, perhaps as much as by other factors influencing their prevailing mood. For most studies, the important conclusion is that the position of the measure in the interview schedule should be standardised and that mood measures should come first if they are to reflect mood minimally influenced by the study. On the other hand, the very act of engaging them in a study may have already influenced mood, and it will be essential to maintain similar methods of administration over conditions that are being compared. As a minimum standard, the position of mood measures within a clinical interview should be reported.

WHAT FACTORS INFLUENCE HOW DISTRESSED PEOPLE BECOME?

The most obvious factor influencing distress is the type of disease and its severity. As indicated above, having the disease is not neces-

TABLE 2
Comparison of HADS Anxiety in women completing the test before and
after other interview material

Order	N	HADS Anxiety		
		Mean	S.D.	
HADS before	25	4.76	2.44	
HADS after	24	6.58	3.11	$t = 2.28, p < .05$

sarily the major factor, as partners were at least as distressed as patients. However, one might still hypothesize that the severity of the
disease and its symptoms would influence the levels of distress as
more severe disease might be expected to require more adjustment.

In addition, a large number of psychological factors have been associated with distress with mental representations, coping, and social
support being amongst the most commonly investigated. Mental representations (Leventhal et al., 1997) of the *identity* or the label for the
condition, of its *cause*—especially if the individual attributes the condition to their own behavior or to other people (Macleod, in press), of
its *timeline* as an acute, chronic, or cyclic condition, of the *consequences* of the condition, and of its *control* or *cure* have all been
found to be related to the emotional impact of chronic conditions.
Further, ways of coping have also been implicated and a meta-analysis
(Suls and Fletcher, 1985) pointed to the importance of contrasting
attentional and avoidant methods, concluding that avoidant methods
were more adaptive for short-term stressors and that attentional methods were more effective for enduring stressors such as chronic disease.
For social support, there are two dominant hypotheses (Cohen and
Wills, 1985), first that social support is generally beneficial and second that it serves a buffering effect and is primarily beneficial under
conditions of stress as might be experienced during chronic disease.

Taken together, these theoretical approaches and the related findings suggest that people with chronic disease will be more distressed if
the disease is more severe, they perceive it to be severe and to have
many symptoms, they attribute it to themselves, it is seen as chronic,
they anticipate little control or cure, they experience or expect undesirable consequences, they use avoidant coping, and they have little social support.

Many studies use cross-sectional research designs, and it is virtually
impossible to draw conclusions from these. If there is no association

between the postulated influence factor and distress, then one can conclude that it is not influencing distress. Otherwise, it is impossible to ascertain whether the factor influences distress or if increased distress exacerbates the disease, influences cognitions, affects coping, and alters social support.

Study 4: Factors Influencing Distress: Predicting Distress in Acute Stroke and Chronic Disability

There are various conceptualisations of severity, including indices of the underlying impairment or pathology and measures of the degree of functional limitations, and both were employed for the stroke sample. Control cognitions were assessed, over recovery for the stroke group and over future disability for the community disabled group. For the community disabled group, coping was measured using two of the currently most widely used measures. For both groups, measures of satisfaction with services were assessed as an index of perceived social support from formal helping agencies, and the community disabled group also completed a more general measure of social support.

Three questions were examined:

1. Is disease severity associated with levels of distress?
2. Which psychological factors predict distress?
3. Which combination of variables best predicts distress?

Method. HADS assessments were completed by a representative, population-based sample of one hundred people with disabilities (Knight and Johnston, 1995) and by the Study 1 cohort of seventy-eight people suffering an acute stroke one and six months after discharge from hospital (Morrison et al., in submission). Assessments of disease severity were the OPCS Disability Scales (Martin et al., 1988) completed near the time of the interview by the patients' general practitioners for the community disability sample. For the stroke patients, a Neurological Index (Orgogozo et al., 1983) was assessed by a hospital clinician, and a researcher completed an index of observed disability based on standardised ratings.

Psychological measures for the community disabled group included Perceived Control over future Disability (PCD) (Partridge and Johnston, 1991), the Ways of Coping (WOC) (Billings and Moos, 1981), Significant Others Scale (SOS) (Power et al., 1988) and measures of

Satisfaction with services. For the stroke patients, the measures were Recovery Locus of Control (RLOC) (Partridge and Johnston, 1989), Confidence in Recovery (Lewin et al., 1992), and ten-point ratings of Satisfaction with advice and treatment.

All measures were taken at the same time for the community disabled group. For the stroke group, the Neurological Index was assessed within days of the stroke; the observer assessed disability and the psychological measures were taken one month after discharge; and the HADS was completed at one and six months after discharge from hospital.

Results. Correlations between the measures of distress and severity were non-significant for the community disability sample and for the Neurological Index for the stroke group. The observer assessed disability measure was not correlated with anxiety, but correlated concurrently and predictively with HADS depression [r =.36 and .50 respectively].

Control cognitions and social support measures were correlated with distress for both groups, and coping was correlated with distress for the community disabled group. For the community disabled group, multiple regression analyses were used to examine the variance in distress (combined anxiety and depression) accounted for by disease severity and psychological variables. Coping (active-cognitive, avoidance and problem-focused) and Internal control accounted for 43 percent of the variance in distress. For stroke, one month measures of disease severity and psychological factors were used to predict six month mood. Satisfaction with treatment and confidence in recovery predicted 26 percent of the variance in anxiety. Satisfaction with advice and treatment and observer assessed disability predicted 40 percent of the variance in depression. When the analyses took account of mood assessed at the same time as the predictor variables, anxiety was predicted by the same two psychological predictors, but depression was predicted by a combination of satisfaction with advice and confidence in recovery; observer assessed disability no longer accounted for a significant amount of unique variance.

Discussion. The results for the community disability group are incompatible with the hypothesis that disease severity causes distress. Beyond this, it is difficult to draw firm conclusions from the cross-sectional design used with the community disabled group. The correlation and multiple regression analyses indicate variables which may account for distress, but it is equally plausible that distress leads to the pattern of cognitions, coping, and social support observed, or even that some over-riding variable, such as negative affectivity, determines both the levels of disability observed by the GP and the responses to psychological measures.

For stroke, levels of distress are not determined by degree of neurological disorder. However, it is possible from the concurrent correlations and from the simple predictive regression analyses, that the extent of functional limitation contributes to patients' depression. These analyses still allow alternative explanations (e.g., the possibility that one month after discharge, patients levels of depression determine their performance on the observer assessed disability); if levels of depression persist, then one would obtain the correlation and simple predictive results found. Results of the predictive regression taking account of earlier mood are consistent with this explanation. They are also consistent with an interpretation based on an enduring trait such as negative affectivity or optimism; the same pattern of results would be obtained if those low on negative affectivity or high on optimism reported low depression on both occasions and performed well on the disability assessment. Thus, data such as these cannot ascertain whether disease severity *determines* distress.

For both samples, psychological variables were associated with distress. If causal, then they would offer an attractive target for intervention as, unlike disease severity, variables such as control cognitions can readily be altered with potential therapeutic benefit. Demonstrations of their causal role in depressive disorder is also relevant, as, although depression in stroke may be directly associated with the brain damage incurred, it is still possible that some stroke-related depression is influenced by the same factors as other forms of depression. Such interventions might allow one to establish whether the psychological variables were indeed causal.

DO MORE DISTRESSED INDIVIDUALS HAVE POORER DISEASE OUTCOMES?

Distress is clinically important if individuals have high enduring levels of emotional disorder or if levels of distress predict or cause other important outcomes such as survival or levels of disability. Like the above analyses of factors influencing distress, predictive analyses of consequences of distress require care in controlling for confounding factors. For example, demonstrating that distress predicted poor survival would be of only limited interest if levels of distress were determined by disease severity. There are now a number of studies where mood predicts survival, notably the finding of Frasure-Smith et al. (1993) that depression following MI accounted for a similar amount of unique variance in survival rates to indices of disease severity.

Even with the most stringent efforts to control extraneous and confounding variables, however, there are limits to the conclusions that can be drawn from non-experimental studies. Two main kinds of experimental investigation can be conducted with people with chronic disease. In the first, distress is manipulated and effects on functional limitations are recorded. Very few studies of this kind have been conducted, and one is reported below. To date, the results are limited to short term effects. Where longer term outcomes are investigated, more complex therapeutic interventions rather than simple mood manipulations are used and, therefore, it is more difficult to attribute outcome effects to the influence of changing mood.

Mood may affect disease outcomes in a number of ways. It may act psychophysiologically, influencing neuroendocrine, cardiovascular, and immune mechanisms, or it may influence the individual's self-care and health-related behaviors such as diet and smoking; or it may affect the behavior of others such as informal carers and health professionals and thereby determine the quality of care, such as levels of nutrition or access to aggressive treatment regimens. All of these mechanisms may be relevant for both survival and functional limitation outcomes.

Three investigations are reported: the first examines prediction of survival; the second examines prediction of functional limitations from mood and other psychological variables; and the third study examines the effects of mood manipulation on short term changes in disability.

Study 5: Predicting Survival from Measures of Distress in People with MND

McDonald et al. (1994) found that poor psychological status predicted poor survival in patients with MND. Their sample was a large group of patients who had had MND for periods from one month to over twenty-nine years. While they controlled for disease severity, disease duration, and age, it is still possible that distress was predictive simply because patients experiencing a fast rate of decline were more distressed. Thus, distress might have been the result of the same process that determined survival and the result would then be of limited importance. In order to investigate this further, we examined the same hypothesis in a consecutive cohort of people with newly diagnosed MND (Johnston et al., in press, b).

Method. Thirty-eight patients (27 men and 11 women; mean age 64) with MND were followed up for six months from the time of diagnosis and ten people died within that time. They completed psychological assessments [HADS; Rosenberg Self-Esteem Scale (Rosenberg, 1965); Bradburn Affect Balance Scale (Bradburn, 1969)] and disability measures (OPCS disability; Martin et al., 1988) at the time of diagnosis, six weeks and six months later where possible. The three psychological measures were used to create an overall positive mood measure by summing standard scores as MacDonald et al. had done.[1]

Results. Using mood data at six weeks which was incomplete for some participants, those who survived to six months had higher scores than those who died ($t = 2.08$, $df=27$, $p<.05$). Survivors did not differ from non-survivors on OPCS disability at six weeks ($t=0.83$, $df=28$, ns); and neither OPCS disability nor age was significantly correlated with mood.

Discussion. This study was able to replicate and extend the findings of MacDonald et al. by controlling duration of disease and including an index of disability to indicate the experience of the condition. The study does, therefore, rule out some of the more obvious spurious explanations of the findings. It is still possible that patients with poorer mood are later in getting the diagnosis and, therefore, at a later stage in the disease. Since people with poor mood are more likely to attend to physical symptoms, this interpretation is unlikely, but this research design cannot rule it out.

Study 6: Predicting Disability from Distress Following Acute Stroke

This study parallels the work with the stroke group in Study 4 by using a longitudinal predictive study to tease out the possible patterns of influence. It uses the same subjects and some of the same measures in the same research design, but to examine the consequences rather than the precursors of distress.

In predicting functional limitations, the main competing psychological predictors are mental representations, especially perceived control over the condition (Partridge and Johnston, 1989). Therefore, the relationship between distress and perceived control in predicting disability is examined.

Method. Participants were seventy-one patients who had had an acute stroke and survived to complete disability measures six months after discharge. The HADS and a measure of perceived control over recovery, the Recovery Locus of Control scale (RLOC; Partridge and Johnston, 1989), were completed one month after discharge. Two measures of disability, the Barthel Index (Mahoney and Barthel, 1965) which used self-report and the observer assessment discussed in Study 4, were completed at 1 and 6 months after discharge.

Results. Both anxiety and depression at one month predicted six month Barthel scores ($r=-.28$, $p<.05$, and $r=-.30$, $p<.05$ respectively), but only depression significantly predicted observer assessed disability ($r=-.20$, ns, and $r=-.38$, $p<.01$ respectively). When allowance was made for earlier disability, only the correlation between anxiety and Barthel Index remained significant ($r=-.29$, $p<,05$).

However, when both anxiety and RLOC were entered into a stepwise multiple regression equation with six-month Barthel Index, allowing for earlier scores as the dependent variable, only RLOC entered the equation and anxiety did not predict any additional variance.

Discussion. While distress was predictive of disability, most of these correlations became non-significant when earlier levels of disability were allowed for. This suggests that distress is predictive of disability largely because of the relationships between distress and disability at the earlier stage. These results are consistent with the hypothesis that disability caused distress that was then predictive of, but did not cause, later disability. Only one relationship, between anxiety and self-report Barthel disability, is incompatible with this hypothesis as it is sustained when earlier disability is taken into account. Finding a relationship on the self-report but not on the observed measure introduces the possibility that the results are due to reporting biases such as negative affectivity (Watson and Pennebaker, 1989), rather than a true relationship between anxiety and functional limitations.

Perceived control was a stronger predictor than anxiety. Additional results show that perceived control predicted both self-report and the observer assessed disability, allowing for earlier measures, suggesting that this finding is not simply due to patients' reporting styles. The cognitive predictor would appear to be more powerful than the emotional predictor. However, these interpretations are subject to the limits of a non-experimental study, and the following study examined the effects on disability of manipulating mood.

Study 7: Experimental Manipulation of Anxiety and Effects on Disability in People with Chronic Pain

Experimental studies of mood manipulation demonstrate that simple cognitive tasks can affect mood. These effects are brief, but long enough to investigate the consequences for disability assessments. Compared with longitudinal non-experimental studies, this study of the effects of experimental manipulation of mood on disability allows control of extraneous variables and permits the causal hypothesis to be tested. It was therefore hypothesised that a cognitive manipulation which increased anxiety would increase disability while one that reduced anxiety would reduce disability (Fisher and Johnson, 1996).

Method. Fifty patients (21 men, 29 women; mean age 42) with chronic pain (mean duration of pain 6.8 years) were randomly allocated to either an increase or a decrease anxiety manipulation. Mood was manipulated by asking participants to give examples of worrying aspects of their problem (increase anxiety) or of achievements in spite of their problem (decrease anxiety). Anxiety was measured before and after the manipulation using a visual analogue scale (VAS). Disability was assessed on a lifting task which required participants to hold an individually-determined weight for as long as it was comfortable, and the time was recorded; the task was repeated before and after the mood manipulation.

Results. Both anxiety and disability changed in the predicted direction following the mood manipulation. The groups differed significantly in mood change ($F(1,47)$ =12.70, $p<.01$) and in the change in performance on the disability task ($F(1,47)$ = 10.0, $p<.01$), using covariance analyses to control for initial group differences. Change in the time on the disability task was correlated with change in anxiety VAS (r= .43, $p<.01$).

Discussion. These results provide stronger evidence that in patients with chronic illness, distress affects levels of disability. When mood was systematically changed, disability levels changed in parallel. However there are still two major limitations. First, only short term effects have been demonstrated, and it would be difficult to extrapolate to the enduring patterns observed in chronic conditions. Second, it continues to be possible that the effects on disability are the result of the cognitive manipulation rather than the mood effects, i.e., the beliefs about the condition rather than the emotional state may determine the degree of functional limitation. On the other hand, these data are incompatible with explanations in terms of simple response biases or of enduring traits and clearly rule out changes in physical impairment as the sole explanation of functional limitations.

CONCLUSIONS

The studies reported illustrate the methodological problems in investigating the three main research questions concerning the extent, determinants, and consequences of distress in people with chronic disease. Measurement of mood may be influenced by lack of familiarity with the test or by other aspects of the test situation, including other interview material. Thus, in reporting levels of distress or in making comparisons between diseases, such factors need to be controlled or allowed for. The intuitive assumption that the severity of disease affects mood is not supported, nor does the evidence presented demonstrate that patients are more distressed than their healthy relatives. Instead, psychological factors such as coping, perceived control, satisfaction with care, and confidence in recovery explained distress, suggesting that distress in those with chronic disease is subject to the same factors that determine distress in physically healthy individuals. Controlling for disease severity, mood has been found to predict disease outcomes, both in terms of survival and in terms of disability, and the latter has been shown in both longitudinal correlational and experimental studies.

Each of the research paradigms used in investigating mood in chronic disease has limitations, and thus the answers they produce are always subject to question. Much may be achieved by good measurement and design, but answers are dependent on the triangulation of methods, within the limits of what is feasible and ethical. It is not obvious how one might examine the effects of chronic disease on distress other than in non-experimental designs, but the consequences of distress can be studied both experimentally and non-experimentally. In addition to increasing understanding of the relationships between chronic disease and distress, such investigations inform the design of therapeutic interventions which can, in turn, offer a useful test of the hypothesised relationships.

NOTES

I would like to thank my collaborators on the research described here: Cecily Partridge, Louise Earll, Val Morrison, Beth Pollard, Keren Fisher, Jane Knight and Ron MacWalter. Kristina Moodie and Carol Rennie conducted Study 2 and Study 3 respectively as part of the requirements for their undergraudate degrees. I also wish to acknowledge funding from: Chest Heart and Stroke Scotland, the Motor Neurone Disease Association and the Chief Scientist Office of the Scottish Office.

1. Their composite measure of psychological status included the Beck Depression Inventory, the Beck Hopelessness Scale, the Perceived Stress Scale, and the Anger Expression Scale as well as two other measures which are less directly measures of mood.

REFERENCES

Billings, A.G. and Moos, R.H. (1981). The role of coping responses and social resources in attenuating the stress of life events. *Journal of Behavioral Medicine, 4,* 139–157.

Bradburn, N.M. (1969). *The Structure of Psychological Well-being.* Aldine.

Clark, D.M. and Fairbairn, C.G. (Eds.) (1996). *Science and Practice of Cognitive Therapy.* Oxford: Oxford University Press

Cohen, S. and Wills, T.A. (1985). Stress, social support and the buffering hypothesis. *Psychological Bulletin*, 98, 310–357.

Fisher, K. and Johnston, M. (1996). Emotional distress as a mediator of the relationship between pain and disability: an experimental study. *British Journal of Health Psychology, 1,* 207–218

Frasure-Smith, N., Lesperance, F. and Taljic, N. (1993). Depression following myocardial infarction: impact on 6 month survival. *Journal of the American Medical Association, 270,* 1819–1825

Johnston, M. (1980). Anxiety in surgical patients. *Psychological Medicine, 10,* 145–152.

Johnston, M. and Wallace, L. (Eds.) (1989). *Stress and Medical Procedures.* Oxford: Oxford University Press.

Johnston, M. Earll, L., Mitchell, E., Morrison, V., and Wright, S. (1996). Communicating the diagnosis of motor neurone disease. *Palliative Medicine, 10,* 23–34.

Johnston, M., Morrison, V., MacWalter, R., and Partridge, C.J. (1999). Perceived control, coping and recovery from disability following stroke. *Psychology and Health.*

Johnston, M., Foulkes, J, Johnston, D.W., Pollard, B., and Gudmundsdottir, H. (in press). The impact on patients and partners of inpatient and extended cardiac counseling and rehabilitation: a controlled trial. Psychosomatic Medicine

Johnston, M., Earll, L., Giles, M., McClenahan, R., Morrison, V., and Stevens. D. (in press, b). Mood as a predictor of disability and survival in patients newly diagnosed with ALS/MND. *British Journal of Health Psychology.*

Knight, J. and Johnston, M. (1995). Physical disability, services and social support: the impact on families. Report to the SHHD, K/OPR/2/2/D10.

Leventhal, H., Benyamini, Y., Brownlee, S., Diefenbach, M., Leventhal, E., Patrick-Miller, L., and Robitaille, C. (1997). Illness representations: theoretical foundations. In Petrie and Weinman.

Lewin, B., Robertson, I.H., Cay, E.L., Irving, J.B., and Campbell, M. (1992). A self-help post MI rehabilitation package—the heart manual: effects on psychological adjustment, hospitalisation and GP consultation. *Lancet, 339,* 1036–1040.

Ludwick-Rosenthal, R. and Neufeld, W.J. (1988). Stress management during noxious medical procedures: an evaluation review of outcome studies. *Psychological Bulletin, 104,* 326–342.

Macleod, M. (in press). [paper in this volume]

Mahoney, F.J. and Barthel, D.W. (1965). Functional evaluation: the Barthel Index. *Maryland State Medical Journal, 14,* 61–65.

Martin, J., Meltzer, H., and Elliot, D. (1988) *The prevalence of disability among adults. OPCS surveys of disability in Great Britain.* Report I. London: H.M.S.O.

McDonald, E.R., Wiedenfeld, S.A., Hillel, A., Carpenter, C.L., and Walter, R.A. (1994). Survival in amyotropic lateral sclerosis: the role of psychological factors. *Archives of Neurology, 51,* 17–23.

Moodie, K. (1995). Support groups for breast cancer patients: likely uptake and impact of the offer. Unpublished master's thesis: University of St Andrews.

Moorey, S., Greer, S., Watson, M., et al. (1991). The factor structure and factor stability of the Hospital Anxiety and Depression Scale in patients with cancer. *British Journal of Psychiatry, 158,* 255–259.

Morrison, V., Johnston, M., and MacWalter, R. (in submission). Predictors of distress following an acute stroke: Disability, control cognitions, and satisfaction with care.

Orgogozo, J.M., Capildeo, R., Anagostou, C.N., et al. (1983). Development of a neurological scale of middle cerebral artery (MCA) infarction [translation]. *La Presse Medicale, 48,* 3039–3044.

Partridge, C. and Johnston, M. (1989). Perceived control and recovery from stroke. *British Journal of Clinical Psychology, 28,* 53–60.

Partridge, C., Johnston, M., and Morris, L. (1991). Disability and health services: perceptions, beliefs and experiences of elderly people. Report to the Nuffield Provincial hospitals Trust.

Petrie, K. and Weinman, J. (Eds.) (1997). *Perceptions of Health and Illness.* Amsterdam: Harwood.

Power, M.J., Champion, L.A., and Aris, S.J. (1988). The development of a measure of social support: the Significant Others Scale (SOS). *British Journal of Clinical Psychology, 27,* 349–358.

Rennie, C. (1994). Quality of life in breast cancer patients: does the perceived quality differ between clinical and home measurement? Unpublished master's thesis: University of St. Andrews.

Rosenberg, M.I. (1965). *Society and adolescent self-image.* Princeton, NJ: Princeton University Press.

Steptoe, A. (1998). Psychophysiological Bases of Disease. In *Health Psychology,.* edited by D. W Johnston and M. Johnston (eds.), Volume 8 of *Comprehensive Clinical Psychology.* Oxford: Elsevier.

Suls, J. and Fletcher, E. (1985). The relative efficacy of avoidant and nonavoidant coping strategies: a meta-analysis. *Health Psychology, 4,* 249–288.

Taylor, S. (1990). Health psychology: the science and the field. *American Psychologist, 45,* 40–50.

Watson, D. and Pennebaker, J. (1989). Health complaints, stress and disease: exploring the central role of negative affectivity. *Psychological Review, 96,* 234–254.

Zigmond, A.S. and Snaith, R.P. (1983). The Hospital Anxiety and Depression Scale. *Acta Psychiatrica Scandinavica, 67,* 361–370.

The Emotional Impact of Faces (But Not Names): Face Specific Changes in Skin Conductance Responses to Familiar and Unfamiliar People

HADYN D. ELLIS, ANGELA H. QUAYLE
Cardiff University

and

ANDREW W. YOUNG
York University

Skin Conductance Responses (SCRs) to familiar and unfamiliar names and faces were recorded from independent groups of subjects, using two different presentation designs: the first employing fewer familiar than unfamiliar items (Tranel, Fowles, and Damasio, 1985) and the second employing equal numbers of familiar and unfamiliar items. In both designs, familiar faces were responded to significantly more strongly than unfamiliar faces, whereas for names there was no difference in responses to familiar and unfamiliar stimuli. Faces produced significantly larger overall SCRs than names in the unequal familiar/ unfamiliar ratio design, but this effect was not observed in the equal ratio design. The results are discussed with particular reference to those previously published by Tranel et al. (1985) and in relation to work both on covert recognition in prosopagnosia and on one of the delusional misidentification syndromes known as the Capgras delusion.

Though we can identify people from a variety of different sources of information, including voice, gait, and name, the most significant means is undoubtedly from the face (Ellis, 1981). Not surprisingly, then, most research into person identification has concentrated on the

113

normal human ability to quickly and accurately recognize faces (Goldstein and Chance, 1971; Ellis, 1975; Bruce, 1988; Young and Ellis, 1989). From this research, together with observations on those with neurological impairments that impair face recognition (prosopagnosia), various models have been published to explain how we recognize familiar faces (Damasio et al., 1982; Bauer, 1984; Bruce and Young, 1986; Ellis, 1986; Burton et al., 1990).

Tranel and Damasio (1988) pointed out, however, that although most models of familiar face recognition have heuristic value in accounting for conscious face recognition, only some are sufficiently flexible easily to allow for non-conscious or covert processes (Damasio et al., 1982; Bauer, 1984; Burton et al., 1991). The existence of such activity has been inferred from studies of prosopagnosic patients, who, as we have indicated, have an inability to consciously recognize previously familiar faces. Despite the absence of overt recognition, some of these patients, nonetheless, make differential autonomic responses to faces measured by skin conductance responses; that is, they show larger responses to faces they knew prior to their brain injury, despite not revealing any conscious recognition (Bauer, 1984; Tranel and Damasio, 1988). Studies of subjects without brain damage have also revealed elevated skin conductance responses (SCRs) to familiar faces compared with unfamiliar faces (Tranel et al., 1985; Ellis et al., 1993). In the study of Ellis et al., identical differential SCRs were found even when subjects were unable consciously to identify the faces, confirming the importance of covert processing in the intact brain.

Two recently published studies have made use of the familiar face/SCR phenomenon to examine patients with Capgras delusion (Ellis et al., 1997; Hirstein and Ramachandran, 1997). In this delusion patients (psychiatric, neurological, or medical) assert that others, often but not always close to them, have been replaced by doubles, robots, etc. (Capgras and Reboul-Lachaux, 1923). Ellis and Young (1990) suggested that the Capgras delusion may represent the mirror image of covert recognition of faces in prosopagnosia that sometimes is indicated by the autonomic discrimination of faces that cannot be consciously identified. Ellis et al. (1997) tested the hypothesis that patients with Capgras delusion will show the opposite pattern by examining the skin conductance responses (SCRs) to famous and unfamiliar faces from ten psychiatric patients—five with the Capgras delusion and five without—and normal controls. The latter groups responded as expected: each revealed higher SCRs to familiar faces. The Capgras group, however, as predicted from the theory of Ellis and Young (1990), did not show such differential SCRs. Hirstein and Ramachandran (1997) noted similar results with a single, neurological patient with Capgras-like symptoms and also showed them using faces personally familiar to the patient. These independent results provide fairly strong support for the prediction made by Ellis and Young (1990).

The fact that, under normal circumstances, familiar faces yield greater autonomic activity than do unfamiliar faces raises the question as to why this should occur. Tranel et al. (1985) argued that known faces are more "significant" stimuli than unknown faces and that this attribute induces greater autonomic activity. But they did not address the issue as to whether it is only familiar faces that have such signal value in person perception. What about the other means of recognizing people such as names and voices? The following experiment, based on an adaptation of the method employed by Tranel et al. (1985), is aimed at determining whether familiar names generate comparable autonomic responses to familiar faces. This should help us decide whether the phenomenon of autonomic recognition arises somehow from a central acknowledgment of the stimulus person's significance or whether, instead, it is specific to the face processing mechanism.

Before addressing this theoretical question, however, we should mention a methodological problem that potentially may have influenced the data of Tranel et al. (1985) and Tranel and Damasio (1988). Dawson, Schell, and Filion (1990) pointed out a possible artifact in these experiments when they noted that the ratio of familiar to unfamiliar faces was always low. Dawson et al. (1990) argued that this arrangement could simply produce a novelty response to the less frequent familiar faces. Ellis et al. (1993), however, did report an experimental verification in which there were equal numbers of familiar and unfamiliar faces shown. The differential SCRs occurred to familiar and unfamiliar faces not only when the stimuli were consciously perceived, but also when they were displayed subliminally—implying the results cannot be attributed to any conscious awareness of novelty. This replication and extension suggests that Tranel and his colleagues have discovered a robust phenomenon in normal subjects that seems to parallel covert recognition in prosopagnosic patients. The fact that it remains, even when normal subjects are prevented by a masking technique from fully analyzing the stimulus, further supports the notion that facial familiarity may be registered at a level below consciousness of the person's identity.

In the first experiment we, therefore, explore the question of whether the finding of differential SCRs for familiar and unfamiliar faces extends to names as well. Here we employ methods that approximate those used by Tranel et al. (1985) before we subsequently examine how the data may be influenced by a paradigm change in which the ratio of familiar to unfamiliar stimuli is equal.

EXPERIMENT 1

Method

Subjects. Ten male and ten female right-handed student volunteers were paid to take part in one of the two stimulus conditions. Half were randomly allocated to see faces and half to view printed names.

Stimuli.

FACES: Twenty-nine faces of males and females were chosen from a set of 328 faces. They were scanned into a Macintosh LC computer as grey-scale PICT images using Desk Scan II, so that each filled a 7.5 cm × 10 cm area at the center of the monitor. All 328 faces had been previously rated for familiarity by eleven independent judges using a seven-point Likert Scale. For the present experiment twenty faces rated 1 (i.e., unknown) by all judges were used for the unfamiliar set; and five with an average of 6 or over (min: 6.3; max: 6.9) were selected as the familiar set. Four unfamiliar faces acted as buffer items; two occurred before and two after the experimental set.

NAMES: Twenty-nine first name and surname combinations were used as stimuli; five of these were the names of the people in the set of familiar faces. The unfamiliar name set comprised twenty invented names. These names were constructed to each share the same prosodic quality as one of the familiar target names: four unfamiliar names were constructed to match one of each of the five target familiar names. Four unknown names acted as buffer items; two occurred before and two after the experimental set. The names were displayed centrally in twenty-four-point Helvetica font.

Skin Conductance Response. SCRs were recorded on a MacLab/8 device using MacLab software. Recordings were made via 1 cm^2

Ag-AgCl electrodes fixed to the thenar and hypothenar eminences of the non-preferred hand with adhesive collars which allowed a 0.5 cm contact area with the electrolyte. The electrolyte was made up of 0.050 molar NaCl in a Unibase cream medium (Fowles et al., 1981). Subjects' hands had first been thoroughly cleaned with a liquid soap before electrodes were attached. During testing the relaxed arm was supported by a chair rest.

A latency window of 1–3 s from stimulus onset was used to determine an amplitude measure. All responses that did not have their initial deflection within this window were ignored. Tranel and colleagues used a 1–5 s latency window in their investigations. The present, more conservative latency window has been recommended by Venables and Christie (1980) who argue that larger windows are more likely to include non stimulus-specific SCRs.

Procedure. Subjects who had given prior consent to the procedure were seated in an adjustable chair so that their eyes were approximately 100 cm from the center of the display computer monitor. The room was dimly lit and extraneous noises were eliminated. They were told that they would see a series of faces or names, each for 2 s followed by a 20 s interval, and were asked to attend to the stimuli while remaining relaxed throughout. There followed a 5 m period during which electrodes were placed in position and baseline SCR levels recorded. Then the two buffer items, twenty-five experimental stimuli, and two further buffers were presented. The experimental stimuli occurred in a different random order for each subject.

After the experiment, subjects were shown all stimuli again to check that they correctly knew each to be familiar or unfamiliar. They did this without error, and no adjustment to the data was necessary.

The amplitude of the largest SCR within each stimulus latency window was then measured by one E. who was blind as to which stimulus gave rise to each. Magnitude measures (Prokasy and Kumpfer, 1973) were employed: the single largest amplitude response to each relevant stimulus was taken (a value of zero was recorded when no discernible response occurred), and these values were used to create two averages—one relating to the five latency windows for familiar stimuli and the other to the twenty latency windows for unfamiliar stimuli. Only after blind scoring were the calculated SCR magnitude measures related to stimulus familiarity.

Results

The SCR magnitudes, measured in microSiemens, for each subject's responses to familiar and unfamiliar names and faces were compared by ANOVA (split-plot design; Kirk, 1968). This revealed a significant main effect for stimulus type, $F(1, 18) = 6.49$, $p < .05$; and a main effect for stimulus familiarity, $F(1,118) = 9.94$, $p < .01$. There was also a significant interaction between stimulus type and stimulus familiarity, $F(1, 18) = 6.40$, $p < .05$. (Figure 1)

The stimulus type × familiarity interaction was further examined by simple effects analysis that revealed four things: the mean SCRs to faces and names differed significantly for familiar items, with responses to faces being higher, $F(1,18) = 7.151$, $p < .02$; there was no significant difference between mean SCRs to faces and names when they were unfamiliar, $F(1,18) = 3.13$; mean SCRs to familiar faces were significantly greater than for unfamiliar faces, $F(1,18) = 16.14$, $p < .001$; and familiar and unfamiliar names produced equivalent SCRs, $F(1,18) < 1$.

In summary, the results indicate that SCRs to faces are significantly greater than those to names, and the differentially larger responses to familiar stimuli occur only for faces.

Discussion

The findings of this experiment show that the result reported by Tranel et al. (1985) and Ellis et al. (1993), which indicated greater autonomic reactivity to familiar compared with unfamiliar faces, does not extend to names. There is no significant differential SCR responsiveness to familiar names compared with unfamiliar names. Moreover, the overall SCR magnitude to names is significantly lower than those for faces—though this is largely due to the large responses to familiar faces.

It would appear then that, although possible familiarity responses to other aspects of people (e.g., voice) were not examined in the present experiment, it is clear that not all forms of representations of people—here, presentations of their names—lead to measurably different autonomic activation for familiar compared with unfamiliar stimuli.

There are two aspects of the experiment, however, that may raise some doubts about the validity of that conclusion. First, there is the

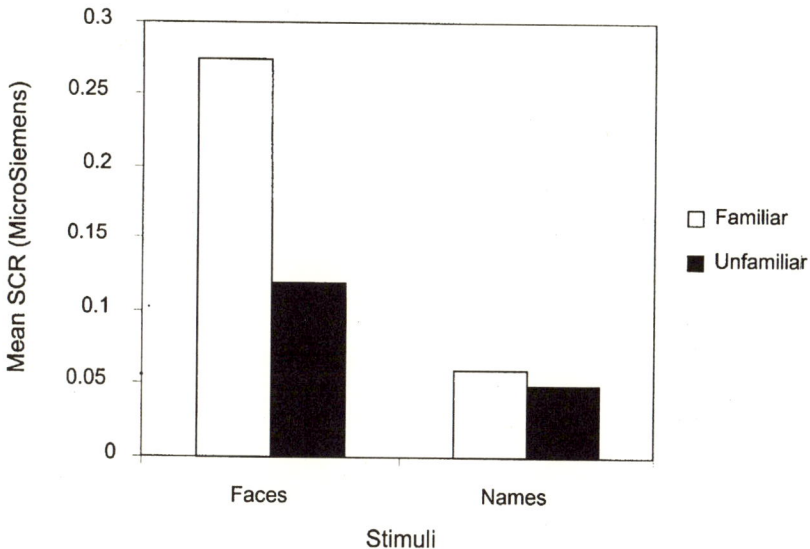

FIGURE 1
Mean Skin Conductance responses (microSiemens) to familiar and
unfamiliar names and faces in Experiment 1

issue raised by Dawson et al. (1990) concerning the unequal incidence
of familiar and unfamiliar faces. This could not explain, of course, the
fact that there were no such differential SCRs for names. But, second,
it could be argued, the mean response magnitude to the names was too
low to easily reveal any familiar/unfamiliar stimulus effect. This re-
duced-magnitude compared with faces is not so easy to address. It
may simply reflect a fundamental difference in stimulus complexity,
but without more data this is a premature inference.

Experiment 2 therefore replicated Experiment 1 in every respect
except that the ratio of familiar to unfamiliar stimuli was equal.

EXPERIMENT 2

Method

Subjects. Twenty-four subjects (12 males and 12 female students)
were paid to take part in the experiment. They were randomly assigned either to the faces task (7 males, 5 females) or the names task
(5 males, 7 females).

Stimuli.

FACES: A total of forty-four faces was used. These comprised twenty familiar faces with ratings between 5.4 and 6.9 on the seven-point familiarity rating scale described earlier; and twenty-four unfamiliar faces with familiarity ratings of 1. Four of these were buffer items, two of which were shown at the beginning, and two at the end. The data from these four buffer stimuli were not used.

NAMES: The names of the twenty familiar faces were used as the familiar set. The unfamiliar names were first name and surname combinations constructed in the same way as in Experiment 1: each familiar name had an unfamiliar comparison, matched for its prosodic qualities. Four unknown names acted as buffers, two before and two after the experimental set.

Skin Conductance Response. SCRs were measured exactly as in Experiment 1.

Procedure. The procedure for preparing and testing subjects was the same as that described for Experiment 1.

As before subjects' knowledge of the familiar stimuli they had seen

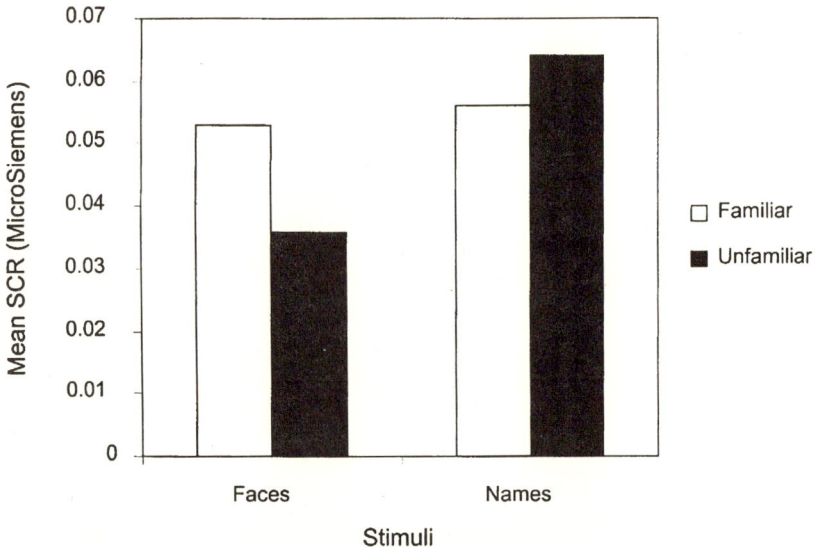

FIGURE 2
Mean Skin Conductance responses (microSiemens) to familiar names and faces in Experiment 2

was checked and as in Experiment 1, all of them correctly knew the familiar from the unfamiliar ones.

Similarly, SCRs were scored by someone blind to the origin of each response.

Results

Owing to unequal-variance for different stimulus conditions the log mean peak SCRs for every subject's response to familiar and unfamiliar stimuli in each of the two stimulus conditions were used for analysis by a 2 × 2 mixed-design ANOVA. This revealed a significant familiarity by stimulus type interaction, $F(1,22) = 5.70$, $p < .05$; and no significant main effects. Exploration of simple effects within this interaction revealed only one significant contrast, which was the effect of familiarity at the level of the faces task, $F(1, 22) = 5.39$, $p < .03$. The F value of the effect of familiarity at the level of the names task was less than 1. The mean SCRs are shown in Figure 2.

Discussion

The results of principal interest in Experiment 2 are essentially the same as those found in Experiment 1, although it should be noted that the overall level of response in Experiment 2 is somewhat weaker.

Eleven subjects produced larger SCRs to familiar compared with unfamiliar faces, and only one showed a very slight opposite tendency. In contrast for name stimuli, only five subjects revealed a bias towards familiar stimuli and the remaining seven produced an opposite bias. We may be confident, therefore, not only that familiar faces do create differential autonomic activity (Tranel and Damasio, 1988; Ellis et al., 1993), but that the effect cannot be attributed simply to some undifferentiated novelty response.

Another notable feature of the data from Experiment 2 was not expected: unlike those from Experiment 1, where, overall, SCRs to names were much lower than those to faces, no such difference was found when the ratio of familiar to unfamiliar stimuli was equal. This means that we can be reasonably confident that the lack of differences in SCRs to familiar and unfamiliar names observed in both experiments cannot be attributed to some artifact of differentially low responding.

GENERAL DISCUSSION

These two experiments serve to confirm that the larger SCR to familiar compared with unfamiliar faces is a robust and reliable phenomenon. Moreover, the same effect does not occur when the names of familiar and unfamiliar people are presented. Although this may not be sufficient to demonstrate that it is an entirely face-specific property of the nervous system, it is clear that differential SC responding is not found for all possible forms of representations of a familiar person. Note that each of the representations used in these experiments (faces and names) were visual representations of the person—yet only faces generated differential SCRs. We should like to pursue the argument that there may be compelling reasons to believe that this does manifest something essential to the way we process faces.

Faces, after all, are probably the most significant socio-biological stimuli in our environment (Ellis, 1981). For our ancestors, the rapid and accurate reaction to them was a matter of crucial importance. Social animals need to distinguish in-group from out-group members and to discriminate high- from low-status members, as well as recognize those who are kin from those unrelated. The face not only provides the richest source of identity information, of course, but also conveys details of health, age, attractiveness, intentions, mood, etc. The systems supporting face recognition are also linked to those that interpret expression, assist oral language comprehension, and make various attributions concerning factors such as race (Bruce and Young, 1986; Ellis, 1986). The rich interaction among subsystems means that face recognition is not simply a cognitive faculty. Instead, it automatically co-triggers emotional responses that may serve to signal the personal relevance of the face (Van Lancker, 1991). Those faces that are known to us trigger a set of interrelated reactions based upon our attitudes towards their owners and, presumably, this is what underlies the increased autonomic responses that familiar faces engender. In those with Capgras delusion, the absence of such autonomic responses is associated with or leads to quite bizarre belief systems regarding the identity of others (Ellis et al., 1997; Hirstein and Ramachandran, 1997).

One could argue that names, too, may trigger similar high-level associated responses. But our data show that there is no difference in SCRs to familiar and unfamiliar names, suggesting that the name recognition system—which has obviously been developed much later than that for faces in evolutionary terms, and is most likely dependent on other language abilities—does not automatically trigger autonomic activity. That seems to be domain specific.

Whether or not the above speculation proves valid, there is no denying the fact that stimuli failing in one domain may cause increased autonomic activity whilst functionally similar stimuli that are within a different domain do not. This domain specificity is consistent with ideas concerning the modular arrangement of mental functions and implies that a module, such as the face-processing one, can have associated with it autonomic activity which another, such as the one serving word recognition, may not—even though each has a parallel function in person identification.

NOTE

This study was carried out with generous support from the EJLB Foundation (Canada) and the Wellcome Trust.

REFERENCES

Bauer, R.M. (1984). Autonomic recognition of names and faces: A neuropsychological application of the Guilty Knowledge Test. *Neuropsychologia, 22,* 457–469.

Bruce, V. and Young, A. (1986). Understanding face recognition. *British Journal of Psychology, 77,* 305–327.

Bruce, V. (1988). *Recognizing Faces.* Hillsdale, N.J.: Lawrence Erlbaum Associates.

Burton, A.M., Bruce, V., and Johnston, R.A. (1990). Understanding face recognition with an interactive activation model. *British Journal of Psychology, 81,* 361–380.

Burton, A.M., Young, A.W., Bruce, V., Johnston, R. and Ellis, A.W. (1991). Understanding covert recognition. *Cognition, 39,* 129–166.

Damasio, A.R., Damasio, H., and Van Hoesen, G.W. (1982). Prosopagnosia: Anatomic basis and behavioral mechanisms. *Neurology, 32,* 331–341.

Dawson, M.E., Schell, A.M., and Filion, D.L. (1990). The electrodermal system. In T. Cacioppo and L.G. Tassinary (Eds.), *Principles of Psychophysiology,* pp. 295–324. New York: Cambridge University Press.

de Pauw, K.W. (1994). Psychodynamic approaches to the Capgras delusion—A historical review. *Psychopathology, 27,* 154–160.

Ellis, H.D. (1975). Recognizing faces. *British Journal of Psychology,* 409–426.

Ellis, H.D. (1981). Introduction. In G.M. Davies, H.D. Ellis and J.W. Shepherd. *Perceiving and Remembering Faces.* London: Academic Press.

Ellis, H.D. (1986). Processes underlying face recognition. In R. Bruyer (Ed), *The Neuropsychology of Face Perception and Facial Expression.* Hillsdale, N.J.: Lawrence Erlbaum.

Ellis, H.D and Young, A.W. (1990). Accounting for delusional misidentifications. *British Journal of Psychiatry, 157,* 239–248.

Ellis, H.D., Young, A.W., and Koenken, G. (1993). Covert face recognition without prosopagnosia. *Behavioural Neurology, 6,* 27–32.

Ellis, H.D., Young, A.W., Quayle, A.H., and de Pauw, K.W. (1997). Reduced autonomic responses to faces in Capgras delusion. *Proceedings of the Royal Society,* London B, *264,* 1085–1092.

Fowles, D.C., Christie, M.J., Edelberg, R., Grings, W.W., Lykken, D.T. and Venables, P.H.

(1981). Publication recommendations for electrodermal measurements. *Psychophysiology*, *18*, 232–239.

Goldstein, A.G. and Chance, J.E. (1971). Visual recognition memory for complex configurations. *Perception and Psychophysics*, *9*, 237–241.

Hirstein, W. and Ramachandran, V.S. (1997). Capgras syndrome: A novel probe for understanding the neural representation of the identity and familiarity of persons. *Proceedings of the Royal Society*, London B, *264*, 437–444.

Kirk, R.E. (1968). *Experimental Design: Procedures for the Behavioural Sciences*. Belmont, California: Brooks/Cole Publishing Company.

Prokasy, W.F. and Kumpfer, K.L. (1973). Classical conditioning. In W.F. Prokasy and D.C. Raskin (Eds.), *Electrodermal Activity in Psychological Research* (pp. 157–202). New York: Academic Press.

Tranel, D. and Damasio, A.R. (1988). Non-conscious face recognition in patients with face agnosia. *Behavioural Brain Research*, *30*, 235–249.

Tranel, D., Fowles, D.C., and Damasio, A.R. (1985). Electro-dermal discrimination of familiar and unfamiliar faces: A methodology. *Psychophysiology*, *22*, 403–408.

Van Lancker, D. (1991). Personal relevance and the human right hemisphere. *Brain and Cognition*, *17*, 64–92.

Venables, P.H. and Christie, M.J. (1980). Electrodermal activity. In I. Martin and P.H. Venables (Eds.), *Techniques in Psychophysiology* (pp. 3–67). New York: Wiley and Sons.

Young, A.W. and Ellis, H.D. (1989). Childhood prosopagnosia. *Brain and Cognition*, *9*, 16–47.

Average Faces
Are Average Faces

JIM POLLARD
University of Canterbury, New Zealand

JOHN SHEPHERD and JEAN SHEPHERD
University of Aberdeen, Scotland

Photographs of faces of young adult male and female Scots were measured on nineteen frontal dimensions. Measures in each dimension were converted to z-scores and summed for each face. For each sex, the ten faces closest to the average summed z-score and the ten most distant from it were rated for attractiveness by white male and female New Zealand undergraduates. Raters agreed significantly in ordering the faces in attractiveness, but did not rate faces close to the "population" average differently from those distant from it. Tested for the first time with actual rather than contrived faces, the commonly reported hypothesis that faces representing the average of a population are attractive is not supported.

The first account we have of the attractiveness of the average face comes from Albert Duncan Austin. He was District Engineer for Otago, New Zealand, when he wrote to Charles Darwin to tell him of his discovery that when viewing different faces together in a stereoscope "the faces blend into one in a most remarkable manner, producing in the case of some ladies' portraits, in every instance, a decided improvement in beauty" (1877).

Darwin passed Austin's letter to Galton who was the first, in 1878, to claim that the composite portrait is an average, although Pearson, in 1924, records that Galton recognised later that it was an "aggregation" rather than an average. In 1886, Stoddart also questioned the composite as an average, especially the "deep-eyed, earnest expression, which is the result of superposing all the eyes of the components on exactly the same points. . . . The deep dark eyes do not represent the average, but rather a summation, and hence an exaggeration of earnest expression" (1886).

Not until 1952 do we find the general claim, made by David Katz, that the composite is both average and beautiful and that it is beautiful because it is average. "Evidemment, en opposition aux tests d'intelligence, où ce qui estmoyen caractérise la médiocrité, la moyenne représentée dans le portrait composite représente la norm de beauté" (Katz, 1952).[1]

In 1990, Langlois and Roggman described the first systematic study to support the claim that faces representing the average of the population are consistently judged as attractive. They digitised photographs of student faces and arithmetically averaged groups of the resulting matrices of numeric grey values to construct composite portraits. The composites were judged more attractive than the individuals from which they were constructed. Langlois and Roggman interpreted their results as evidence of an evolutionary process of stabilizing selection towards averageness that governs our perception of facial attractiveness and gives it an important role in mate selection. As a proximal mechanism, Langlois and Roggman invoked the cognitive process of prototypicality. The Langlois and Roggman interpretation continues to be reported, most recently by Young and Bruce (1998) in an exhibition at the Scottish National Portrait Gallery.

Responses to Langlois and Roggman's findings (Alley and Cunningham, 1991; Pittenger, 1991; Alley, 1992; Benson and Perrett, 1992; Ridley, 1992) questioned their interpretation, suggesting variously that composites are preferred because they appear more youthful, more symmetrical, or more familiar, or that the attractiveness of the composite can be attributed to stretching, distortion, smoothing, blurring, or the presence or absence of blemishes. Langlois, Roggman, and Musselman (1994) replied to these critics, concluding that none of the alternatives could explain their results adequately. A study of the attractiveness of digitized composite faces by Grammer and Thornhill (1994) suggested to them that the symmetry of the composite face may be more important than its averageness in determining attractiveness. Further evidence contradicting the claim that averageness is attractive came from Perrett, May, and Yoshikawa (1994). Using a composite process that does not result in feature enhancement, they found that the mean shape of a set of attractive faces differs from and is preferred to the mean shape of the larger sample from which the attractive faces were selected. In addition, they found that attractive composites could be made more attractive by warping shape differences away from the sample mean.

When Jones (1995) presented a substantial case for neoteny (youthfulness) as an important component, at least of female facial attractiveness, Musselman, Langlois, and Roggman, in their invited comment on this thesis, continued to defend the definition of attractive faces "as those whose facial configurations are closest to the average population configuration."

More recent support for the "average is attractive" hypothesis came in a study by Rhodes and Tremewan (1996) using line drawings produced by a computerized character generator, which are not subject to feature enhancement. They found that attractiveness increased with averageness and was negatively correlated with distinctiveness, a subjective measure of the converse of averageness.

Empirical evidence both for and against the "attractiveness is averageness" hypothesis has come entirely from studies using artificially contrived faces (photographic, average bit mapped, warped morphed, or caricatured faces). The extent to which these processes produce "average" faces is not always clear (Pollard, 1995). The present study sought, therefore, to test the hypothesis more directly by using photographs of normal human faces that differ in distance from their population mean.

METHOD

Subjects

Subjects for the attractiveness judgements were twenty male and twenty female volunteer white New Zealand undergraduate psychology students in their late teens or early twenties. Each was paid a small sum for taking part in the rating exercise of about forty minutes.

Materials

The faces were drawn from a "population" of photographs of 240 clean shaven male and 99 female faces accumulated to develop an interactive computer system for retrieving faces (Shepherd, 1986; Ellis et al., 1989). All the faces used were of caucasians in their late teens or early twenties, and were frontal views presented as individual mono-chrome prints measuring 93mm × 122mm.

Each face was measured on nineteen linear dimensions, chosen because they were those most commonly used by people asked to describe faces from memory (Ellis et al., 1989). Distances between facial extremities comprised seven of the dimensions, five involved eyes and eyebrows, three involved the nose, three involved the mouth, and one measured hair length.

Separately for each sex, values on each dimension were converted to z scores about the population mean for that dimension. For each sex, the ten faces with the highest combined z score ("distant" faces) were selected as were the ten having the lowest combined z score ("near" faces). The only limitation placed on selection was that the faces be without skin blemishes. This procedure provided two sets of faces from each sex, one of faces close to the "population" mean on the nineteen parameters and the other of faces distant from that mean.

Procedure

Male and female faces were presented to subjects separately in shuffled packs of twenty prints. Half first rated the female faces and half first the male faces. Subjects were asked to distribute the faces from each pack into seven categories with Category 1 containing the least attractive and Category 7 the most attractive faces. Subjects were requested to place at least one face in each category.

RESULTS

Analysis of variance of the ratings was carried out with gender of subject as a between subject factor and sex of face and distance from population mean as within subject factors. The analysis yielded no significant main effects or interactions (Subject gender, $F(1,38) = 1.89$, $p = .18$; Sex of photograph, $F(1/38) = 0.30$, $p = .59$; Distance from population mean $F(1/38) = 0.01$, $p = .90$; Subject gender × Distance, $F(1/38) = 2.44$, $p = .13$; Subject gender × Sex of photo, $F(1,38) = 0.27$, $p = .61$; Distance × Sex of photo, $F(1/38) = 2.20$, $p = .15$; Subject gender × Sex of photo × Distance. $F(1/38) = 0.05, p = .82$).

TABLE 1
Attractiveness ratings by young men and women of male and female faces
varying in distance from their population mean

	Mean attractiveness rating	
	Distant faces	Near faces
Male subjects looking at female faces	3.54	3.80
Male subjects looking at male faces	3.66	3.66
Female subjects looking at female faces	3.82	3.81
Female subjects looking at male faces	4.01	3.80

Table 1 presents the mean attractiveness ratings of male and female subjects judging male and female faces near to and distant from their population mean.

An indication of the reliability of the attractiveness ratings was gained by correlating the mean ratings for women with the mean ratings for men. For both male and female faces, the correlations are significant and very high. Judging male faces, men's and women's ratings correlated + .863 ($p = .0002$, $df = 19$); while judging female faces they correlated + .902 ($p < .0001$, $df = 19$).

To check the possibility that selecting arithmetically deviant faces had yielded a mix of very attractive and very unattractive faces, Cochran's test for homogeneity of variance was applied to the attractiveness ratings of the four sets of faces. With a critical value of $C = 0.5017$ ($p = .05$) the observed value of 0.372 ($k = 4$, $df = 9$) provides no support for this hypothesis. Means and standard deviations of the ratings in each category are shown in Table 2.

DISCUSSION

Men and women subjects showed significant agreement in their attractiveness rankings, but contrary to what might be expected from the Langlois and Roggman hypothesis, there were only slight and non-significant differences in perceived attractiveness between the average and the deviant faces, whether male or female.

It might be claimed that the test was insensitive because the method for selecting the average and the deviant faces was unsophisticated, with the facial dimensions all given equal weight in the combined z

TABLE 2
**Means and standard deviations of attractiveness ratings of male and female
faces varying in distance from their population mean**

	Mean	Standard deviation
Male faces		
Distant	3.84	1.17
Near	3.73	1.56
Female faces		
Distant	3.68	0.99
Near	3.81	1.33

scores. This is true, but the same might be said of the composite portrait technique that gives indiscriminate weightings to different features, yet does produce robust enhancement of perceived attractiveness. Despite the crudity of the z score selection, one would have expected from the Langlois and Roggman hypothesis that faces that differed so markedly in relation to their population average would also differ in perceived attractiveness.

Tested for the first time with actual rather than contrived faces, the hypothesis that average faces are attractive faces is not supported. This still leaves the undoubted and cross-culturally validated attractiveness of the composite face (Pollard, 1995) to be explained. If the composite is not attractive because it is average, why is it attractive? Yet to be investigated, is Pollard's proposal that the photographic composite is in no sense an average, and that the attractiveness of the photographic and digital composites is a result of feature enhancement with artifactually larger features being perceived as more attractive than smaller ones.

NOTE

1. "Apparently, in contrast with intelligence tests, where what is average characterizes mediocrity, the average represented in the composite portrait represents the norm of beauty."

REFERENCES

Alley, T.R. (1992). Perceived age, physical attractiveness and sex differences in preferred mates' ages. *Behavioural and Brain Sciences*, *15*, 92.
Alley, T.R. and Cunningham, M.R. (1991). Averaged faces are attractive, but very attractive faces are not average. *Psychological Science*, *2*, 123–125.

Austin, A.D. (1883). In Galton, F. *Inquiries into human faculty and its development* (p. 226). London: MacMillan.

Benson, P. and Perrett, D. (1992). Face to face with the perfect image. *New Scientist, 133,* 32–35.

Berry, D.S. (1991). Attractive faces are not all created equal: Joint effects in of facial babyishness and attractiveness on social perception. *Personality and Social Psychology Bulletin, 17,* 523–531.

Ellis, H.D., Shepherd, J.W., Shepherd, J., Flin, R., and Davies, G.M. (1989). Identification from a computer-driven retrieval system compared with a traditional mug-shot album search: a new tool for police investigations. *Ergonomics, 32 ,* 167–177.

Galton, F. (1878). Composite portraits. *Journal of the Anthropological Institute, 8,* 132–142.

Galton, F. (1883). *Inquiries into human faculty and its development.* London: MacMillan.

Horvath, T., Szmigelsky, L., and Fenton, L.A. (1987). Some attractiveness parameters from birth to four years. *Perceptual and Motor Skills, 64,*1243–1248.

Jones, D. (1995). Sexual selection, physical attractiveness, and facial neoteny. *Current Anthropology, 36,* 723–747.

Katz, D. (1952). Le portrait composite et la typologie. *Ikon (Revue internationale de Filmologie), 2,* 207–214.

Korthase, K.M. and Trenholme, I. (1982). Perceived age and physical attractiveness. *Perceptual and Motor Skills, 54,* 1251–1258.

Langlois, J.K. and Roggman, L.A. (1990). Attractive faces are only average. *Psychological Science, 1,* 115–121

Langlois, J.H., Roggman, L.A., and Musselman, L. (1994). What is average and what is not average about attractive faces. *Psychological Science, 5,* 214–220.

Lorenz, K. (1943). Die angeborenen formen moglicher arfahrung. *Zietscrift Fur Tierpsychologie, 5,* 233–409.

Pearson, K. (1924). *The life, letters and labours of Francis Galton.* Cambridge: Cambridge University Press.

Perrett, D.I., May, K.A., and Yoshikawa, S. (1994). Facial shape and judgements of female attractiveness. *Nature, 368,* 239–242.

Pittenger, J.B. (1991). On the difficulty of averaging faces: Comments on Langlois and Roggman. *Psychological Science, 2,* 351–353.

Pollard, J.S. (1995). Attractiveness of composite faces: A comparative study. *International Journal of Comparative Psychology, 8,* 77–83.

Rhodes, G. and Tremewan, T. (1996). Averageness, exaggeration, and facial attractiveness. *Psychological Science, 7,* 105–110.

Ridley, M. (1992). No better than average. *Science, 257,* 327–328.

Shepherd, J.W. (1986). An interactive computer system for retrieving faces. In H.D. Ellis, Jeeves, M.A., Newcombe, F., and Young, A.W., *Aspects of face processing,* (p. 398–409) Dordrecht: Martinus Nijhoff.

Sternglanz, S.H., Gray, J.L., and Murakami, M. (1977). Adults preferences for infantile facial features: An ethological approach. *Animal Behaviour, 25,*108–115.

Stoddart, J.T. (1886). Composite portraiture. *Science, 8,* 89–91.

Young, A.W. and Bruce, V. (1998). Pictures at an exhibition: the science of the face. *The Psychologist, 11,* 120–125.

Computer Graphic Studies of the Role of Facial Similarity in Judgements of Attractiveness

I.S. PENTON-VOAK, D.I. PERRETT and J.W. PEIRCE
School of Psychology, University of St. Andrews

Anecdotally, spouses are often said to resemble one another. This study investigates the effects of similarity between participants and stimuli on judgements of facial attractiveness: does "like prefer like"? Using computer graphic techniques, opposite sex facial stimuli were generated from subjects' photographs. Experiment 1 showed a correlation between attractiveness and similarity but the effect can be explained by the attractiveness of average faces. Beyond this, there was a trend for individual subjects to rate opposite sex images with a similar face shape to their own face as more attractive than other subjects. Experiment 2 allowed subjects to interactively manipulate an opposite sex facial image along a continuum from a self-similar shape, through an average face shape, to a face with opposite characteristics. No significant preferences for self-similar or opposite characteristics were found. Preferences for average faces are stronger than preferences for self-similar faces.

Cross-population studies indicate that facial attractiveness reflects features that indicate good genetic quality, reproductive potential, and the likelihood of pro-social parenting behaviours, not arbitrary cultural values (Perrett et al., 1994; Jones 1995; Perrett et al., 1998).

Selection pressures operate against extreme genotypes, leading to the hypothesis that facial attractiveness is "averageness" (Symons, 1979). Composite faces with average features are judged as more attractive than the individual faces from which they are constructed (Langlois and Roggman, 1990; Grammer and Thornhill, 1994). These average faces, although attractive, can be improved upon (Perrett et

133

al., 1994). "Good genes" theories predict that symmetrical, exaggerated secondary sexual characteristics will be found attractive in faces as they indicate developmental stability and immunocompetence in males and youth and fertility in females (Thornhill and Gangestad, 1996). Whilst symmetry is attractive (Grammer and Thornhill, 1994), exaggerated facial secondary sexual characteristics are not always preferred. Recent studies have shown that, although female faces that are artificially feminised are considered more attractive than average faces, masculinised male faces are not (Perrett et al., 1998). In fact, *feminised* male faces are preferred, possibly due to negative personality characteristics attributed to very masculine faces.

Despite cross-subject and cross-population agreement in judgements of attractiveness, individual differences exist in such preferences. One factor that may lead to such variation in attractiveness judgements is the similarity in physical appearance between judge and judged. We briefly review evolutionary theories of *assortative mating*: a mating pattern that occurs when similar phenotypes mate at levels above chance (Partridge, 1983). Data from many species indicate that positive assortment is the most common pattern found among animals (Burley, 1983; Thiessen and Gregg, 1980); it seems mates across many species are indeed more similar than chance predicts. This study investigates, for humans, whether or not like really does *prefer* like with respect to facial similarity.

Theoretical work by evolutionary biologists indicates that phenotypic similarity between partners may increase inclusive fitness (Thiessen and Gregg, 1980; Bateson, 1983). Most of the hypothesized benefits accrue from increasing the coefficient of parent-offspring relatedness, resulting in increased gene duplication and reduced costs of altruism (Thiessen and Gregg, 1980; Epstein and Guttman, 1982; Rushton, 1988, 1989). The advantage of extra-closely related offspring is, however, disputed (Dawkins, 1979).

Rushton presents controversial evidence (based on blood type analysis) that genetic similarity in human partnerships increases fecundity (Rushton, 1988). Clark and Spuhler (1959) proposed a similar link and found small positive correlations between spousal physical similarity and the number of children produced. Bateson (1988) examined fecundity of pairings between Japanese quail with varying levels of relatedness showing that first cousin partnerships produced fertile eggs earlier than unrelated pairs.

Some benefits of assortment may occur at the phenotypic level. For example, mating within local populations results in an assortative mating pattern that is beneficial as individuals avoid the costs of leaving the immediate environment to mate. Hill et al. (1976) found that human couples who were similar on a variety of traits were more likely to remain together than dissimilar partners. An increase in marital satisfaction may lead to an increase in fecundity without the need for any biological increase in fertility.

A limiting factor on any hypothesized increase in fitness associated with assortative mating is the *inbreeding depression*. Assortative mating will, to a greater or lesser extent, increase homozygosity leading to the expression of potentially lethal traits. Such effects have been observed in many non-human species (Partridge, 1983). In humans, the result of incestuous mating is high infant mortality, developmental disorders, and physical defects such as heart abnormalities, deafness, and dwarfism (Seemanova, 1971).

Homozygosity may also prove disadvantageous for passive immune system resistance to parasites and pathogens that are generally best adapted to common proteins in the host population. Heterozygous individuals are more likely to carry rare alleles and may therefore possess more passive genetic resistance to pathogens (Thornhill and Gangestad, 1993). Individuals may seek to maximize heterozygosity in offspring by *negative* assortative mating. Indeed, Wedekind et al. (1995) demonstrate that women respond preferably to male odours that indicate a different major histocompatability complex from their own. Ober et al. (1998) demonstrate that fetuses that share HLA alleles with their mothers are less likely to survive to full term, providing evidence that assortative mating may have fitness costs.

Individuals could optimize the costs and benefits of assortative mating (Wright, 1933). "Optimal outbreeding" requires that individuals must assess the phenotype of a potential mate, estimate the likely genotypic similarity between themselves and the possible partner, and "decide" whether they are too closely or too distantly related to be an "optimal" mate. Processes of kin recognition may be used in mate choice to avoid excessive inbreeding and to allow optimal mate choice, as well as to direct altruistic behavior (Bateson, 1983; Waldman, 1987).

Lorenzian sexual imprinting during a critical sensitive period early in life seems a likely mechanism for establishing later mate preferences, including incest avoidance (Immelman, 1975). Repeated social

interaction between proximate individuals (e.g., nest mates) at early
stages of development seems to foster altruistic acts while inhibiting
sexual interaction (Holmes and Sherman, 1983; Waldman, 1987). Placing infants in surrogate families at appropriate stages of development
and observing kin-directed behavior of these non-related "offspring"
reveal the involvement of learning in the identification of "kin" for
many species including fish, mice, and goats (Holmes and Sherman,
1983).

Evidence for familial characteristics influencing future sexual
behaviour comes from fostering studies of ungulates (Kendrick et al.,
1998), rodents (D'Udine and Alleva, 1983), and birds (e.g., Vos, 1994,
1995a,b). Bateson (1982) attempted to test the optimal outbreeding
hypothesis: that the preferred level of relatedness in a partner for
Japanese quail lies between close relatives and unrelated birds. He
found that quail spent significantly more time in front of first cousins
than unrelated birds and novel or familiar siblings—the first empirical
evidence that birds avoid both excessive inbreeding and outbreeding.

Similar mechanisms that prevent incestuous mating, but promote
some similarity between partners may exist in humans. Westermarck
(1894) hypothesised that children have an innate tendency to learn a
sexual aversion to individuals with whom they live closely in infancy
and early childhood (normally biological siblings and parents). Ethno-
graphic studies have formed natural experiments that support
Westermarck's hypothesis. For example, there are very few cases of
sexual interaction between unrelated peers co-socialised since infancy
in Kibbutzim, even though sexual relationships are not actively dis-
couraged (Talmon, 1964; Rabin, 1965; Spiro, 1965; (Shepher, 1971).
Studies of *sim-pua* marriages in China, in which future husbands and
wives were raised together from childhood (effectively as siblings),
indicate that *sim-pua* marriages are 250 percent more likely to end in
divorce than marriages between partners who have not been raised
together. The fertility of *sim-pua* marriages is 25 percent lower than
other marriages (Wolf, 1993).

The findings of the studies of spousal facial similarity could be
attributed to the development of preferences for family-like facial characteristics. Weak, but significant effects from two studies indicate that
parental characteristics could influence later choice of partner. Small
positive correlations between father's age and husband's age demonstrate that daughters of older men subsequently tend to choose older

husbands (Zei et al., 1981; Wilson and Barrett, 1987). Wilson and Barrett also showed that females chose partners whose eye color resembled their fathers'.

Human partners assort strongly for a wide range of non-biological characteristics such as religion, educational level, and socioeconomic status (Vandenberg, 1972; Thiessen and Gregg, 1980; Epstein and Guttman, 1982; Rushton, 1988, 1989). There seems to be an inverse relationship between the genetic component of a trait and the amount of assortment that occurs for it (Thiessen and Gregg, 1980), although some evidence of assortment for heritable physical characteristics has been found.

Roberts (1977) and Spuhler (1968) review early research of spousal correlations from large-scale measurement studies of anthropometric characteristics (arm length, ear lobe length, etc.). Overall, these studies reveal positive correlations (0.01–0.35) between spouses on many physical features. The validity of these early studies is questionable. Few take into account the age of partners (physical features vary systematically with age), or the effects of environmental coexistence (diet, etc.) on similarity. Recent studies of assortative mating (Malina et al., 1993; Allison et al., 1996), however, have found significant correlations in measures of weight and physical strength between spouses that could not be explained by cohabitation or age. It seems reasonable to conclude that some physical similarity occurs in human marriage.

Three studies have reported facial similarity between couples at the perceptual level. Griffiths and Kunz (1973) found observers could match spouses married for less than ten years or more than twenty years at above chance levels, though subjects failed to match couples married for between ten and twenty years. The small stimuli sets used (*n*=5) may explain the inconsistent results. Zajonc et al. (1987) obtained two photographs (one from the first year and the second from the twenty-fifth year of the partnership) from each individual in married couples. Older, but not young partners were ranked as more similar and more likely to be married than predicted by chance. This indicates that couples do not get together due to similarity, but become more alike over time, perhaps due to shared environmental and emotional experiences. Hinsz (1989) used photographs of individuals from engaged couples and couples who had been married for around twenty-five years. Real couples were rated as more similar than randomly generated couples. Unlike Zajonc et al. (1987), Hinsz (1989) did not find that couples that had been together for longer periods of time were perceived as more similar than new couples.

It is important to note that an assortative *pattern* is not necessarily caused by assortative *preferences* (Burley, 1983). Assuming that "like mates with like" because "like prefers like" is an oversimplification; in a population where a certain characteristic is universally considered attractive (a *type* preference) an assortative pattern can still develop. For example, Berscheid et al. (1971) showed that, although college students prefer to date highly attractive people, (a type preference) they actually find themselves with dates of similar attractiveness to themselves (leading to assortment for attractiveness despite a type preference). Likewise, Shepherd and Ellis (1972) found that married couples have similar attractiveness rating. Thus, one problem with studies assessing perceived facial similarity of real couples is that similarity may be more due to attractiveness matching rather than actual facial similarity.

EXPERIMENT 1

The study of similarity of real life couples has obvious validity in the study of assortative mating for facial appearance, but it also has drawbacks; studying partnerships is not the same as studying preferences (Burley, 1983), and studies can have confounding factors such as a common source of photographs for partners.

FIGURE 1
Average composite images

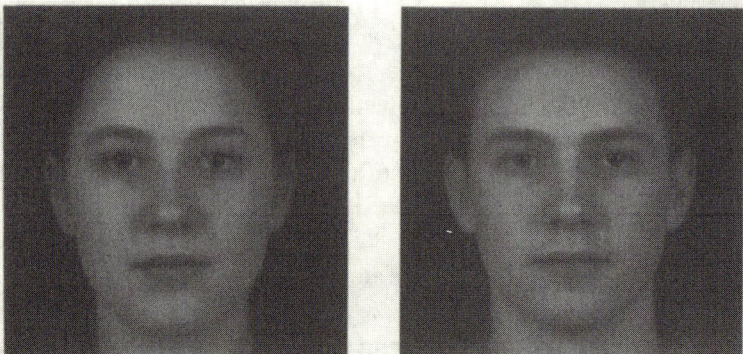

Note: Female average (left, 40 females) and male average (right, 21 males).

FIGURE 2
Examples of original faces and synthetic stimuli

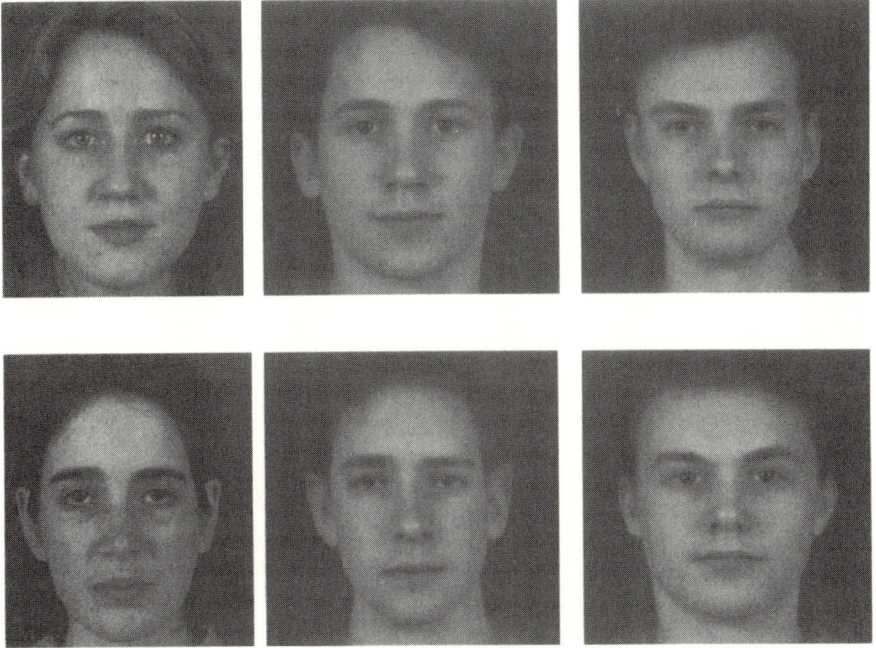

Note: Original female (left), "similar" male face stimuli (centre, experiments 1 & 2) and "opposite" male face stimuli (right, experiment 2).

A computer graphic study is well placed to investigate assortative preferences for facial characteristics. Experiment 1 employs techniques that change the apparent sex of an individual's face, while maintaining their own characteristics (Rowland and Perrett, 1995). This creates an image of a hypothetical opposite sex "sibling." As there can be no Westermarckian impediment to an individual finding a synthesized facial image attractive, these sibling images can be used as test stimuli in studies of similarity and facial attraction.

Method

Stimuli. Fifty-two female and twenty-three male participants (students at St. Andrews University, mean age twenty-one, were photographed and the images digitised. The positions of 174 feature points were marked on each image to define the shape of the eyes, mouth, etc. Component images were then blended to form average or prototype images (Benson and Perrett, 1992; Perrett et al., 1994; Rowland and Perrett, 1995).

An opposite sex image that retained shape information from the individual source faces as generated for each of the fifty-two female participants photographed. The vector difference between the feature points of an individual (e.g., female subject) and the same sex (female) prototype specifies the shape information unique to the individual. This identity information can be added to the shape of the opposite sex (male) prototype to create a synthetic male with a "similar" face type to the subject (Figure 2, left versus centre; Rowland and Perrett, 1995).

Attractiveness Judgements. Thirty-six of the original fifty-two female subjects photographed rated the attractiveness of fifty-two transformed "male" faces on a seven-point Likert scale (1 = "very unattractive," 7 = "very attractive"). The order of presentation was randomised.

Similarity Assessment. Six different subjects rated the similarity (on a six-point Likert scale) of each of the synthetic male faces to each of the original photographs of the thirty-six female subjects making attractiveness judgments. Each subject rated the similarity of the complete set of fifty-two male faces to one original face before proceeding to repeat the task for a different original face (randomly chosen from the thirty-six). Ratings were self-paced in sessions spaced over several days.

RESULTS

None of the subjects spontaneously recognized the stimuli as being derived from the face of themselves or their peer group. This might mean that the attempt to construct stimuli similar to subjects was unsuccessful. Analysis of similarity ratings showed this was not true. For each original female face, the fifty-two male faces were ranked by the average similarity rating across the six raters. For all but four of the thirty-six original faces, the male face constructed as an opposite sex version (Figure 2, center images) ranked highest in similarity from the set of fifty-two. Two synthetic male faces ranked fifth and two ranked second most similar to the original face from which they were derived.

Figure 3a plots the relationship between similarity of stimuli to the subjects and the subjects' judgments of stimulus attractiveness. Attractiveness and similarity ratings were transformed to allow comparisons among subjects. The thirty-six subjects' ratings of the male face most similar to themselves were averaged to give the extreme right data point. The extreme left point gives the average of the thirty-six subjects' ratings of the face least similar to themselves. Points in-between reflect the averaged attractiveness ratings of faces with intermediate rated levels of similarity.

The point on the extreme right appears an outlier, with a much higher similarity level than the average similarity of the second most similar face. This is not an artifact, but an indication of the success of the stimulus construction. The sex transformed stimulus was on average much more similar to the subject from which the face shape information was derived than any of the stimuli constructed to look like the fifty-one other female students.

The graph shows a clear relationship between similarity of faces to subjects and the subjects' ratings of attractiveness of the faces. Linear regression accounts for 58 percent of the variance in the data. Regression with a second order polynomial equation provides a better fit to the data and accounts for 65 percent of the variance. This indicates that although attractiveness ratings increase with similarity, this relationship asymptotes or declines when faces become very similar to the subject. This finding is consistent with the optimal outbreeding hypothesis, which postulates that intermediate levels of similarity should be most attractive.

Figure 3b plots the attractiveness ratings of subjects in isolation from the views of others. A critical question is whether subjects rate self-similar faces differently to other members of the population. This can be assessed by taking the difference between each subject's ratings of a face and the average rating of everyone else for the same face. This value (subject's view—others' view) gives the subject's "unique view" and is presented in Figure 3b. The graph displays no consistent relationship between the similarity of stimuli to subjects and their unique view of attractiveness.

The most exacting test of assortative preferences concerns the subject's ratings of the face most similar to themselves. This is analogous to testing whether the extreme right point in Figure 3b has a rating that is higher than zero. For each of the thirty-six subjects, two ratings were compared. The first of these was the rating given by a

FIGURE 3
Facial similarity and judgements of attractiveness

3a

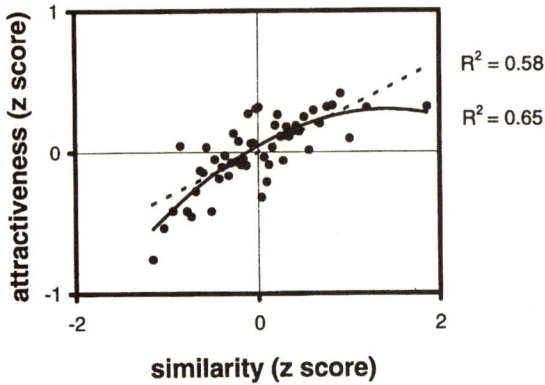

3b

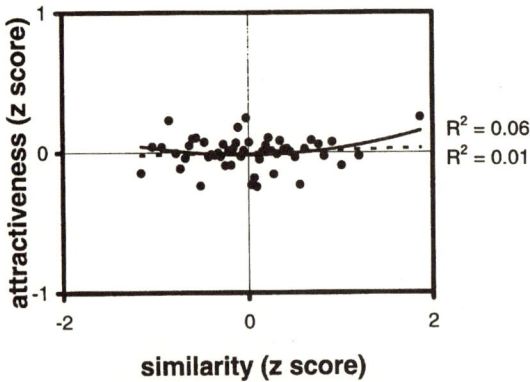

Notes: (a) Average of attractiveness scores assigned by thirty-six subjects to fifty-two face stimuli ranked according to their similarity to each subject (for Method see text). Trend lines calculated by regression analyses using both linear (dashed line, accounting for 58% of the variance in the data) and second order polynomial models (solid line, accounting for 65% of variance). (b) Subjects' "unique view" of attractiveness, displaying the average difference between an individual's attractiveness rating of a face and the average ratings of all other subjects of that face. Linear and polynomial regression account for 1% and 6% of the variance respectively.

subject to the image rated as most similar to that individual (the "self-similar" rating). In thirty-two of the thirty-six cases, this was the opposite-sex image generated from the subject's own face. The second was the median of all the other subjects' ratings of that face (the "others" rating). A Wilcoxon signed ranks test showed a non-significant trend for self-similar ratings to be higher than others' ratings of that image ($Z = -1.692$, $p = 0.091$, $n = 36$).

DISCUSSION

Figure 3a indicates that (a) subjects are attracted to others with similar faces and (b) preference peaks or asymptotes at a moderate level of similarity. Such evidence might be taken as support for the notion of optimal outbreeding and assortative mating. Figure 3b appears to contradict this.

It is not obvious how to reconcile Figure 3b with Figure 3a, in that it is not intuitive as to why subjects should be attracted to similar faces, but no more so than other members of the population. The results can be explained in terms of a preference for average face shapes. Consider faces that are very different from average; highly unusual faces are likely to receive low ratings of attractiveness but, by definition, such unusual faces are unlike most people. Subjects are not attracted to faces that look very different from themselves, but neither is anyone else. Now consider faces with an average shape that are viewed as attractive (Langlois and Rogman, 1990). A given subject's face will be more similar to an average face shape than to a face shape randomly chosen from the population. This means that average face shapes will have moderate levels of similarity to most subjects and will be rated relatively highly for attractiveness.

From these arguments, it can be seen that optimal outbreeding, positive assortative mating, and the averageness hypothesis all converge to make the same prediction: that like will prefer like (i.e., subjects will be attracted to similar looking others). While Burley (1983) notes that an assortative mating pattern need not be caused by assortative preferences, our data indicate that the corollary is also true: a *preference for similarity* (i.e., averageness) need not translate into a *pattern of similarity* in partners' faces. Consider a population of individuals of varying attractiveness (averageness) in which each individual competes to get the most attractive partner. The result is partnerships of equivalent levels of attractiveness (Berscheid et al., 1971). While highly attractive individuals should end up with similar (average) looking partners, there is no reason for unattractive couples to look alike: each partner may have a face shape that differs from average in unique ways. Thus, the averageness hypothesis predicts a preference for similar partners, but game theory predicts that this will not translate into a pattern of physical similarity in partners (positive assortative mating).

Figure 3b provides a measure of attractiveness relative to the opinion of others. Subjects may find faces that are slightly similar to themselves (i.e., average faces) attractive and faces very different from themselves (i.e., faces far from average) unattractive, but other members of the population are likely to have similar views about these same faces. From this analysis subjects will not have extra motivation (above other members of the population) to seek out partners with a similar face.

In summary, Experiment 1 found evidence for a positive relationship between facial similarity and judgements of attractiveness across a range of face stimuli (Figure 3a). This preference could simply reflect the relationship between averageness and attractiveness. There was, however, a trend for an assortative preference, i.e., subjects rated faces with the shape most similar to their own slightly higher than other subjects.

EXPERIMENT 2

A more direct test of positive assortative preferences is to compare a subject's ratings of an opposite sex face that is constructed to have the same shape as that subject and an average face of the opposite sex. Experiment 2 was designed to allow this direct comparison. In addition, Experiment 2 addresses the concept of optimal similarity and investigates the possibility of negative assortative preferences for facial appearance. Negative assortative mating can be predicted from theories of parasite driven sexual selection since preference for partners with a dissimilar genotype should increase heterozygosity in offspring and, thereby, improve immunity (Thornhill and Gangestad, 1993). Human preferences for odour suggest negative assortative mating (Wedekind et al., 1995).

Novel interactive computer techniques allow warping between two different faces in real time giving subjects opportunity to select an optimum blend along a smooth continuum (Perrett et al., 1998). By constructing a continuum from an individual's sex transformed face through an average face to a face with dissimilar characteristics, the relative influence of similarity, averageness, and dissimilarity can be assessed. Thus, three competing hypotheses based on evolutionary concepts of fitness can be tested.

(1) Individuals will be attracted to some optimal degree of self-similarity in a face to realize the possible fitness benefits of positive assortative mating—the "like prefers like" hypothesis;

(2) Individuals will be attracted to facial shapes dissimilar to their own to maximise heterozygosity—the "opposites attract" hypothesis; and

(3) Individuals will prefer average faces to self-similar or dissimilar face shapes as selection acts against extreme, non-average genotypes—the averageness hypothesis.

Method

Subjects and Procedure. Forty female and twenty-one male (mean age 21) participants were photographed and the images digitized as in Experiment 1. The identity information used to create the similar face type (Figure 2, centre) can be subtracted from the male prototype to create a synthetic male with an "opposite" face type (Figure 2, right). If the original female had a small nose and thick lips, the similar male face would have both characteristics, but the opposite male face would have a large nose and thin lips.

These two new face shapes (the similar and opposite face types) formed the end points of an interactive continuum, in which participants could manipulate the face shape displayed by moving a mouse controlled pointer left or right. Colour information from the appropriate sex prototype was rendered into the face shape in real time. Moving the computer mouse to the left or the right of the image showed the similar or the opposite face. Between these two points, the image displayed a face shape in proportion to the position of the pointer. The centre of the range displayed a prototype image (50% of the similar and 50% of the opposite face shape—mathematically equal to the average). The interactive software ran on a Silicon Graphics Indigo[2] Maximum Impact workstation, in twenty-four-bit color. Two examples of the end-points of face continua are shown in Figure 2.

Seventeen females and six males took part in testing, all of whom had been photographed. Subjects were instructed to move the mouse left and right to view the continuum and press the space bar when the image on the screen was, in their opinion, most attractive. The software recorded responses in terms of the proportion of the transform selected by the subjects. After a short training period using continua of the same sex as the subject, the experimental stimuli proper were presented.

Male subjects performed sixty-three trials in total. The stimuli (female faces generated from the 21 male photographs) were grouped into three blocks of twenty-one trials; within each block the order of stimulus presentation was randomized. Similar and the opposite face shapes had an equal probability of appearing at the right or left end of the continua. Female participants performed ninety trials in total, in three blocks of thirty trials. Ten of the original forty continua generated were not included in testing to reduce the duration of the testing. Order and left/right presentation was randomized as for male subjects.

Subjects were naïve as to the source of the stimuli; they were at no point informed that their own faces were used to generate the images.

RESULTS

The face shape selected by subjects in the continuum generated from their own facial characteristics is of primary interest. Subjects could select a face shape anywhere between a 100 percent similar to 100 percent opposite in shape. The mean level of similarity selected from this range was compared to the null hypothesis that the face shape selected would, on average, be neither similar nor dissimilar to the subject's own face (i.e., that the optimal face would be the prototype and 0% similar).

A one-sample t-test against a hypothesized mean of 0 percent similarity preferred demonstrated that subjects did not generate responses that were significantly different from the prototype when presented with a continuum generated from their own face (mean preference = 2% similar, $t(22) = -0.44$, $p = 0.67$). Separate analyses for each sex also yielded non-significant results (females, mean = 4.4% similar,

$t(16) = -0.90$, $p = 0.38$; males, mean = 4.4% opposite, $t(5) = 0.35$, $p = 0.74$).

DISCUSSION

Experiment 2 found no preference for any significant level of self-similarity in opposite sex partners. The design of this study placed it in a position to investigate the relative importance of two processes in preferences for facial shape: preference for average characteristics and preference for self-similar characteristics. Research has shown that average faces are, in general, more attractive than the individual faces from which they are synthesised. This effect remains when skin texture and blurring are controlled in both original and average face shapes (Langlois and Roggman, 1990; Benson and Perrett, 1992). It appears hard to improve on faces with average characteristics. It may be that the fitness benefits associated with averageness (e.g., immuno-competence and fertility) far outweigh the hypothesised fitness ben-efits that accompany an optimal amount of self-similarity in a partner.

Our current experiments failed to reveal strong support for assorta-tive preferences. One qualification of our studies is that they focused on female judgments of male attractiveness. Studies of sexual imprint-ing suggest stronger effects of early rearing on male subjects (Vos 1994, 1995a; Kendrick et al., 1998). Previous studies of spousal facial similarity have reported sporadic positive results; one possibility for these findings is that subjects have matched partners on attractiveness rather than physical resemblance.

Perhaps a better test of assortative mating theory would be to allow subjects to choose between faces that differ from average by equal amounts, but vary in similarity to the subject. If similarity between partners does correspond to a fitness advantage, and preferences for self-similar partners have evolved, subjects should prefer faces similar to themselves from a selection of equivalent non-average faces.

ACKNOWLEDGMENTS

This work was supported by project grants to DP from Unilever Research and the ESRC-ROPA. IPV was supported by an ESRC Ph.D. studentship. We thank R. Edwards for help collecting similarity data, Dr. K. Lee, Dr. D. Rowland, and M. Burt for help in stimuli and test construction.

REFERENCES

Allison, D.B., Neale, M.C., Kezis, M.I., Alfonso, V.C., Heshka, S., and Heymsfield, S.B. (1996). Assortative mating for relative weight: genetic implications. *Behavior Genetics, 26,* 103–111.

Bateson, P. (1982). Preferences for cousins in Japanese Quail. *Nature 295,* 236–237.

Bateson, P. (1983). Optimal outbreeding. In: *Mate Choice,* P. Bateson (ed.). Cambridge: Cambridge University Press, p. 257–277.

Bateson, P. (1988). Preferences for close relations in Japanese Quail. H. Ouellet. Ottawa: University of Ottawa Press. *Acta XIX Congressus Internationalis Ornithologici, 1,* 961–972.

Benson, P.J. and Perrett, D.I. (1992). Face to face with the perfect image. *New Scientist, 133,* 32–35.

Berscheld, E., Dion, K., Walster, E., and Walster, G.W. (1971). Physical attractiveness and dating choice: a test of the matching hypothesis. *Journal of Experimental Social Psychology, 7,* 173–189.

Burley, N. (1983). The meaning of assortative mating. *Ethology and Sociobiology, 4,* 191–203.

Clark, P.J. and Spuhler, J.N. (1959). Differential fertility in relation to body dimensions. *Human Biology, 31,* 121–137.

Dawkins, R. (1979). Twelve misunderstandings of kin selection. *Zeitschrift fur Tierpsychologie, 51,* 184–200.

D'Udine, B. and Alleva, E. (1981). Early experience and sexual preferences in rodents. In: *Mate Choice,* P. Bateson (ed.). Cambridge: Cambridge University Press, 311–330.

Epstein, E. and Guttman, R. (1982). Mate selection in man: Evidence, theory, and outcome. *Social Biology, 31,* 243–276.

Grammer, K. and Thornhill, R. (1994). Human (*homo sapiens*) facial attractiveness and sexual selection: the role of symmetry and averageness. *Journal of Comparative Psychology, 108,* 233–242.

Griffiths, R.W. and Kunz, P.R. (1973). Assortative mating: A study of physiognomic homogamy. *Social Biology, 20,* 448–453.

Hill, C.T., Rubin, Z., and Peplau, L.A. (1976). Breakups before marriage: The end of 103 affairs. *Journal Social Issues, 32,* 147–168.

Hinsz, V.B. (1989). Facial resemblance in engaged and married couples. *Journal of Social and Personal Relationships, 6,* 223–229.

Holmes, W.G. and Sherman, P.W. (1983). Kin recognition in animals. *American Scientist, 71,* 46–55.

Immelman, K. (1975). Ecological significance of imprinting and early learning. *Annual Review of Ecology and Systematics, 6,* 15–37.

Jones, D. (1995). Sexual selection, physical attractiveness, and facial neoteny. *Current Anthropology, 36,* 723–748.

Kendrick, K.M., Hinton. M.R., and Atkins, K. (1998). Mothers may irreversibly determine male social and sexual preferences. *Nature, 395,* 229–230.

Langlois, J.H. and Roggman. L.A. (1990). Attractive faces are only average. *Psychological Science, 1,* 115–121.

Malina, R.M., Selby, H.A.. Buschang, P.H., Aronson, W.L., and Little, B.B. (1983). Assortative mating for phenotypic characteristics in a Zapotec community in Oaxaca, Mexico. *Journal of Biosocial Science, 15,* 273–280.

Ober, C., Hyslop, T., Elias, S., Weitkamp, L.R., and Hauck, W.W. (1998). Human Leukocyte antigen matching and fetal loss—results of a ten year prospective study. *Human Reproduction, 13,* 33–38.

Partridge. L. (1983). Non-random mating and offspring fitness. In: *Mate Choice,* P. Bateson (ed.). Cambridge: Cambridge University Press, p. 227–256.

Perrett, D.I., Lee, K.J., Penton-Voak, I.S., Rowland, D.R., Yoshikawa, S., Burt, D.M., Henzi, S.P., Castles, D.L., and Akamatsu, S. (1998). Effects of sexual dimorphism on facial attractiveness. *Nature, 394,* 884–887.

Perrett, D.I., May, K.A., and Yoshikawa, S. (1994). Facial shape and judgements of female attractiveness. *Nature, 368*, 239–242.

Rabin, I.A. (1965). *Growing up in a Kibbutz*. New York: Springer.

Roberts, D.F. (1977). Assortative mating in man: Husband/wife correlations in physical characteristics. *Supplement to the Bulletin of The Eugenics Society, 2*.

Rowland, D.A. and Perrett, D.I. (1995). Manipulating facial appearance through shape and color. *IEEE Computer Graphics and Applications, 15*, 70–76.

Rushton, J.P. (1988). Genetic similarity, mate choice, and fecundity in humans. *Ethology and Sociobiology, 9*, 329–333.

Rushton, J.P. (1989). Genetic similarity, human altruism, and group selection. *Behavioral and Brain Sciences, 12*, 503–559.

Seemanova, E. (1971). A study of the children of incestuous matings. *Human Heredity, 21*, 108–128.

Shepher, J. (1971). Mate selection among second generation Kibbutz adolescents and adults: Incest avoidance and negative imprinting. *Archives of Sexual Behavior, 1*, 293–307.

Shepherd, J.W. and Ellis, H.D. (1972) The role of physical attractiveness in selection of marriage partners. *Psychological Reports, 30*, 1004.

Spiro, M.E. (1965). *Children of the Kibbutz*. New York: Schocken Books.

Spuhler, J.N. (1968). Assortative mating with respect to physical characteristics. *Eugenics Quarterly, 15*, 128–140.

Symons, D. (1979). *The evolution of human sexuality*. Oxford: Oxford University Press.

Talmon, Y. (1964). Mate selection in collective settlements. *American Sociological Review, 29*, 491–508.

Thiessen, D. and Gregg, B. (1980). Human assortative mating and genetic equilibrium: An evolutionary perspective. *Ethology and Sociobiology, 1*, 111–140.

Thornhill, R. and Gangestad, S.W. (1993). Human facial beauty: Averageness, symmetry, and parasite resistance. *Human Nature, 4*, 237–269.

Thornhill, R. and Gangestad, S.W. 1996). The evolution of human sexuality. *Trends in Evolution and Ecology, 11*, 98–102.

Vandenberg, S.G. (1972). Assortive mating or who marries whom? *Behavior Genetics, 2*, 127–157.

Vos, D.R. (1994). Sex recognition in zebra finch males results form early experience. *Behaviour, 128*, 1–14.

Vos, D.R. (1995a). The role of sexual imprinting for sex recognition in zebra finches: a difference between males and females. *Animal Behavior, 50*, 645–653.

Vos, D.R. (1995b). Sexual imprinting in zebra-finch females: Do females develop a preference for males that look like their father? *Ethology, 99*, 252–262.

Waldman, B. (1987). Mechanisms of kin recognition. *Journal of Theoretical Biology, 128*, 159–185.

Wedekind. C., Seebeck, T., Bettens, F., and Paepke, A.J. (1995). MHC-dependent mate preferences in humans. *Proceedings of the Royal Society of London B., 260*, 245–249.

Westermarck, E. (1894). *The History of Human Marriage*. London: Macmillan.

Wilson, G.D. and Barrett, P.T. (1987). Parental characteristics and partner choice: Some evidence for Oedipal imprinting. *Journal of Biosocial Science, 19*, 157–161.

Wolf, A.P. (1993). Westermarck Redivivus. *Annual Review of Anthropology, 22*, 157–175.

Wright, S. (1933). The roles of mutation, inbreeding, crossbreeding, and selection in evolution. *Proceedings of the VIth International Conference on Genetics*, New York: Brooklyn Botanic Garden.

Zajonc, R.B., Adelmann, P.K., Murphy, S.T., and Niendenthal, P.M. (1987). Convergence in the physical appearance of spouses. *Motivation and Emotion, 11*, 335–346.

Zei, G., Astofli, P., and Jayakar. S.D. (1981). Correlation between father's age and husband's age: A case of imprinting? *Journal of Biosocial Science, 13*, 409–418.

One Extreme or the Other, or Perhaps the Golden Mean? Issues of Spatial Resolution in Face Processing

DENIS M. PARKER
Glasgow Caledonian University

and

NICHOLAS P. COSTEN
University of Manchester

The findings of some of the key studies that have examined the contribution of different bands of spatial information, specified in terms of cycles per face, to face recognition, and identification are reviewed. Based on findings from studies of low-, high-, and band-pass filtering, it is concluded that neither low facial scales nor high facial scales are optimal. Instead, a center range of facial scales, approximately 8–16 cycles per face, appears to make the greatest contribution to the recognition process. A study of identification of band-pass filtered faces is reported that reinforces the view derived from the literature. This indicated that a band with a harmonic mean of 11.1 cycles per face provided the most efficient recognition, with speed and accuracy declining at lower and higher bands.

Sergent (1986) was probably the first to explicitly suggest that different levels of resolution might be involved in the performance of different facial processing tasks. Coarse scale information (low spatial frequencies) might be involved in registering the presence of a head or face, intermediate levels of detail might allow the discrimination of whether the face or head was male or female, and fine scales (high spatial frequencies) would allow the identification of an individual.

Although it is clear that object resolution (in Fourier terms, cycles per picture/object width) rather than retinal resolution (cycles per degree of visual angle) is the crucial metric (Riley and Costall, 1980; Bruce, 1988), the idea of different levels of object resolution subserving different tasks was an intriguing one. The idea fits nicely with the temporal ordering of spatial scale processing in vision; the lowest spatial frequencies in an image are processed relatively quickly while progressively finer spatial information is processed more slowly (Breitmeyer, 1975; Parker and Salzen, 1977; Parker and Dutch, 1987; Watt 1988; Parker et al., 1996). There is then a satisfying symmetry in the proposed relationship between the precision of the psychological task, the spatial resolution required to accomplish it, and the time to extract the required resolution level from the image.

When we look at the experimental support for such an idea, problems arise immediately. Even before Sergent (1986) had made her proposal, evidence appeared to conflict with it. Harmon (1973) had suggested that very low levels of resolution, indeed, were sufficient to allow facial identification, as low as 2.5 cycles per face, measured at eye level. In looking at the way the tasks were carried out in Harmon's investigations, it is certainly questionable whether the subjects were performing true face identification. The responses were untimed, and it was also possible to use experiences with other pictorial versions of the face in order to guide a judgement of identity; radical differences in hairstyle, e.g., bald versus not bald, were also available as cues to differentiate the set of faces. Just how little information is available at 2.5 cycles per face can be seen by looking at the top set of images in Figure 1, although it is clear that it is possible to make an educated guess, especially if one knows that one is dealing with a group of public figures. The fact that one can link a name with a blurred picture of a face, particularly when no time pressure is applied, may say more about the inferential capabilities of humans than about true face recognition. The issue of timing may be as important as any other aspect of the task in drawing conclusions about what the task tells us about the nature of face processing. So, although Harmon's results imply that very low resolution may allow face recognition, it may be best to withhold judgement.

A study more in accord with Sergent's (1986) ideas was that of Hayes, Morrone, and Burr (1983) that claimed that relatively high facial frequencies were best for recognition. They looked at facial images that were bandpassed at a range of facial frequencies, with 1.5 octave wide envelopes, centered between 3.2 and 31.2 cycles. They found accuracy was best at a band centered on 25 cycles per face. While this quite fine level of resolution implies that a fairly high level of facial detail is most important for recognition, a careful look at the details of the study raises some doubts. Peak performance at 25 cycles per face occurred for both normal and negative facial images, the latter finding being a little surprising given that photographic negatives of faces impair recognition (Galper, 1970; Phillips, 1972). It was also the case that a set of target faces and names was always immediately available as subjects performed the task. The task seems to be much more like a matching than a recognition task. Interestingly, Parker, Lishman, and Hughes (1996), in a successive matching task using faces, found that images with facial frequencies above 32 cycles were better cues than those with only information below 5 cycles. Matching tasks, which rely on information in primary or short-term memory, may force the use of different strategies to those necessary for recognition or identification, where long term stores must be accessed.

An investigation by Fiorentini, Maffei, and Sandini (1983), using an identification rather than a matching measure, produced a pattern of results that, broadly speaking, has been confirmed by a number of other investigators. They examined identification with low-pass and high-pass filtered facial images. Their results indicated that when low-pass filtering was applied to faces, lowering the highest facial frequency in the image from 8.0 cycles to 5.0, it significantly depressed identification accuracy. When the low facial frequencies in the images were removed, by high-pass filtering, there was also a decline in accuracy when the range between 8 and 12 cycles was removed. Fiorentini et al. (1983) made the point that we can recognize faces that are low- or high-pass filtered, so there is no question of a specific range being absolutely necessary for recognition. The system used for facial processing is obviously extremely tolerant, and even line drawings with their very restricted spatial content may be recognized, although with a significant decrement in accuracy (Davies et al., 1978).

The main finding to emerge from the study by Fiorentini et al. (1983), that there appears to be a central range of facial frequencies that are more important for recognition than either extreme, was partly confirmed in a study by Bachmann (1991), which used block averaged versions of frontal views of faces. Bachmann found that once the resolution level reached eighteen pixels per face, then it made little difference whether or not resolution was further refined since performance, at least as measured by accuracy, had become asymptotic. A resolution level of eighteen pixels per face is approximately 9 cycles in facial frequency terms, although by using square pixels with clearly visible edges, a range of added noise is introduced into the image that partially masks the face (Harmon and Julesz, 1973; Morrone et al., 1983; Costen et al., 1994). Unfortunately, neither the study of Fiorentini et al., nor that of Bachmann took any account of processing time and it is possible that this may interact with the range of available information. For example, one may, indeed, get an improvement in accuracy as one moves from a resolution of 2.5 cycles per face to 8–12 cycles, but there may be an associated increase in processing time, and so the overall efficiency of facial processing, if one takes rate of processing into account, may be relatively uniform.

Face identification or recognition under normal conditions, subjectively at least, appears to be a fast process, and certainly we are not conscious of pondering slowly about whether a face is familiar or not, although providing the name or semantic information about the individual may sometimes be slow and problematic. Trying to separate a "natural" quick process from a slow inferential pattern-matching process may be important in defining what normal face processing is. As an example of what we are referring to here, we can look at some results of Parker, Lishman, and Hughes (1996), which involved using spatially filtered pictures of faces or objects to cue a successive matching process. The sets of filtered pictures were first screened, without any time pressure being applied, by getting groups of subjects to match the filtered versions to the full bandwidth versions. Accuracy was found to be 98 percent for the faces and 100 percent for the objects. However, when the experiments proper were run and time pressure applied, it was clear that responses with the filtered versions were slower and more error prone than with the full bandwidth versions. It was only the application of time pressure that revealed the significant effects of spatial filtering on processing efficiency. Thus, carrying out a face identification or recognition task without the application of time pressure may conceal significant variations in efficiency.

Two sets of experiments (Costen et al., 1994, 1996) that measured reaction times (RTs), as well as accuracy, in face identification tasks confirm the results of both Fiorentini et al. (1983) and Bachmann

(1991) in implying that a central range of facial frequencies is dominant in face recognition. These studies looked at Fourier filtering as well as block averaging, and found that accuracy reached asymptotic heights and RTs reached asymptotic lows once resolution had reached 10.5 cycles per face in low-pass filtered images. There was also a hint with high-pass image versions (Costen et al., 1996) that exclusion of information below 6 cycles per face impaired identification efficiency. Two further studies by O'Toole, Millward, and Anderson (1988) and Peli, Young, Goldstein, and Trempe (1991) reinforce the notion that a central range of spatial scales plays the major role in recognition. The former used a learning technique and showed greater transfer of training for those images low-passed, rather than high-passed at 11 cycles per face, while the latter found a fall in performance on a familiar-unfamiliar task when facial frequencies above 6 cycles were attenuated. It seems that a number of studies, including two that combine accuracy and speed measures, imply that a central range of spatial scales is more important than either extreme in carrying information subserving recognition and identification. In the experiment described briefly below, bandpass filtered facial images, in combination with accuracy and speed measures, are used to look at the identification of faces.

Band-Pass Spatial Filtering of Faces and Identification

Subjects. Thirty-six undergraduates in the Psychology Department of the University of Aberdeen, who were paid for their participation, provided data for the experiment.

Stimuli. Six clean-shaven faces of males in their early to mid-twenties, who were judged not to have any strikingly distinctive facial or hair features, were photographed at five angles of rotation by a digital camera. The angles were 0° (fronto-parallel), 22°, 45° (three quarter view), 67°, and 90° degrees (full-profile), with the sitter looking towards his right for non-0° portraits. The pictures of the faces were digitized and Fourier-filtered with second-order exponential roll-off band-pass filters that were one octave wide. The five spatial bands had center frequencies of 2.46, 5.22, 11.1, 23.6, and 50.15 cycles per face. Examples of similar filtering operations applied to the face of a well-known public person is shown in Figure 2. When displayed in monochrome on a Phillips 35 cm color monitor and viewed from a

FIGURE 1
Low-pass Fourier filtered images with a cut-off of 2.5 and 8.0 cycles per face.

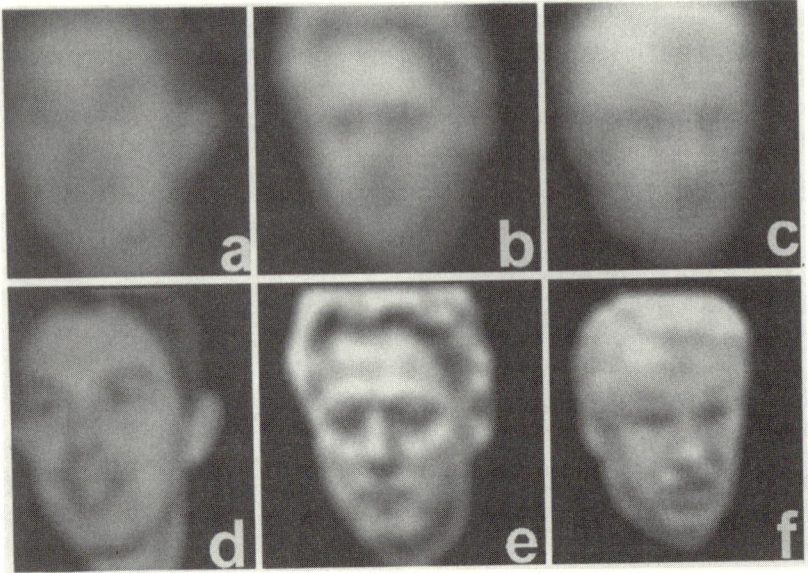

Note: The top row of the figure shows three portraits of political leaders, Blair, Clinton, and Yeltsin, low-pass Fourier filtered with a cut-off at 2.5 cycles per face. The lower row shows the same portraits filtered with a cut-off at 8.0 cycles per face.

distance of 1 meter, the experimental images subtended 6.02×9.74 degrees.

Procedure. Three sets of images, fronto-parallel (0°), three-quarter (45°) and full-profile (90°) were used as training images, with a group of twelve subjects assigned to a particular training view. Each subject used a response pad with six buttons to make his or her responses. Each button corresponded to a particular face and during the training phase a display containing the six faces and the button number corresponding to that face, having the same layout as the response pad, was available. Each subject was instructed to respond as accurately and as quickly as possible during the 48 training trials. There was a slight improvement in response accuracy, with hit rates increasing from 97.99 percent in the first 18 trials to 99.16 percent in the last 18 trials, and a significant fall in response latency, $F(2, 22) = 79.22$, $p < 0.001$ over the training trials. No effect at all of the three angles of face view was found ($F < 1.0$). Following the training trials, the set of cue images was removed, and subjects were told they would be seeing the six faces again during the testing session, but that the angle of view could be any one of five, and the faces would be filtered so that could appear fuzzy or faded. When each subject understood what the nature of the testing was to be, then the 450 randomised test trials, in three blocks of 150, were completed.

RESULTS

Response accuracy is shown in Figure 3, where it can be seen that performance is best for the band centered at 11.1 cycles per face, although the band centered at 5.22 cycles per face is almost as good, closely followed in turn by the 23.6 centered band. An ANOVA shows that while there was no significant effect of training angle, $F(2, 33) = 1.05$, $P = 0.36$, there was a significant effect of spatial frequency band, $F(4, 132) = 67.26$, $p < 0.001$. Tukey HSD tests, with $p = 0.05$, indicate that the three center bands, 5.22, 11.1, and 23.6 were significantly better than the lowest and highest bands, although the latter was significantly better than the former.

Response time data mirrored the accuracy results, with a minimum at 11.1 cycles per face, but with the two neighboring bands being close and the high and low extremes being worst. An ANOVA indicates a significant effect of spatial frequency band, $F(4, 132) = 57.29$, $p < 0.001$, but no effect of training angle, $F < 1.0$. Tukey HSD tests, with $p = 0.05$, indicate that while RTs to the band centered at 11.1 did not differ significantly from those to the 5.22 band, they are significantly faster than those to the 23.6 band; the latter band yields RTs significantly faster than those to either the 2.46 or the 50.15 bands.

DISCUSSION

The pattern of these results suggests quite strongly that, for an identification task, the middle range of facial frequencies is the most useful. Accuracy measures, as well as RTs, point to best performance being found in a band with its harmonic mean at 11.10 and a range from 7.85 to 15.69 cycles per face. The test session in this investigation consisted of filtered faces being presented at five different angles, yet the significant effect of bandwidth still emerges, suggesting that

FIGURE 2
Five portraits of the American president, A–E, that have been bandpass
filtered with center frequencies at 2.46, 5.22. 11.1, 23.6, and 50.15 cycles
per face respectively

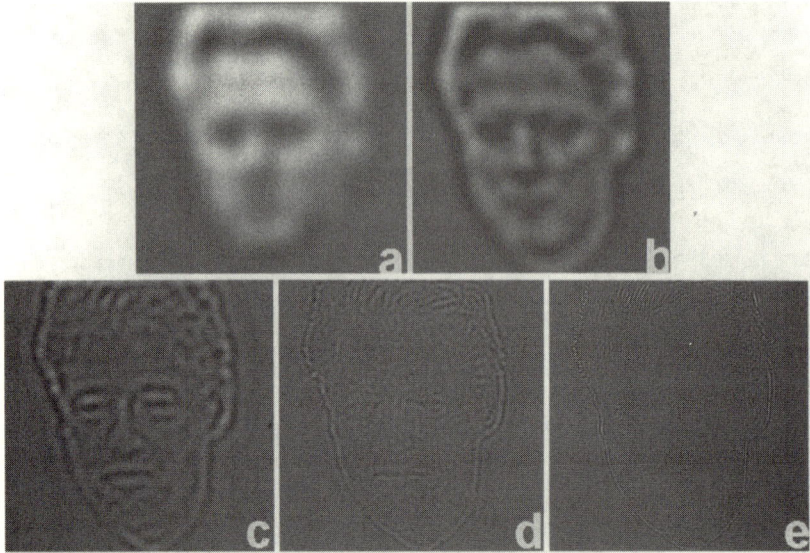

what we are seeing is a true face identification, rather than a picture identification, effect. Most interestingly, it is not the highest facial frequency bands that give the best identification results, even though the highest bands may give the best feature locations and, thus, the most accurate feature distance measures. Of course, if we look at the illustration of the filtered examples of the face in Figure 2 it is evident that the higher the spatial band, the less surface information is available to the viewer. In the 11.10 band, some surface information survives, particularly local surface information, but it is dropping out rapidly in the higher bands. The low bands, in contrast, provide very good global surface information, but are much weaker on local feature shape. The band centered on 11.10 appears to provide the best compromise from the available set.

We cannot, of course, state that this 11.10 band contains the spatial information that is critical for face identification, because it provides only an indication of what might be important. Even the band, centered at 2.46 cycles per face, in which performance is poorest, yields a

FIGURE 3
Response accuracy for five bandpass filtered versions of the set of faces
used in the identification experiment

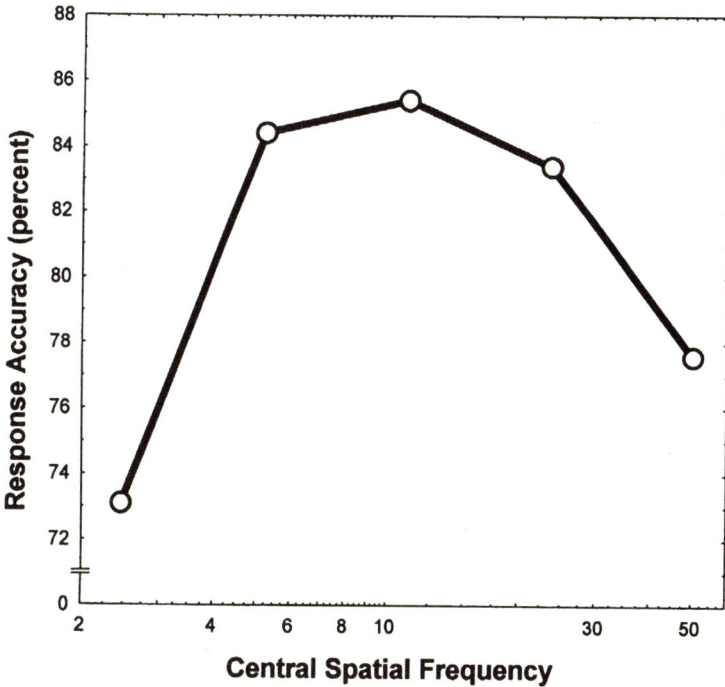

mean accuracy of over 70 percent and an RT performance that is approximately 120 msec slower that the 11.10 band; effective performance is not abolished under the worst condition of this experiment. However, previous reports (Bachmann, 1991; Costen et al., 1994, 1996) indicate that, when identification performance is being measured, and low-pass filtered faces are being used, accuracy and speed asymptote when resolution reaches about 8 cycles per face, i.e., the inclusion of finer scale information does not improve efficiency. With high-pass spatial filtering, there is also an indication that, once the inclusion of the band in the region of 11 cycles per face has been reached, accuracy becomes asymptotic (Costen et al., 1996). Results from high-pass, low-pass, and band-pass filtering then converge to suggest that when spatial information is restricted, the inclusion of a central band of face frequencies significantly improves performance. We can also reject the view that processing information at a finer scale necessarily leads to an increased cost in processing time. It may well be true that there is a monotonic increase in processing/scanning time with spatial frequency (Parker, 1980), but over the range of bands from 2.46 to 11.10, accuracy is increasing and processing time is failing. Once the spatial window moves above this central band then accuracy falls and processing times rise. It does not seem to be any simple aspect of the way spatial frequencies are processed that determines the pattern of results. This implies that it is crucial configural information held at intermediate scales that is driving performance.

It is important to remember, however, that we have not exhausted the range of possibilities in the experiment described and the other studies reviewed above. Remember that in the identification experiment described, at the end of the training interval, accuracy was almost 100 percent, but careful inspection of the data indicates that performance dropped even for the optimal band of the five tested, e.g., for the group trained on the fronto-parallel view performance fell to below 90 percent for the band centered on 11.10 cycles per face, even when these were presented in the same view (0°) as during training. When we look at low-pass identification results, it is apparent that performance can be as good once a resolution level of about 10 cycles per face has been reached as it is for the unprocessed, full band-width image (Costen et al., 1994), although how similar the faces are can modify these results (Costen et al., 1996). There is an indication, then, that identification performance is likely to be better if a band extending out from the most important central facial band, particularly towards the low facial frequencies (Costen et al., 1996), is added into the available spatial spectrum. The additional low facial frequency information gives a good impression of global face shape or mass (Figure 3). This implies that combinations of several spatial bands may be important, in the sense that they add to overall efficiency, but we do not in fact know which band combinations may be most advantageous. How would removal of the apparently important 8–16 cycle central band (band reject filtering), leaving the low and high spatial spectrum intact, affect the identification process? Such images would provide information about gross face shape/mass and fine local edge detail, but would omit shape information about local features such as the three dimensional shape of the nose or the eye socket. Knowing the answer to this question would be helpful in reaching a conclusion about the relative importance of local feature shape, as opposed to global face shape/mass with a smattering of local detail (this would be adequately provided by an image with the central 8–16 cycles per face rejected). In fact, some suggestive data on this question were provided by Bruce, Hanna, Dench, Healey, and Denton (1992), who used the Pearson and Robinson (1988) algorithm to provide a combination of crude facial mass and fine edge detail. They found that this combination produced identification accuracy almost as high as unprocessed images.

In conclusion, one can say there is strong evidence pointing to the relative importance of a central range of facial frequencies, between 8 and 16 cycles, in recognition and identification. This evidence is particularly good because, in part, it is provided by studies that combine processing time and accuracy measures. Does this indicate that there is a golden mean of facial scales that is necessary and sufficient for the job? Unfortunately not. Identification is possible from a range of information about the face, including line drawings and very low or very high facial frequencies, and there is even a possibility that the combination of low and high extremes may be quite efficient. The extent to which information in the non-central range is optimal for the task, however, remains unresolved: it is possible that, although subjects can use a variety of spatial information ranges when enough time is given for the task, pondering for several seconds over a degraded image before inferring the likely candidate may not be the same process as the quick decision that we commonly think of when talking about recognising a face. However, the fact that spatial bands centered on 2.46 or 50.15 cycles per face can produce accuracy levels of over 70 percent, only 15 percent below the optimal band, and the fact that response latencies that are circa 100 msec slower than peak performance, point to an extremely flexible identification system.

REFERENCES

Bachmann, T. (1991). Identification of spatially quantised tachistoscopic images of faces: How many pixels does it take to carry identity? *European Journal of Cognitive Psychology*, *3*, 85–103.

Breitmeyer, B.G. (1975). Simple reaction times as a measure of the response properties of transient and sustained channels. *Vision Research*, *15*, 1411–1412.

Bruce, V. (1988). *Recognising faces*. London: Erlbaum.

Bruce, V., Hanna, E., Dench, N., Healey, P., and Burton, M. (1992). The importance of mass in line drawings of faces. *Applied Cognitive Psychology*, *6*, 619–628.

Costen, N.P., Parker, D.M., and Craw, I.G. (1994). Spatial content and spatial quantisation effects in face recognition. *Perception*, *23*, 129–146.

Costen, N.P., Parker, D.M., and Craw, I.G. (1996). Effects of high-pass and low-pass filtering on face identification. *Perception and Psychophysics, 58*, 602–612.

Davies, G.M., Ellis, H.D., and Shepherd, J.W. (1978). Face recognition accuracy as a function of mode of representation. *Journal of Applied Psychology, 63*, 180–187.

Fiorentini, A., Maffei, L., and Sandini, G. (1983). The role of high spatial frequencies in face perception. *Perception, 12*, 195–201.

Galper, R.E. (1970). Recognition of faces in photographic negative. *Psychonomic Science, 19*, 207–208.

Harmon, L.D. (1973). The recognition of faces. *Scientific American, 229*, 70–83.

Hayes, T., Morrone, M.C., and Burr, D.C. (1986). Recognition of positive and negative bandpass-filtered images. *Perception, 15*, 596–602.

O'Toole, A.J., Millward, R.B., and Anderson, J.A. (1988). A physical system approach to recognition memory for spatially transformed faces. *Neural Networks, 1*, 179–199.

Parker, D.M. (1980). Simple reaction times to the onset, offset and contrast reversal of sinusoidal grating stimuli. *Perception and Psychophysics, 28*, 365–368.

Parker, D.M., Lishman, J.R., and Hughes, J. (1996). Role of coarse and fine spatial information in face and object processing. *Journal of Experimental Psychology: Human Perception and Performance, 22*, 1448–1466.

Parker, D.M. and Salzen, E.A. (1977). Latency changes in the human visual evoked potential to sinusoidal gratings. *Vision Research, 17*, 1201–1204.

Pearson, D.E. and Robinson, J.A. (1985). Visual communication at very low data-rates. *Proceedings of the IEEE, 73*, 795–811.

Peli, E., Young, G.M., Goldstein, R.B., and Trempe, C.L. (1991). The critical spatial frequency for face recognition. *Noninvasive Assessment of the Visual System, Technical Digest, Vol. 1, Optical Society of America*, Washington D.C., pp. 105–108.

Phillips, R.J. (1972). Why are faces hard to recognise in photographic negative? *Perception and Psychophysics, 12*, 425–426.

Riley, D. and Costall, A. (1980). Comment on "Recognition of faces in the presence of two-dimensional sinusoidal masks" by Tieger and Ganz. *Perception and Psychophysics, 27*, 373–374.

Sergent, J. (1986). Microgenesis in face perception. In: H.D. Ellis. M.A. Jeeves, F. Newcombe, and A. Young (eds.), *Aspects of face processing* (pp. 17–73). Dordrecht, The Netherlands: Martinus Nijhoff.

The Impact of Character Attribution on Composite Production: A Real World Effect?

GRAHAM DAVIES
Leicester University, United Kingdom

and

HEIDI OLDMAN
Middlesex University, United Kingdom

Facial memory draws upon both veridical detail and beliefs based upon prior knowledge and stereotypes. Shepherd, Ellis, McMurran, and Davies (1978) demonstrated that subjects' perception and subsequent reconstruction of a face using the "Photofit" kit was significantly influenced by whether they believed the person to be a multiple murderer or a local hero. The current study explored whether similar effects would occur when the face involved was one of four male celebrities about which subjects held pronounced positive or negative views and where reconstruction was accomplished using the computerised "E-fit" composite system. Semantic differential ratings showed significant influences of liking on subjects' perception and reconstruction of the faces involved, though the pattern of effects was not always readily predictable. Liking also influenced accuracy of reconstruction; ranking and naming data showed that the best composites were made by subjects who disliked the target and made their reconstructions with the aid of a photograph.

Theories of memory emphasise the selective nature of the process and the role that reconstruction, based on prior knowledge and experience, plays in recall (Bartlett, 1932; Neisser, 1966; Schank and Abelson, 1977). Memory for faces is unlikely to be exempt from these processes. This raises the possibility that forensic tools like Photofit and Identikit, which demand witnesses provide complete recall of all facial features of a suspect's face may draw on attributions and beliefs as well as real memories. This was explored in a pioneering study by Shepherd, Ellis, McMurran, and Davies (1978) who reported significant distortions in the perception and subsequent reconstruction of a face using the Photofit kit, depending upon whether the observer thought the person was a multiple murderer or a local hero. The current study seeks to explore this effect in a real-world context and, further, to see whether negative stereotyping differentially influences the accuracy of facial reconstruction.

There is now considerable evidence that memory for facial appearance is often fragmentary and selective. When observing and describing faces, greater attention appears to be paid to the upper regions of the face, particularly the hair and eyes, relative to the lower regions, such as the mouth and the chin (Shepherd et al., 1977; Haig, 1986). In making judgements of facial similarity, more attention is paid to hair, face shape, and age cues than other information (Shepherd et al., 1981). As faces become more familiar, so knowledge grows of the internal, expressive features (Ellis et al., 1979; Young et al., 1985). Even partial knowledge of facial appearance is sufficient for effective everyday recognition of other persons, but it can break down when the person appears in an unfamiliar context or where a stranger shares key facial cues with the familiar person (Young et al., 1985).

If memory for faces is selective, then it is likely that any gaps will be filled in by the perceiver, relying upon attributions and stereotyping. Shepherd (1981, 1989) has reviewed the abundant evidence for social influences on face perception and recognition: we do not just describe someone as having "dark hair and a long nose," we go on to say that they were "attractive" or "looked dishonest." This was acknowledged in one of the first analyses of person perception by Warr and Knapper (1968), who distinguished between "episodic judgements" and "dispositional impressions," a theme taken up by Klatsky, Martin, and Kane (1982) with their distinction between "physical/structural codes" and "semantic judgements" in face recognition. Curiously, the most influential of contemporary theories of face processing, the Bruce and Young (1986) model, has little to say about the role of extra-stimulus information, beyond recognizing its importance and ascribing it to the "cognitive system" (Bruce, 1988).

The role of semantic judgements is not only of theoretical, but also practical interest. Witnesses to crime are frequently called upon to construct a facial composite of the appearance of a suspect, from a library of possible features. In order to construct a total face, it is necessary for the witness to select an example of all of the major features: hair, eyes, nose, mouth, and chin. Traditional procedures such as Identikit and Photofit have involved the selection and physical assembly of the components into a composite face. Laboratory research suggested that such systems achieved a very low degree of likeness, in part because the range of features was limited, and the division of the face was arbitrary (Clifford and Davies 1989; Shepherd and Ellis, 1996). However, with the growing power and availability of personal computers, a new generation of computerised facial composite systems has become available, which offer a greatly enhanced range of features and versatility in construction methods. Yet, research results to date have been unable to demonstrate any marked improvement in composite quality relative to traditional composite kits when witnesses construct faces from memory (Koehn and Fisher, 1997; Kovera et al., 1997; Davies et al., in press).

One of the other reasons for the poor quality of composites may be that they make demands upon a witness' facial memory that exceed their recall abilities. In these circumstances, subjects may fall back upon expectations and social stereotypes to complete the total face. This possibility was explored in a study by Shepherd et al. (1978). In it, subjects were informally shown a photograph of a man who was variously described as being a Glaswegian multiple murderer or a lifeboat captain who had been recently decorated for bravery at sea. Subsequently, subjects were asked to make a series of judgements on his face using semantic differential scales (Osgood et al.,   1957), before going on to construct a likeness using the Photofit kit. Subjects in the "murderer" condition showed significant differences from those in the "lifeboat man" condition on eight of the nine scales employed. Further, when the resulting composites were shown to independent judges who rated them using the same scales, "lifeboat man" composites were judged as significantly more good-looking and attractive than were "murderer" composites. Such results could have important implications for the general quality of composites made by witnesses to actual crimes who must construct likenesses of persons for whom they have strongly negative feelings, but the researchers did not examine the impact of the judgements on the quality or accuracy of the likeness. Moreover, it could be argued that the changes in the face ratings were driven by strong demand characteristics; subjects could have simply furnished them on the basis of the Experimenter's descriptions, rather than attributing characteristics to the face, as such.

In order to explore these issues, the current study replicated the main features of the Shepherd et al. (1978) experiment with a number of significant departures. The current study used the face of a celebrity as a target, about whom the subject was known to hold negative or positive views, rather than a stranger. Composites were constructed first from memory and then in the presence of a reference photograph of the celebrity concerned. The reason why the subject was asked to make this particular face was not explained prior to the experiment, and all semantic differential ratings on the target face were made subsequent to the construction phase. In addition to rating the resulting composites on the same semantic scales, judges also made assessments of the accuracy and quality of the composites. Finally, composites were constructed using E-fit, a computer-based system in wide use by the police in the United Kingdom (Aspley, 1993), rather than Photofit, which it has replaced.

It was hypothesised that: (a) ratings of the actual faces of the targets made by the group of subjects who disliked them would differ systematically from those who liked them; (b) liking would also influence the ratings subsequently provided by judges for composites produced by the same subjects; and (c) such effects would be stronger for composites made from memory compared with those made with the aid of a reference photograph, which might be expected to rely more on veridical information. No specific prediction was made regarding the possible impact of liking on composite accuracy.

METHOD

Subject Selection

In order to select appropriate subjects, it was necessary to identify persons who had clear negative and positive feelings about well-known public figures. A list was compiled of eight persons about whom student opinion might be polarised. As only a male E-fit system was available, choice of celebrities was restricted to that gender. The list consisted of: Roger Cook, Jarvis Cocker, Rowan Atkinson, Jim Davidson, Noel Edmonds, Paul Merton, Tony Blair, and Terry Venables. A total of ninety-four female and fifty-one male undergraduate students taking first year psychology courses at Leicester University were approached and agreed to complete five-point rating scales concerning how much they liked (point 1: strong liking; point 5: strong dislike) each of the eight target celebrities. In addition, subjects also completed a five-point rating of their familiarity with each member of the list (point 1: very familiar; point 5: very unfamiliar), as previous research had shown that familiarity significantly influenced composite quality (Davies et al., in press).

The distribution of extreme ratings across targets made it possible to select four targets (Jarvis Cocker, Jim Davidson, Noel Edmonds, and Tony Blair) for each of whom there were three subjects who expressed either liking or strong liking (scale points 1 and 2) and three who expressed disliking or strong disliking (scale points 4 and 5). Familiarity ratings for all targets were high and did not differentiate between the like and dislike group, $t(22) < 1$. Three weeks after the rating task, these twenty-four subjects, eighteen female and six male, were approached individually and agreed to take part in an experiment on face reconstruction. They were offered either course credit or a small honorarium for participation.

Overview of Design of the Main Experiment

A balanced design was employed, whereby each of six subjects (three of whom liked and three disliked the target), constructed composites of one of four targets, first from memory and then from a photograph, generating a total of forty-eight composites. All subjects subsequently rated their target face on nine semantic differential scales. The sets of twelve composites corresponding to each target were rank ordered for degree of resemblance by a group of independent judges. A further group of judges rated the composites on these same nine semantic differential scales and attempted to name any of the persons they believed they recognised. The resulting data were then analysed using a series of 2 (like/dislike) × 2 (memory/photo) mixed ANOVAs.

Procedure

Construction Phase. Subjects were seen individually by the experimenter in a small room containing two chairs, a computer, and monitor. She began by reminding them that they had recently indicated they were familiar with the appearance of the particular target celebrity and that they would now have the opportunity to try to construct his face using E-fit. The experimenter, who was an experienced operator of the system, then introduced E-fit to the subject, following the standard procedure laid down in the training manual. This first involved a demonstration of the format and capabilities of the system, including scrolling through or resizing features. Subjects were instructed that they could commence construction with any feature they wished and that they should not select descriptors for features they could not recall.

Subjects then selected descriptors appropriate to the target, which in turn generated an approximate composite. Subjects then exchanged, enlarged, reduced, or moved features until an acceptable composite was achieved. This "from memory" image was then saved on disc, and the process of exchange and refinement repeated, this time with continuous reference to a life-size, full-face monochrome photograph of the target. This additional "from photo" image was also saved on disc.

Subjects took up to thirty minutes to compile the "from memory" image and an additional ten minutes for the "from photo" composite. Subsequently, all subjects rated the photograph of the target using the nine semantic differential scales originally employed by Shepherd et al. (1978). These were: intelligent/unintelligent; passive/quick-tempered; pleasant/unpleasant; soft/hard; good/bad; sociable/unsociable; kind/unkind; humorous/humorless; and good-looking/ugly. The adjectives served as anchors on five-point scales with some scales reversed to avoid positive attributes always being associated with the same end point. On completion of the tasks, subjects were debriefed and thanked for their participation.

Evaluation Phase. All stored composites were printed out using a high-definition laser printer and mounted individually on thin card. A total of eighteen undergraduate students from Leicester University, twelve female and six male, all of whom were familiar with the appearance of the targets, agreed to act as judges of resemblance. They were given a set of four folders, each containing a picture of one of the targets and the twelve composites, six from memory, six from view, of that target. They were required to scrutinise each composite relative to the picture of the target and then to rank order them from the best to the worst attempt. This was repeated for each of the four targets and the composite rankings were recorded for each judge.

An additional thirty-six judges, twenty-one females and fifteen males, who were also undergraduate volunteers, rated the forty-eight composites on the same nine semantic differential scales as had originally been used by the subjects themselves. These thirty-six judges were split into three groups of twelve, and each group was responsible for rating a different set of sixteen composites structured so that all combinations of target, liking, and construction condition (memory/photo) were represented in each set. Each judge was told to work through their set of composites, rating each in turn on the five-point semantic differential scales. Finally, the judges were informed that the composites were of "well known public figures" and were required to go through the set of composites and to name any that they identified. Judges were permitted to work at their own pace on all tasks and were thanked and debriefed on completion.

RESULTS

Semantic Differential Ratings

Constructors' own ratings. The mean ratings given by the twelve constructors for their target face were computed as a function of liking. On all nine scales, constructors who liked the target rated the target more favorably than those who did not, but in all instances the size of the difference was quite small and reached statistical significance for only two scales. These were *humorous/humorless* where those who liked the targets rated their faces as more humorous ($M =$ 2.75) than did those who did not ($M = 1.67$), $t(22) = 2.60$, $p < .02$, and *pleasant/unpleasant* where likers rated their face as more pleasant ($M = 3.08$) than did dislikers ($M = 2.08$), $t = 2.18$, $p < .05$. The strong effect for humor may be explained by the presence of two entertainers among the four targets. These, overall, rather modest effects may be contrasted with the much larger differences for constructors' ratings reported by Shepherd et al. (1978).

Judges' Ratings. The mean ratings on each of the nine scales given

FIGURE 1
Mean Ratings on the 9 Semantic Differential Scales for Composites as a function of Liking and Method of Construction[a]

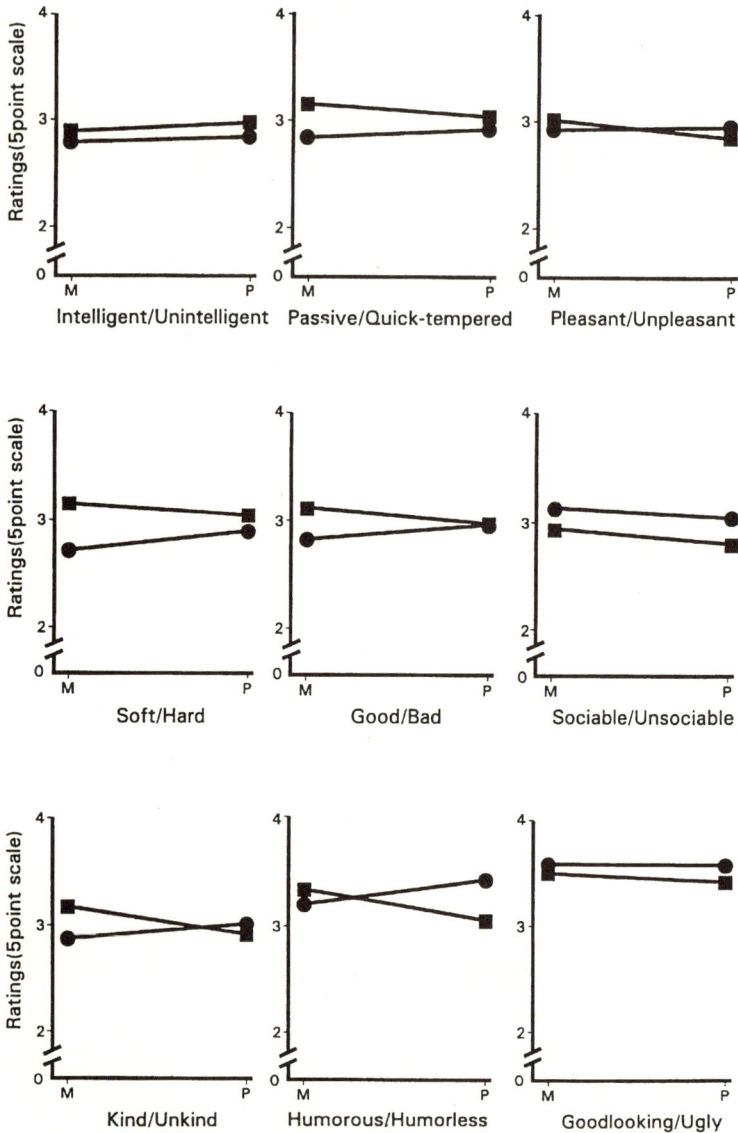

[a] Each mean based on thirty-six observations. Lower rating indicates more positive perceptions. M = from memory; P = from photo; circles = liked target; squares = disliked target.

by judges as a function of liking and construction condition are shown in Figure 1. The hypothesis was that liking would interact with construction condition such that semantic influence would be likely to be more pronounced when faces were constructed from memory, compared with those made in a presence of a photograph of the target. Ratings were analysed both in terms of individual scales and a pooled score based on all nine scales. Constructors' liking for the targets influenced performance on six of the nine individual scales, though the impact did not always take the form predicted. In addition, the pooled scale scores showed the expected pattern.

The predicted interaction was present to some extent for three of the nine scales. The strongest effect was on *kind/unkind*, with a interaction between Liking and Construction Condition, $F (1,286) = 6.95$, $p < .01$, and no other significant main effects. A Simple Effects analysis confirmed that while ratings of images made from photographs were very similar, $F < 1$, ratings of composites made from memory by subjects who liked the targets were perceived as more kind than those who disliked them, $F (1, 286) = 8.30$, $p < .01$. For *good/bad*, the predicted interaction fell just short of significance, $F (1, 286), = 3.62$, $p < .06$, with again, composites produced from memory by likers being more favourably judged than those made by dislikers, $F (1,286) = 7.20$, $p < .01$, and no difference on ratings from photographs, $F < 1$. For *soft/hard*, the interaction again just missed significance, $F (1, 286) = 3.21$, $p < .10$, with the same pattern present: a significant difference due to liking on composites made from memory, $F (1, 286) = 9.68$, $p < .01$, and none when made from photographs, $F (1,286) = 1.04$.

In addition, constructors' attitude toward the targets influenced performance on a further three scales, though not always in the form predicted by the hypothesis. For *passive/quick-tempered* composites made by constructors who liked the targets were generally rated more positively than those made by those who disliked them, $F (1, 286) = 4.62$, $p < .05$. Conversely, on *sociable/unsociable,* constructions made by subjects who liked the targets were perceived as less sociable than those who disliked them, $F (1, 286) = 4.92$, $p < .05$. Finally, on *humorous/humorless,* liking entered into a significant interaction with construction condition, $F (1,286) = 10.57$, $p < .001$, such that composites made from photographs by those who disliked the targets were

TABLE 1
Mean Rank for Resemblance to the Target for Composites as a
Function of Liking and Construction Condition[a]

	Condition	
Construction	From memory	From photograph
Liking		
Like target	7.94	7.38
	(3.77)	(3.59)
Dislike target	7.54	6.09
	(3.62)	(3.43)

[a] Each mean based on 18 observations. Lower rank indicates better resemblance.

rated as more humorous than those who liked them, F (1, 286) = 11.67, $p < .001$, with no corresponding effect for composites made from memory, F (1, 286) = 1.39. There were no other significant findings for any of these analyses.

Three scales produced no significant effects: *pleasant/unpleasant, intelligent/unintelligent* and *good-looking/ugly*. Interestingly, it was the latter two scales which proved significant in the Shepherd et al. (1978) study.

As a final test of the hypothesis, each judge's ratings for all nine scales were summed and a further ANOVA conducted. This pooled analysis showed stronger support for the hypothesis: the interaction was present, F (1, 286) = 4.35, $p < .05$, and took the form predicted: the mean total ratings for composites made from memory by subjects who liked the targets (M = 28.26) differed significantly from those who made by subjects who disliked them (M = 26.86), F (1,286) = 4.30, $p < .05$; while for those made from photographs, mean ratings for likers (M = 27.60) did not differ significantly from dislikers (M = 27.01), $F < 1$.

Accuracy of Construction

Mean ranked accuracy. The mean ranking achieved by composites as a function of Liking and Construction Condition is displayed in Table 1.

Analysis of these data showed significant main effects both for Liking, F (1,430) = 7.77, $p < .01$, and for Construction Condition, F

TABLE 2
Number of Spontaneous Correct (and Incorrect) Identifications of
Composites as a Function of Liking and Construction Condition[a]

	Condition	
Construction	From memory	From photograph
Liking		
Like target	8	10
	(40)	(37)
Dislike target	8	18
	(35)	(33)

[a] Incorrect identifications in parentheses. All correct scores out of a maximum of 144.

(1, 430) = = 36.56, $p <$ 001, which in turn were qualified by an interaction between these two factors, F (1, 430) = 7.24, $p <$ .01. A Simple Effects analysis confirmed that, while liking had a marginal impact on the assessed quality of composites made from memory, F (1, 430) = 2.84, $p <$ .10, it had a major influence on those made from photographs, F (1, 430) = 30.15, $p <$ .001. In both instances, the direction of the effect was the same: composites made by persons who expressed dislike for the targets were judged to be better likenesses than those who liked them. In addition, the same analysis confirmed that composites made from photographs were of better quality than those made from memory, though this effect applied only to constructors who disliked the targets, F (1, 430) = 17.69, $p <$ .001, and not to those who liked the targets, F (1, 430) = 2.84, ns.

Identification. The number of spontaneous correct and erroneous identifications of targets made by judges and totalled as a function of Liking and Construction Condition is shown in Table 2.

As can be observed from Table 2, the rate of spontaneous correct identifications was low overall but mirrored the general pattern for the ranking data. Of the four targets employed, Noel Edmonds was most readily named (23 correct identifications), followed by Jarvis Cocker (12), Tony Blair (8) with Jim Davidson hardly ever recognized (1). Subjects achieved a rate of correct naming of 7.6 percent overall, rising to 12.5 percent for composites made from photographs of the targets by those who disliked them. Rates of correct recognition need to be placed in the context of misidentifications, which were generally high (25.2%) and again were lowest in the condition combining dislike of the target and construction from a photograph (23.0%).

DISCUSSION

The current study demonstrates that the attitude of the subject toward the target does have significant and pervasive effects on the way the target's face is perceived and remembered, though the precise pattern of influence is not entirely as predicted. First, the influence of positive and negative attitudes toward the target had only modest effects upon the subjects' ratings of the targets actual appearance. While all scales were in the expected direction, significant effects were observed on only two of the nine scales, compared to eight out of nine for the related study by Shepherd et al. (1978). One explanation for the difference in the size of the observed effect could be that the use of actual politicians and TV personalities in the current study did not generate such extreme reactions as the multiple murderer/local hero contrast used in the earlier study. Another would be that the demand characteristics were stronger in the earlier study, because the rating task followed so shortly after the negative and positive information about the target.

Second, positive and negative attitudes toward the targets did influence the subsequent construction of composites. Significant effects for liking were observed on four of the nine scales, with a further two approaching significance. As in the Shepherd et al. (1978) study, the absolute sizes of the rating differences were modest, and where effects for liking occurred, the pattern was by no means always in accord with expectation. It is understandable that those who think positively about someone might invest their composites with characteristics like sensitivity, goodness, even-temper, and kindness. It is less clear why they should also believe their heroes to be unsociable and humorless, especially given the presence of three entertainers in the target list. One explanation may be that these latter contrasts are caused not so much by the positive views of their protagonists as by the negative views of their detractors: those who think ill of Messrs. Edmonds, Davidson, and Cocker may have been trying to tell us something! It is also interesting that two of the three scales that produced no effects—intelligence and attractiveness—were precisely those that produced significant results in the Shepherd et al. (1978) study. One explanation for this anomaly may lie in the choice of targets: as politicians and television personalities, they may have been grudgingly perceived by their detractors as possessing the necessary minimal physical attractiveness and intelligence to do their jobs, but to be glaringly deficient in other areas of character.

While liking had a demonstrable influence on performance, stronger effects when the face was being retrieved from memory as opposed to being constructed from a photograph were by no means the norm. There was an overall effect when all ratings were pooled, but only one of the nine scales showed a strong effect, with two others showing a marginal impact. One reason for this failure of prediction may have been the high familiarity of the faces involved that may have restricted the opportunity for what Read (1995) terms "context-driven judgements" to prevail over "perceptual knowledge." The original design of the study called for the inclusion of subjects who were unfamiliar with the target's appearance but who nevertheless disliked them, but the familiarity and liking judgements were so highly correlated as to preclude this. For faces, it seems, contempt is inexorably linked to familiarity.

Third, while liking had a demonstrable effect on how faces were perceived, it also influenced how well the targets were identified. Composites made by those who disliked the targets were ranked higher overall and elicited more spontaneous correct identifications than those made by those who liked them. While the effect was again quite modest in absolute terms, the results are reassuring for the use of such systems in criminal detection; suggesting that negative affect toward a suspect is likely to aid rather than hinder the construction of a likeness. It is unclear why dislike should engender improved recall. One explanation may lie in the nature of positive and negative judgements: positive judgements may encourage rather more global evaluations of faces, a process known to improve recognition of faces (Winograd, 1981), but impair composite reconstruction (Wells and Hryciw, 1984). If this is the case, one might predict that positive attitudes toward persons would facilitate recognition, but impair recall: an expectation in line with the anecdotal observation that husbands and wives show surprisingly poor recall for each other's personal appearance.

Finally, the relatively low rates of spontaneous identifications combined with high rates of false alarms in the naming condition are entirely in accord with earlier findings (Koehn and Fisher, 1997; Kovera et al., 1997; Davies et al., in press) in demonstrating the difficulties of constructing a recognisable composite face. The basic sensitivity of the E-fit system is demonstrated by the superiority of faces made from photographs compared with memory, an effect not always found with the earlier generation of manual systems like Photofit (Ellis et al., 1975). It appears that composite images, however sophisticated, rarely elicit the spontaneous recognition processes triggered by photographs. Perhaps future research should explore the degree to which subjects could be assisted in relating composites more readily to their stored information on faces, perhaps through semantic priming, which is known to have facilitative effects on face recognition in other contexts (Bruce, 1988).

NOTE

This experiment was conducted while Ms. Oldman was acting as a Research Assistant for Professor Davies as part of the Middlesex University Student Work Placement Programme. This paper was written while the first author was on study leave granted by Leicester University. Information on E-fit may be obtained from Aspley Identifying Solutions, 82a Town Centre, Hatfield, Herts. AL10 0JW, United Kingdom.

REFERENCES

Aspley Limited (1993). *E-fit*. Hatfield, UK: Aspley Limited.
Bartlett, F. C. (1932). *Remembering: A study in experimental and social psychology*. Cambridge: Cambridge University Press.
Bruce, V. (1988). *Recognising faces*. Hove, UK: Erlbaum.
Bruce, V. and Young, A. W. (1986). Understanding face recognition. *British Journal of Psychology, 77*, 305–327.
Clifford, B. R. and Davies, G. A (1989). Procedures for obtaining identification evidence. In D. C. Raskin (Ed.), *Psychological methods in criminal investigation and evidence* (pp. 47–96). New York: Springer.
Davies, G. M., van der Willick, P. and Morrison, L. J. (in press). Facial composite production: A comparison of mechanical and computer-driven systems. *Journal of Applied Psychology*.
Ellis, H. D., Shepherd, J. W., and Davies, G. M. (1975). An investigation of the use of the Photofit technique for recalling faces. *British Journal of Psychology, 66*, 29–37.
Ellis, H. D., Shepherd, J. W., and Davies, G. M. (1979). Identification of familiar and unfamiliar faces from internal and external features: Some implications for theories of face recognition. *Perception, 8*, 431–439.
Haig, N. D. (1986). Investigating face recognition with an image processing computer. In H. D. Ellis, M. A. Jeeves, F., Newcombe, and A. Young (Eds.), *Aspects of face processing* (pp. 410–425). Dodrecht, The Netherlands: Nijhoff.
Klatsky, R., Martin, G. L., and Kane, R. A. (1982). Semantic interpretation effects on memory for faces. *Memory and Cognition, 10*, 195–206.
Kovera, M. B., Penrod, S., Pappas, C., and Thill, D. (1997). Identification of computer-generated facial composites. *Journal of Applied Psychology, 82*, 235–246.
Koehn, C. and Fisher, R. P. (1997). Constructing facial composites with the Mac-a-Mug Pro system. *Psychology, Crime and Law, 3*, 209–218.

Neisser, U. (1966). *Cognitive Psychology*. New York: Appleton-Century-Crofts.

Osgood, C. E., Suci, G. J., and Tannenbaum, P. H. (1957). *The measurement of meaning*. Urbana, Il: University of Illinois Press.

Read, J.D. (1995). The availability heuristic in person identification: The sometimes misleading consequences of enhanced contextual information. *Applied Cognitive Psychology, 9*, 91–121.

Schank, R. C. and Abelson, R. P. (1977). *Scripts, plans, goals and understanding: An enquiry into human knowledge structures*. Hillsdale, NJ: Erlbaum.

Shepherd, J. W. (1981). Social factors in face recognition. In G. M. Davies, H. D. Ellis and J. W. Shepherd (Eds.), *Perceiving and remembering faces* (pp. 55–79). London: Academic Press.

Shepherd, J. W. (1989). The face and social attribution. In A. W. Young and H. D. Ellis (Eds.), *Handbook of research on face processing* (pp. 289–320). Amsterdam: North Holland.

Shepherd, J. W., Davies, G. M., and Ellis, H. D. (1981). Studies in cue saliency. In G. M. Davies, H. D. Ellis and J. W. Shepherd (Eds.), *Perceiving and remembering faces* (pp. 105–131). London: Academic Press.

Shepherd, J. W. and Ellis, H. D. (1996). Face recall—Methods and problems. In R. Sporer and G. K. Malpass (Eds). *Psychological issues in eyewitness identification*. Mahwah: Erlbaum.

Shepherd, J. W., Ellis, H. D, and Davies, G. M. (1977). *Perceiving and remembering faces*. (Report POL/73/1675/2411). London: The Home Office.

Shepherd, J. W., Ellis, H. D., McMurran, M. and Davies, G. M. (1978). Effect of character attribution on Photofit construction of a face. *European Journal of Social Psychology, 8*, 263–268.

Warr, P. B. and Knapper, C. (1968). *The perception of people and events*. London: John Wiley and Sons.

Wells, G. L. and Hryciw, B. (1984). Memory for faces: Encoding and retrieval operations. *Memory and Cognition, 12*, 338–344.

Winograd, E. (1981). Elaboration and distinctiveness in memory for faces. *Journal of Experimental Psychology: Human Learning and Memory, 7*, 181–190.

Young, A. W., Hay, D. C., and Ellis, A. W. (1985). The faces that launched a thousand slips: Everyday difficulties and errors in recognising people. *British Journal of Psychology, 76*, 495–523.

Young, A. W., Hay, D. C., McWeeny, K. H., Flude, B. M., and Ellis, A. W. (1985). Matching familiar and unfamiliar faces on internal and external features. *Perception, 14*, 737–746.

Repetition Priming of Face Gender Judgments: An Instance Based Explanation

DENNIS C. HAY
Lancaster University

Earlier studies of repetition priming using faces have been interpreted as indicating that such effects are confined to the processing of known faces. The experiment reported here employed eight rather than the more usual two presentation trials and required subjects to make gender decisions (is it a male or is it a female face?) to both familiar and unfamiliar faces. This allowed the currently favored recognition unit theories of face processing to be compared with the Logan (1988) instance model. Equivalent repetition priming effects were observed for both familiar and unfamiliar faces and were well fitted by power functions. It is argued that the findings are consistent with the strong predictions made by Logan's model and pose problems for recognition unit based theories.

Current theoretical models of face recognition distinguish between the sets of processes needed to extract basic information common to all faces (e.g., gender, age, expression, transformations across pose, etc.) and the processes required to recognise and retrieve information about known faces. For example, in the Hay and Young (1982) model, the Bruce and Young (1986) model, and the Burton, Bruce, and Johnson (1990) neural network simulation, knowing that a face is familiar requires activation of a face recognition unit (FRU), which in turn allows access to semantic information and finally access to name retrieval. Common to these serial access models is the concept of an FRU; a device containing both the "essence" of a known face and a set of procedures for matching incoming facial information with this stored internal representation. These can best be described as *abstraction* models in which the "essence" of a face is abstracted from the variety of exposures to this face and requires the discarding of the individuating characteristics of any particular instance of a known face. FRUs, therefore, are direct equivalents of the logogens proposed by Morton (1979) to explain how words are recognized.

One of the main sources of evidence that has been used to examine the validity of FRU-based functional models has come from experiments using a repetition priming methodology (Bruce and Valentine, 1985; Ellis et al., 1987). The results from these studies and the finding that expression and gender decisions to photos of famous and unfamiliar faces speeded subsequent familiarity decisions, led Ellis, Young, and Flude (1990) to conclude that repetition priming is confined to the processes involved in processing familiar faces and not other forms of face processing. In a recent integrative study Ellis, Flude, Young, and Burton (1996) identified two loci at which repetition priming in processing faces operates. The first involves perceptual recognition of a face as familiar and is, in their view, domain specific by which they mean that it is restricted to classes of stimuli having a specialized recognition system (Baddeley, 1982). That is, previous exposure to a famous face will prime later presentations of the same photograph or other similar views, but will fail to prime the name of that celebrity. The second locus is at the stage of name retrieval and is domain independent. Thus, previously reading aloud the name of a celebrity will prime the subsequent naming of the face of that celebrity. In a series of experiments, Ellis et al. showed that tasks involving familiarity or occupational decisions are susceptible to locus 1 priming effects, while locus 2 priming is observed in tasks involving face naming.

Ellis et al. (1996) argue that the existing face priming data support what they term to be *structural theories* of face repetition priming, in which response time speed-up on the second viewing of a known face is a reflection of the structural change in the activation unit threshold, which is lowered by the initial presentation of the face. They also argue that the data pose significant problems for alternative theoretical accounts in which the internal representation are not FRU abstractions, but are based on the storage of instances or episodes (Jacoby, 1983; Jacoby and Brooks, 1984) and suggest repetition priming results from a process of *perceptual enhancement* where the memory of a previous encounter with a stimulus facilitates its recognition. Ellis et al. direct their criticisms towards one particular instance-based account, that of Logan (1990), which attempts to draw parallels between repetition priming and the development of automaticity in task performance following large amounts of practice.

In the Logan model there exist a basic set of algorithms capable of processing stimuli and the algorithm used to process a novel face has an associated response time (RT) distribution. Each encounter with a face generates a stored representation, and each of these *instances* also has an associated RT distribution. Subsequent recognition is accomplished by a processing race in which all existing instances race against one another and the basic algorithm. Logan (1988) has shown that simulating the race model over a range of algorithm and instance parameters always leads to RT functions that are well fitted by power functions of the form;

$$RT = a + b \, (\text{Instance})^{-c}$$

where a is the function asymptote, b a measure of the difference between initial and asymptotic performance, and c the learning rate.

Hay (in press) extended these findings by showing that RT data from a face repetition priming task in which subjects made familiarity decisions (deciding if a stimulus face was of a famous celebrity or of a previously unknown person) to the same faces on eight trials, also produced power functions of this form. In addition, the data also supported a number of strong predictions made by the Logan instance model, namely:

(a) that mean correct RT performance and the variability in performance, as measured by the standard deviation, reduce as the number of trials increase and that both are well fitted by power functions with the above form;

(b) that the mean and the standard deviation power functions share the same exponent; and

(c) that different quantiles of the RT processing distribution are also well fitted by power functions and that these also share the same exponent as the mean and standard deviation functions.

These data offer strong support for an instance based account of face repetition priming, pose serious problems for the abstraction models based on FRUs, and explain priming as due to the lowering of an FRU activation level on the first encounter with a known face. These are not well enough specified to make any predictions about the amount of speed-up in RT that should result. In addition, Hay found power function RT speed-up for both the familiar and the initially unknown faces. The latter speed-up is particularly problematic for current abstractive accounts as priming is based on the functioning of FRUs that only exist for known faces.

However, Ellis et al. (1996) also point out that certain properties of locus 1 priming (i.e., recognizing that a face is familiar) are difficult for Logan's instance model to explain. For example, they cite the Ellis, Young, and Flude (1990) study, showing that only certain types of face decision are subject to repetition priming. Gender decisions (is this a male or female face?) show no priming, even when the same photo of a familiar face is seen minutes earlier. Instance models, they argue, predict priming as the second presentation should lead to the activation of the previous instance leading to better performance. There are, however, a number of reasons why Logan's instance model can explain and even predict when such tasks should and should not produce priming. First, in the Logan scheme, an instance relates not to the stimulus alone, but to the context in which it is experienced and the response made. Only instances that are sufficiently similar are accessed. In the Ellis et al. (1990) study, subjects generated semantic statements to the stimulus faces on the first occasion, while making speeded binary-choice, sex, or expression decisions on the second occasion. Thus, the two instances require different types of decision and different response outcomes, making it debatable whether the prior instance was useful and thus accessed.

Even in the Ellis et al. experiments, when the context was identical it is still possible to define the conditions under which the instance model predicts priming. At the core of the model is a race between an algorithm—a base set of processes—and a set of instances residing in memory. The more instances existing in memory, the greater the chance that an RT sample from one of the instance distributions will be the minimum value and win the race. However, it could be argued that the gender algorithmic processing is fast—in the Ellis et al. study, gender decisions on the first occasion were below 650 ms—so priming by a single previous instance is only likely if the instance RT distribution mean is lower. The instance model does predict that speed-up will be observed with increasing numbers of instances irrespective of the distributional parameters (Logan, 1988).

The present study sets out to examine certain predictions made by the Logan instance model. In particular, whether priming does occur with more than one repetition and whether the strong predictions made concerning the observation of power curves for the indices of performance RT and their relationship hold for making gender decisions for faces.

METHOD

Subjects

Fifteen psychology students from Lancaster University acted as subjects. All had normal or corrected vision, and had been exposed for a minimum of five years to the British media. They ranged in age from nineteen to thirty-two years and were paid for participating in this experiment.

Stimuli and Materials

Video clips of a range of celebrities were collected from TV productions. Each was around two minutes in duration and contained a range of head movements and expression changes. From these twenty-three celebrities, a sample with as wide a range of interests as possible were selected. Twenty celebrities, ten males and ten females, were used as experimental stimuli, and three were used on the lead-in trials. Similarly, clips of unfamiliar faces were collected from German and Dutch TV programs and films in an attempt to equate the quality and range of faces. Twenty of these were selected to match the chosen celebrities on age, facial hair, and spectacle use and three for the lead-in trials.

These video clips yielded eight monochrome images that were "frame-grabbed" using the QuickImage system. The images selected for each individual ranged from three-quarter right, through full face, to three-quarter left pose and contained a variety of facial expressions. The selected images were then standardized by first cropping the image to maximise the amount of facial information while minimising the amount of background and clothes. Images were then standardised in size (6.5 cm × 4 cm) and equated in brightness and contrast using Adobe Photoshop software on a Macintosh computer.

The stimuli were presented on Macintosh LCII computers with color monitors. These were viewed at approximately eye level (i.e., the center of the screen was 35 cm above the height of the desk at which subjects were seated) and situated behind a black screen situated approximately 60 cm from the subject that allowed only the monitor to be viewed. Subjects made their response by pressing one of two buttons on a box positioned on the desk in front of the subject. The buttons were interfaced to the computer and simulated a single key press of two particular keys (in this case lower case t and o). A filler task was used between experimental blocks to ensure subjects had short breaks. This task involved rating words and non-words presented in a booklet. Each of the eight pages contained eight letter strings to be rated on several scales.

Experimental Design

The experimental design and stimulus presentation was handled by the SuperLab application for Macintosh computers. Subjects first viewed two screens of instructions before completing four practice trials, two of which presented images of celebrities and two of unfamiliar persons. These were followed by a screen, listing the key instructions for the experiment and informing subjects that they now had an opportunity to ask questions.

There then followed an experimental block consisting of six lead-in trials (the data from which did not enter into the analyses) and forty experimental trials. Both the lead-in trials and the experimental trials were randomized before each presentation, and subjects viewed the experimental block eight times. After each experimental block, subjects were required to complete one of the pages of the word booklet.

The background color of the screen for each of the lead-in and experimental trials was a pale blue upon which the word "ready" appeared in red letters approximately 1.5 cm tall. This was displayed for 2000 msecs in the center of the screen and replaced after a 500 msecs blank screen with a central red dot. This was presented for 500 msecs and again followed by a 500 msecs blank screen. A stimulus face was then presented centrally for 2500 msecs and subjects responded by pressing one of the two buttons. A further 1000 msecs blank preceded the presentation of the next "ready" signal that indicated the start of the next block. After each block, instructions appeared instructing the subjects to fill in the one of the pages of the word booklet.

TABLE 1
**Mean and standard deviation of the correct response times for each
trial block for all types of face**

Trial Block	Mean RT	S.D. RT
1	562	92.1
2	553	86.4
3	532	71.7
4	534	69.3
5	530	65.9
6	529	74.8
7	525	73.2
8	530	63.6

Procedure

Subjects sat at a desk facing the monitor and were instructed to
place the index finger of each hand on the two buttons and to locate
the button box in a comfortable position. They were then asked to read
the instructions presented on the screen. These indicated that the experiment was designed to investigate how male and female faces are
processed and that a series of faces was to be presented, some of
which would be of famous faces and some of unfamiliar faces. Subjects were instructed to decide if a particular face was male or female
and to indicate their decisions by pressing the appropriate button. They
were asked to make decisions as quickly and as accurately as possible
and to complete the practice trials. At the end of these, the experimenter indicated what the correct responses were for the practice trials
and asked if subjects had any questions. The experimenter then orally
repeated the instruction to be as fast and as accurate as possible before
allowing subjects to start the experiment proper. Each subject then
completed eight consecutive experimental blocks separated by one
page of the filler task booklet.

For half the subjects, pressing the right button was used to indicate
the image was of a celebrity and for half the mapping was reversed.

RESULTS

The analyses were of two forms. First, analyses of variance
(ANOVAs) were conducted on the response time (RT) data, as this

has been the primary method used in previous face research to analyse differences in face processing. Second, power curve parameters were fitted to the data as a means of examining the validity of the instance-based model and to allow comparisons between the forms of analysis presented in this study and the series of studies, following Logan (1988).

ANOVAs of the Response Time Data

For each subject the RTs from the twenty male, of which ten were famous faces and ten were unfamiliar, and the twenty female faces, and the errors were collected. These were processed to yield the mean correct RT and the standard deviation for each subject for each experimental condition. This generated a $2 \times 2 \times 8$ within design (gender of face $\times$ familiarity of face $\times$ experimental block) and subsequent ANOVAs revealed the main effect of gender to be significant with it taking 526 ms to identify a face as male compared to 548 ms to identify a face as female, $F(1,29) = 7.51$, $MSE = 14852.84$, $p < 0.05$. In addition, performance over the experimental blocks showed a practice curve decrease $F(7,203) = 3.928$, $MSE = 5387.97$, $p < 0.001$ (see Table 1). In order to compare these data with previous priming studies a number of additional planned comparisons were conducted. The data from Ellis et al. (1990) indicate no priming of gender decisions on a second gender decision trial. The current data indicate a drop in RT performance but in line with the Ellis et al. study this was found not to be significant. However a significant priming effect was found between trials 2 and 3, $F(1, 203) = 4.191$, $MSE = 22581.3$, $p < 0.05$. No other significant main effects or interactions were observed.

Power Curve Parameter Estimation

The instance theory detailed by Logan (1988, 1992) makes two strong predictions. First, that data from conditions in which subjects make the same decision to the same stimuli in repeating blocks of trials are well fitted by power functions of the form:

$$RT \text{ measure} = a + b(\text{Trial Block})^{-c}$$

Secondly, the mean and standard deviation power functions of the data from each type of face should be well fitted by power functions and

TABLE 2
Estimated parameters and measure of goodness of fit

	a	b	c	R2	rmsd	F	p
Mean RT	509	54	−0.56	0.905	116.03		
Constrained							
Mean RT	511	52	*−0.61*	0.905	116.28	0.004	> 0.05
S.D. RT	58	36	−0.65	0.777	151.79		
Constrained							
S.D. RT	57	36	*−0.61*	0.778	151.81	0.002	> 0.05

Note: Parameter estimates for the unconstrained and the constrained power functions ($RT = a + b (Block)^{-c}$) fitted to the means and the standard deviations of the correct response times. Also given are the goodness-of-fit measures and tests of the reduction in variance explained by the unconstrained and constrained fits.

have the same c parameter (Logan 1988).

The analysis strategy used to examine these predictions involved fitting power functions to various RT summaries. A number of different algorithms were employed, including using the STEPIT algorithm (Chandler, 1965) used by Logan (1988, 1990), Newton, Quasi-Newton, Steepest Descent algorithm (Raner, 1994), and the Levenberg-Marquard algorithm (Press et al., 1992). These all produced similar solutions. The prediction of common rate exponents was examined by constraining the c parameter to be equal across functions while allowing the other parameters to vary freely, and to select the common exponent that minimised the error fit statistics for the functions under consideration. The constrained fits could then be compared with the unconstrained fits as a means of examining the validity of the instance theory predictions (Logan 1988).

Power functions were fit to the overall mean correct RT and standard deviation data (see Figure 1) and the estimated parameters and the measures of goodness of fit are presented in Table 2. These clearly show that the data are well fitted by power functions of the form specified by Logan, which explain the majority of the observed variance. Moreover, when the exponents for means and standard deviations were constrained to be the equal and to minimise the resulting error measures, the decrease in explained variance was found to be minimal and non-significant for both the mean and the standard deviation data (see Table 2).

FIGURE 1

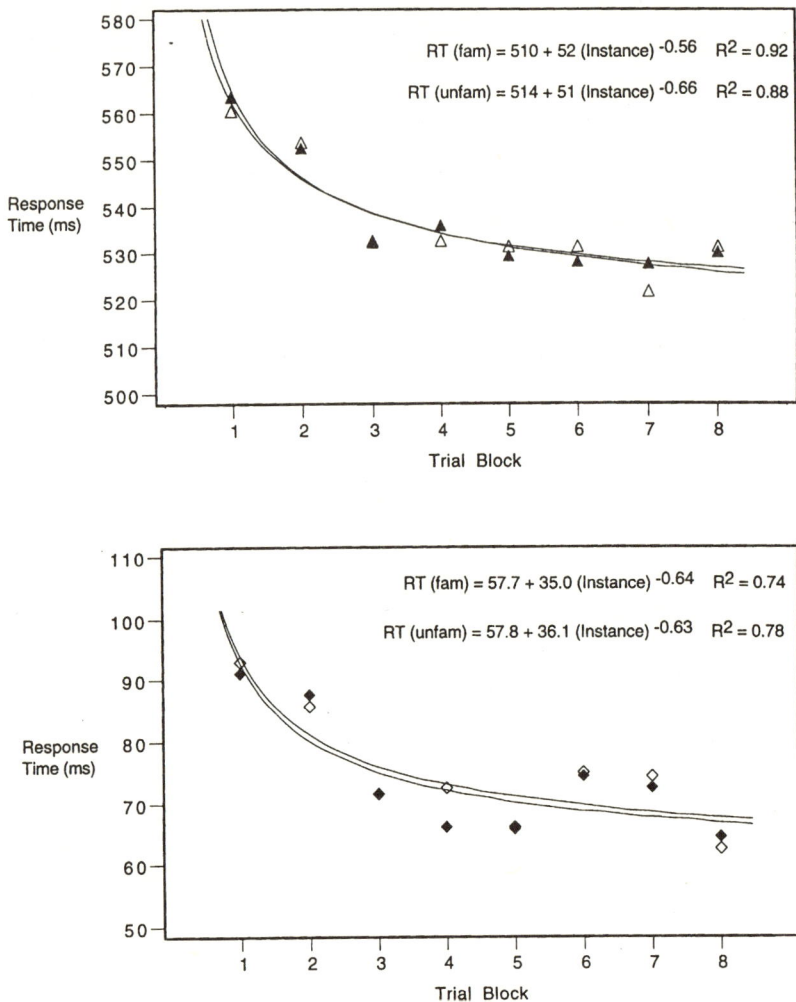

Note: Upper display shows the power curves fitted to the mean correct RT data and gives the associated functions. The lower display is the corresponding standard deviation data. In both cases, the familiar face data are given by the solid symbols and the upper curve and the unfamiliar by the outline symbol and the lower curve.

DISCUSSION

The results from the current experiment are unambiguous. It is clear that repetition priming does not depend solely on the identity processing system, as reductions in processing speed for subsequent items is found for familiar and unfamiliar faces and that the degree of priming is equivalent for both classes of stimulus. In addition, the conditions under which repetition priming can be observed in gender decision making has been clarified. If only the first two trials are considered, then the data replicate the findings of Ellis et al. (1990) by showing no evidence of repetition priming. However, in line with the predictions made by Logan's instance model, priming is in evidence with subsequent repetitions. Thus, a change from algorithmic processing to instance based retrieval in gender decisions is only possible if sufficient instances exist. This, in turn, makes it statistically more likely for one of the instances to be retrieved before the fast algorithmic processing can be accomplished. In fact, performance on trial block one, which reflects only algorithmic processing, was found to be fast (562 ms) and reflects an efficient algorithm that is applied to the processing of all faces.

At a theoretical level, the results are difficult to encompass within current abstraction models which assume repetition priming occurs only within the system that stores abstractions of the appearance of familiar faces (Ellis et al., 1990, Ellis et al., 1996). In this experiment, repetition priming was observed in a gender decision task and to be equivalent for both familiar and unfamiliar faces (Figure 1) confirming previous observations of unfamiliar face priming (Bentin and Moscovitch, 1988; Hay, in press). In contrast, the data are entirely consistent with memory models which are episodic based (Jacoby, 1983) and particularly Logan's (1988) instance model which not only predicts power function repetition priming speed-up, but can predict the conditions under which repetition priming can be observed in gender decision tasks.

Some form of integration, however, may be possible as the Burton et al. (1990) model is based on the interactive activation model suggested by McClelland and Rumelhart (1981). More recent and comprehensive versions of this seek to explain the development of what appear to be abstractive word and concept units as resulting from storage of all instances of the word or concept (McClelland and

Rumelhart, 1985). Models such as these respond strongly to prototypical patterns while also responding strongly to recent instances in the training set. However adopting such a position involves embracing the concept of abstractions based on instances and viewing face priming as being dependent on the number of "appropriate" instances available on any task. This may also be important for attempts to explain how FRU are formed in the first place.

REFERENCES

Baddeley, A.D. (1982). Domains of recollection. *Psychological Review, 89,* 708–729.

Bentin, S. and Moscovitch, M. (1988). The time course of repetition priming effects for words and unfamiliar faces. *Journal of Experimental Psychology: General, 117,* 148–160.

Bruce, V. and Valentine, T. (1985) Identity priming in the recognition of familiar faces. *British Journal of Psychology, 76,* 373–383.

Bruce, V. and Young A.W. (1986). Understanding face recognition. *British Journal of Psychology, 77,* 305–327.

Burton, A.M., Bruce, V., and Johnson, R.A. (1990). Understanding face recognition with an interactive activation model. *British Journal of Psychology, 81,* 361–380.

Chandler, P.J. (1965). *Subroutine STEPIT: An algorithm that finds the values of the parameters which minimise a given continuous function* [Computer program]. Bloomington: Indiana University, Quantum Chemistry Program Exchange.

Ellis, A.W., Young, A.W., and Flude, B. (1990). Repetition priming and face processing: Priming occurs within the system that responds to the identity of a face. *Quarterly Journal of Experimental Psychology, 42A,* 495–512.

Ellis, A.W., Young, A.W., Flude, B., and Hay, D.C. (1987). Repetition Priming of face recognition. *Quarterly Journal of Experimental Psychology, 39A,* 193–210.

Ellis, A.W., Flude, B., Young, A.W., and Burton, A.M. (1996). Two loci of repetition priming of familiar faces. *Journal of Experimental Psychology: Learning, Memory and Cognition, 22,* 295–308.

Hay, D.C. (in press). Testing instance models of face repetition priming. Memory and Cognition

Hay, D.C. and Young, A.W. (1982). The human face. In A.W. Ellis (ed.), *Normality and Pathology in Cognitive Functions.* New York: Academic Press.

Jacoby, L.L. (1983). Perceptual enhancement: Persistent effects of an experience. *Journal of Experimental Psychology: Learning, Memory and Cognition, 9,* 21–38.

Jacoby, L.L. and Brooks, L.R. (1984). Nonanalytic cognition: Memory, perception and conceptual learning. In G.H. Bower (ed.). *The psychology of learning and motivation* (Vol. 18, pp. 1–47). New York: Academic Press.

Logan, G.D. (1988). Toward an instance theory of automatization. *Psychological Review, 95,* 492–527.

Logan, G.D. (1990). Repetition priming and automaticity: Common underlying mechanisms? *Cognitive Psychology, 22,* 1–35.

McClelland, J.L. and Rumelhart, D.E. (1981). An interactive activation model of context effects in letter perception: Part I. An account of basic findings. *Psychological Review, 88,* 375–407.

McClelland, J.L. and Rumelhart, D.E. (1985). Distributed memory and the representation of general and specific information. *Journal of Experimental Psychology: General, 114,* 159–188.

Morton, J. (1979). Facilitation in word recognition: Experiments causing change in the logogen model. In P.A. Kohlers, M. Wrolstad, and H. Bouma (eds.), *Processing of visible language* (vol. 1, pp. 259–268). New York: Plenum.

Press, W.H., Flannery, B.P., Teukolosky, S.A., and Vetterling, W.T. (1992). *Numerical recipes—the art of scientific computing.* Cambridge: Cambridge University Press.

Raner, K. (1994). *MacCurveFit* [Computer program]. Victoria, Australia; Kevin Raner Software.